Do I have to be GOOD to go to Heaven?

A Series of Fresh Pulpit Homilies on the Book of Romans

Roy C. Price

AN IMPRINT OF
GLOBALEDADVANCEPRESS

Do I have to be GOOD to go to Heaven?
A Series of Fresh Pulpit Homilies on the Book of Romans

Copyright © 2019 Roy C. Price

Library of Congress Control Number: 2019941087

Price, Roy Cantrell   1935 -

Do I Have to be GOOD to go to Heaven?

ISBN 978-1-935434-96-2 Print

ISBN 978-1-935434-97-9 eBook

Subject Codes and Description: 1. REL 012070 Religion/Christian Living/Personal Growth 2. REL 006220 Religion/Biblical Studies/New Testament/General 3. REL 006810 Religion/Biblical Commentary/New Testament/Paul's Letters

All rights reserved, including the right to reproduce this book or any part thereof in any form, except for inclusion of brief quotations in a review, without the written permission of the author and GlobalEdAdvancePRESS.

Cover design by Global Graphics NYC

Printed in Australia, Brazil, France, Germany, Italy, Poland, Russia, Spain, UK, USA, and wherever there is an Espresso Book Machine

The Press does not have ownership of the contents of a book; this is the author's work and the author owns the copyright. All theory, concepts, constructs, and perspectives are those of the author and not necessarily the Press. They are presented for open and free discussion of the issues involved. All comments and feedback should be directed to the Email: [comments4author@aol.com] and the comments will be forwarded to the author for response.

Order books from www.gea-books.com/bookstore/
or any place good books are sold.

Published by
POST-GUTENBERG BOOKS
AN IMPRINT OF
GlobalEdAdvance PRESS

Acknowledgments

This series of sermons were first presented to the Christian and Missionary Alliance Church of Paradise, California, and then revised for Monte Vista Chapel of Turlock, California. I further revised the series at the request of John Lane, CEO of Cal.Net in Shingle Springs, California, and Lt. Col. James Ramos, (retired, U. S. Army). It is my honor to share with them and a dozen others in a Friday morning Bible study. John came to a full commitment to Jesus as Lord and Savior during the initial presentation of Romans at Paradise Alliance church. In the fall of 2018, the Camp Fire wild fire devastated the entire town of Paradise. Nearly 12,000 homes were destroyed. The senior pastor of the church had been in place only three months and had to flee with his wife and three young children. Of the 22 employees of the church, 16 lost their homes including 8 of 10 on the pastoral staff. In the middle of that destruction, the Alliance church building was untouched by the fire.

In addition, I am grateful to Luther Rice Seminary where I earned both Th.M. and D.Min. degrees. In those programs, I was taught to outline with a sentence structure. That method is seldom used by pastors today. I am also indebted to further academic rigor acquired in studies at Oxford Graduate School in Tennessee, where I earned a D.Phil. in the sociological integration of religion and society. My academic advisor, mentor and encourager, Dr. Hollis Green, has given confidence to go ahead with this endeavor.

This volume is dedicated to Rev. Brian Long, D.Min., my son-in-law, who faithfully presents the Bible to his congregation and has helped me develop my own skills. Brian is a graduate of Taylor University in Upland, Indiana, where he met his wife, my daughter, Cynthia. He earned both a M.Div. and D.Min. at the Conservative Baptist Seminary, in Denver, Colorado.

Contents

Acknowledgments	5
First Reviews...	13
Publisher's Preface	15
Preface	17
Martin Luther on Romans	19
Augustine and Romans	20

1
Romans 1:1-7   21
Jesus Rose from the Dead—So What?

2
Romans 1:8-15   29
Serving God with Our Whole Heart

3
Romans 1:16-17   37
God's Power is for Everyone

4
Romans 1:18-23   47
What Happens to People Who Haven't Heard About Jesus?

5
Romans 1:24-32   57
Why Do Good People Do Bad Things?

6
Romans 2:1-11   67
Which Way Does the Finger Point?

7
Romans 2:12-29   77
The Religion of the Heart

8
Romans 3:1-20 — 85
The Conclusion: We Are All Guilty

9
Romans 3:21-31 — 95
There's Only One Way, and It's Free

10
Romans 4:1-15 — 105
Did Abraham Get a Paycheck?

11
Romans 4:16-25 — 113
Hope When Everything Seems Hopeless

12
Romans 5:1-5 — 123
Peace in Spite of Pain

13
Romans 5:6-11 — 133
Life for the Powerless

14
Romans 5:12-21 — 143
Lives in Contrast: Adam and Jesus

15
Romans 6:1-11, Part 1 — 153
The Way to Life is Through Death: a Lesson from the Phoenix

16
Romans 6:1-11, Part 2, — 161
God Is Still Changing Me

17
Romans 6:1-11, Part 3 — 173
I'm Confused: Am I Dead or Alive?

Contents

18
Romans 6:12-14   183
The Choice is Ours About What Kind of Life We Live

19
Romans 6:15-23   193
You Can be a Slave to Something that Kills You or to Someone Who Gives Life

20
Romans 7:1-6   203
Marriage as a Picture of the Christian

21
Romans 7:7-25   213
Winning Over the Internal Conflict

22
Romans 8:1-8   225
How We Have Resurrection Power

23
Romans 8:9-11   235
Resurrection Life Is Ours Now

24
Romans 8:12-17   243
Wow! What an Inheritance

25
Romans 8:18-25   251
What a Fantastic Future

26
Romans 8:26-27   261
Help in Prayer

27
Romans 8:28-30   269
God Is Determined That We Will Win

28
Romans 8:31-39   279
We Are Conquerors Plus!

29
Romans 9   289
Is God Unjust?

30
Romans 10   299
Obstinate or Responsive

31
Romans 11   309
Where Do We Fit in God's Plan?

32
Romans 12:1 2   319
Our Most Important Personal Commitment

33
Romans 12:3-8   331
We Need to Think Sensibly About Ourselves

34
Romans 12:9-16   341
Eight Things a Christian Does

35
Romans 12:17-21   351
When You Receive Evil

36
Romans 13:1-7   361
The Christian's Relationship to Government

Contents

37
Romans 13:8-14   371
God's Wakeup Call to His People

38
Romans 14   383
We Are Different, but We Don't Have to Be at Each Other's Throat

39
Romans 15:1-7, 13   393
Learning to Accept One Another

40
Romans 15:14-22   407
The Competence of the Church

41
Romans 15:23-33   417
Looking to the Future

42
Romans 16:1-16   427
The Church is Made Up of Ordinary People

43
Romans 16:17-24   437
God's Ultimate Objective

Conclusion   **449**
Bibliography   **451**
About the Author   **457**

Do I Have to be GOOD to go to Heaven?

First Reviews...

This work on the great treatise of Romans deserves a place in the library of anyone who desires to understand and clearly communicate its profound truths to a lost and hurting world.

I had the privilege of serving under Dr. Roy Price for nearly five years before entering into my M.Div. studies at Denver Seminary and again afterwards. Over the span of my 30-plus years in pastoral ministry, Dr. Price has served as a rich and formative mentor for pastoral ministry through countless transformative theological discussions and coaching conversations.

Students of the Bible will find this work very readable for the laymen, or the pastor who has yet to complete in depth theological training or pastoral preparation, yet even those with terminal degrees will not find Dr. Price's treatment of Romans elementary in the slightest.

Dr. Price bases his practical, common sense approach to Romans on the most highly regarded theological sources and the most well respected theological minds and authors. When critical for understanding the text, Dr. Price includes relevant historical/cultural insight, without getting bogged down in unhelpful details. In addition, this work emphasizes practical application of Romans, and the format of this work will serve as a helpful aid to break down the book and outline its life changing contents.

This work will serve as an excellent resource for teachers/preachers. It includes relatable stories and illustrations for anyone who desires to communicate the truths of the profound book of Romans in plain language. Following each chapter there are questions for reflection and discussion making it an excellent small group study resource.

— Brian Long, Lead Pastor
Foothills Church, Cameron Park, CA
Adjunct Faculty, William Jessup University

Expository preaching, the business of moving faithfully through whole books of Scripture with the goal of helping people to understand what the Bible is saying and then to apply it thoughtfully and carefully to their own situations, is a dying art. Roy Price is a master expositor.

He opens the Book of Romans, which many would identify as the "crown jewel" of all the New Testament Epistles, and carefully explains its meaning to his listeners (and now his readers).

The addition of thought provoking questions at the end of every chapter make it an ideal text for any small group seeking a better understanding of the heart of the Good News and its implications for anyone seeking to live the life that Christ came to give us.

— Dr. John F. Soper, Director, Mission 119
(www.mission119.org)
Former Vice President for Church Ministries
Christian and Missionary Alliance

Roy Price's new book, *Do I have to be GOOD to go to Heaven?* is a wonderful 43 chapter homiletical walk through the book of Romans. Dr. Price accurately addresses the text and then provides commentary to help the student of the Bible think through how to communicate it.

Having preached this series multiple times, Roy's illustrations are timely and fit. Thank you, Dr. Price, for helping us think clearly about Paul's letter to the Romans.

— Rev. Patrick A. Blewett, Ph.D., Dean
A.W. Tozer Theological Seminary

Publisher's Preface

The Letter to the Romans was written before Paul was known to the congregation there; consequently, he wrote to introduce himself and express basic truths about salvation and his desire to visit. Paul's intent was to provide a systematic presentation of basic teachings organized around major themes, not to correct problems. Paul was certain that grace, faith, righteousness, and justification opened the door for Gentile participation in congregational life. His letter makes certain that Gentiles were included in the blessings of grace. However, Paul was convinced that God's merciful forgiveness did not eliminate the requirement to learn and follow basic guidelines codified in the tenets of faith.

After a series of fresh pulpit homilies from Romans, delivered from a pastor's heart with love and spiritual insights, Dr. Price interacted with listeners and followed their encouragement to edit the messages for publication. Because of receptive listeners to these messages and the laborious endeavor to convert a public sermon into a private message, the readers of this book are blessed with an opportunity to gain insights and spiritual strength to increase their stride and enjoy their spiritual journey.

With broad experience, a missional lifestyle and a pastor's concern for believers, Dr. Price extrapolates from Romans spiritual truths and generalizes their certainty to enhance the lifestyle behavior of believers. Roy has enjoyed a lifelong leadership role among his peers and his academic scholarship has enhanced his reputation as a Man of God who shares the Truth with love and tenderness. Welcome to a good read from a scholarly pastor with deep affinity with people and genuine affection for the Word of God.

> *4. Therefore we were identified with Him by baptism into death: that as Christ was raised up from the dead by the power of the Father,* **likewise we should behave in newness of life** *(Romans 6:4 EDNT).*

I have known Roy Price most of my adult life. My association with him includes speaking at his church, hearing his marvelous voice in song, having him as a graduate student in two doctoral programs, knowing him as a missionary, an academic, author, and Churchman. When one understands his pastor's heart and his commitment to a missional lifestyle, his book, *Do I have to be GOOD to go to Heaven?* will assist the reader in discovering "the end is worth the journey."

— Hollis L. Green, ThD, PhD, DLitt

Preface

At this writing, the world has been thrown into chaos largely driven by multiple cases of suicide bombings killing thousands of people and destroying billions in property. Ancient sites and historical artifacts have been wantonly destroyed with no respect for either history or property. The perpetrators interpret their religious text to guarantee heaven with its perceived perks if they give their lives for the cause of their god. On the opposite side is the idea that if a person does enough good things, religiously, socially in helping others, one can earn their way into heaven. Do I have to be good to go to heaven? It comes down to a sound bite phrase: spell religion, d-o; spell Christianity, d-o-n-e. Even within Christianity, the idea of earning one's way by doing the religious thing or being a good person, is a misunderstood position. These sermons on Paul's letter to the Romans seek to answer the basic questions most people wrestle with regarding their relationship to God and life after death. The core theme of Paul's letter to the Roman house churches is that heaven is a free gift we cannot earn and do not deserve but it can be received. We do have to be good to go to heaven. The question is whose goodness qualifies a person.

Another book on Romans? Yes, but this is not in the genre of a commentary. There are many and I have relied on several. This is a pastor seeking to be true to the text and apply it in a specific social and cultural setting. To enhance my content, I chose to provide short excerpts from commentaries and other sources related to the passage of the sermon. These quotes were not part of the original sermon. Why did I include these quotations? It was my intention that the added content would augment the reader's understanding and appreciation of the passage. In sermon preparation I always began with the text of the Bible, reading it through multiple times looking for a central phrase that drove the passage's thought. I developed a main idea with every main point a development of that idea. I was trained to express each point in sentence form. The concept of theme development also applies to the treatment of the Roman letter. It was my desire to conclusively answer the question of how any person, regardless of ethnicity, language, education or culture is qualified and assured of heaven. That is a fundamental question to all humans for as the teacher of Ecclesiastes declared: "He has also set eternity in the hearts of men; yet they cannot fathom what God has done from beginning to end" (Ecclesiastes 3:11). That was Augustine's quest and the issue that haunted a devout Luther who conscientiously worked to be acceptable to God. His attempts ended with no assurance until Romans burst open with kaleidoscopic beauty to him. We'll see a brief description of both Luther and Augustine to set the stage for the forty-three sermons to follow.

A number of years ago, seeking to learn the skill and art of preaching, I read that good preaching has one hand hold of God and the other hold of culture and seeks to bring the two together. The Bible is the preacher's hand holding on to God. Illustrations give windows of light and a hand on the culture and times of which one is a part. Illustrations are often date specific. Nonetheless, they are still relevant although easily replaced by a recent current event in the news or from life experience of the reader or the new communicator.

Martin Luther on Romans

In 1552, Martin Luther (the Reformation's champion of "the just shall live by faith") wrote in his Preface to his commentary on Romans: "This epistle is really the chief part of the New Testament and the very purest Gospel, and is worthy not only that every Christian should know it word for word, by heart, but occupy himself with it every day, as the daily bread of the soul. It can never be read or pondered too much, and the more it is dealt with the more precious it becomes, and the better it tastes."[1]

As a young monk in his late twenties and early thirties, Luther went through intense spiritual struggles trying to "work out his own salvation by careful observance of the monastic rule, constant confession, and self-mortification." He "viewed God as a wrathful judge who expected sinners to earn their own righteousness." It wasn't until 1517-1518 that he came to the settled understanding his right standing with God was by faith alone.[2]

The Reformation was sparked in October 1517, when Luther, appalled by the abuse of the sale of indulgences, posted his Ninety-Five Theses. All of us who enjoy the freedom of God's grace in cleansing, forgiving and receiving sinners by faith in Christ's atoning redemption are indebted to the clarity of Paul's writing in this letter to the Romans.

---

1 Martin Luther, Translated by J. Theodore Mueller, *Commentary on Romans* (Grand Rapids, Michigan: Kregel, 1954), xiii.
2 Walter A. Elwell, ed., *Evangelical Dictionary of Theology*, s.v. "Martin Luther", R. W. Heinze, Grand Rapids, Michigan: Baker Book House, 1984.

Augustine and Romans

"Romans was used by God to effect the conversion of mighty Augustine. As a headstrong youth who had left his North African home for the pleasures of Italy, much to the distress of his mother Monica, he was arrested by this very portion of God's Book. After a conversation with a Christian friend, he resorted to a quiet garden where he might think and pray things through. He was keenly conscious of his divided self. The good that he wanted he could not do and the evil that he did not want he found himself continually doing. His will was maimed and struggling, 'with one part sinking as another arose.' As he was thus torn in spirit and weeping in bitter contrition of heart, he heard from a neighboring house a child's voice—whether it was a boy or a girl he could not tell—sing again and again 'Tolle, lege'—'Take up, and read.' Apparently, it was a snatch of some ditty or perhaps part of a nursery game. But to Augustine it came as the command of God Himself.

He hurried into the house, opened his Bible and read these words from the epistle to the Romans: 'Let us conduct ourselves becomingly as in the day, not in reveling and drunkenness, not in debaucher and licentiousness, not in quarreling and jealousy. But put on the Lord Jesus Christ, and make no provision for the flesh, to gratify its desires' (13:13,14). 'No further would I read,' he tells us, in his Confessions, 'nor needed I' for instantly at the end of this sentence by a light as it were of serenity infused into my heart, all the darkness of doubt vanished away.' Augustine found salvation in Christ through reading in Romans—and the Church was braced to endure the mortal storm when the city of Rome fell."[3]

---

3   A. Skevington Wood, *Life by the Spirit* (Grand Rapids, Michigan: Zondervan Publishing House, 1963),9.

1

Romans 1:1-7

Jesus Rose from the Dead —So What?

"If we begin with God in our theory of values, we end with a God Who provides immortality for men; if we begin with man in our theory, we end with neither God nor immortality, but with pessimism and despair only.

"If Christianity could but make personal immortality secure, it would have done enough to assure it a place in the philosophic hall of fame; but when Christianity goes on and guarantees, not only personal immortality, but the resurrection of our own bodies, then it has done something that none of the ancients even dreamed could be incorporated in a rational world-view. But this is the very hope of the Christian, that since Jesus Christ rose from the grave, we will rise also! With this doctrine of the resurrection we find the final and perfect solution to the soul-sorrow of man...."[4]

Scripture: Romans 1:1-7

Main Idea: Paul's message was the gospel of Jesus, a descendant of David, was proven to be the Son of God by His resurrection from the dead.

Introduction

Kings shall bow and adore,
And nations kneel down before Him,

---

[4] Edward John Carnell, *An Introduction to Christian Apologetics* (Grand Rapids, Michigan: Wm. B. Eerdmans Publishing Company, 1948), 346.

And every tongue confess that Jesus Christ is Lord!

These lines are not fiction or fantasy; this is as sure to happen as we are alive today. The day will come when the whole universe will bow in confession that Jesus of Nazareth is the Lord, the Creator, the Savior, the eternal Son of God. You can join that crowd now and enjoy eternity in the presence God, or you will acknowledge Jesus is Lord later only it will be too late for heaven.

Our nation was jolted in April 1996 by the news of the Air Force 737 that slammed into the mountains of Croatia killing Ron Brown (US Secretary of Commerce) and everyone aboard. Certainly, none of them had any inkling when they got up in the morning that they would be killed that day, but death doesn't usually announce its coming. We must be ready to die and meet God, because that is more certain than taxes.

My view of Easter Sunday was dramatically changed in 1987. I am the youngest of three brothers. All of us entered the ministry. That year, my oldest brother, who was a pastor in Seattle, was stricken with leukemia and died two weeks before Easter. The night following a very large and moving memorial service held in his church in Seattle, Washington, my 82-year-old mother suffered a heart attack and was taken to the same hospital where her son had died. Later, she seemed to be recovering and I asked her if it was all right if I returned home for Easter services and she said by all means.

My wife and I left only to receive news after we arrived home that Mom had died—exactly one week after my brother's death. She lived in southern California, so we immediately left to assist in preparations for her funeral which was held the day after Easter.

We can cruise through life pretty cocky about things when we're making money, are healthy, and things are going well. But none of that gives support and strength when death hits you head-on. On Easter Sunday, the day before we buried Mom, we sang:

> Crown Him the Lord of life:
> Who triumphed o'er the grave,
> Who rose victorious to the strife
> For those He came to save;
> His glories now we sing,
> Who died and rose on high,
> Who died eternal life to bring,
> And lives that death may die.

I had never sung those words with the meaning they carried that day.

One event that transcends all other events in Jesus' life is the final proof of His claims. The single most important proof of who He is was His resurrection from the dead. Jesus of Nazareth was really dead when they buried him. He was raised from the dead by the power of God and is alive today. Take the resurrection from Jesus and Christianity is reduced to simply another religion among hundreds. Take your pick which one suits you best. However, if Jesus really did rise from the dead, Christianity is distinguished from all others, and its claims to be true are vindicated.

Because of the crucial nature of the historicity of the resurrection, Satan has attacked it throughout the ages. This year as last year, both *Time* and *Newsweek* had cover articles that primarily raised doubt about the whole matter. The resurrection of Jesus isn't a casual side-issue, it is the heart of Christian faith and hope. It was the heart of the message of the apostle Paul. Here is how he wrote it in his letter to the Romans:

> *The sacred writings contain preliminary reports [promises] by the prophets on God's Son. His descent from David roots him in history; his unique identity as Son of God was shown by the Spirit when Jesus was raised from the dead, setting him apart as the Messiah, our Master. Through him we received both the generous gift of his life and the urgent task of passing it on to others who receive it by entering into obedient trust in Jesus. You are who you are through this gift and call of Jesus Christ (The Message).*

Paul called his message the gospel because it was good news. No other religion offers the good news of forgiveness of sins and eternal life as a free gift that we cannot earn, do not deserve, but can receive. There are five basic things about the "good news."

I. The Good News Was Promised by Prophets in the Old Testament (2)

The word, "promise", indicates something more than a prediction. It refers to God fulfilling His Word. The last chapter of Luke has two references of Jesus teaching His disciples the numerous OT passages that spoke of His death and resurrection. Those specific promises are not referred to in this paragraph, but in essence the whole Old Testament promised a coming Messiah.

II. The Good News Was About God's Son—Who He Was, What He Did

The message is not a philosophical treatise. It is a person, God's only begotten Son. Two important facts are stated:

First, Jesus received His human nature as a descendant of David. He was a real human being. He knew the full experience of humanity from conception through death. Stuart Briscoe expressed it this way: "He became what we are to make us what He was."

Second, through the Holy Spirit, Jesus was proven to be the Son of God with power by the resurrection. We read: "his unique identity as Son of God was shown by the Spirit when Jesus was raised from the dead, setting him apart as the Messiah, our Master." Another translation reads: He "was openly designated the Son of God in power—in a striking, triumphant and miraculous manner." Let's break it down.

It was the Holy Spirit who enabled Mary as a virgin to conceive a son. The Holy Spirit empowered the entire ministry of Jesus, and the same Spirit gave life to the corpse in the tomb. He is also the source of victory over sin and all of its tangled effects in our personal lives today.

The resurrection of Jesus was a powerful act. Paul wrote to the Ephesians of the power God made available to us as believers. It is, he wrote, the same power that raised Jesus from the dead. He piled one word on top of another in speaking of the power required to raise Christ from the dead.

In Ephesians 1:19-20, Paul prayed that we might experience God's *"incomparably great power [dunamis] for us who believe. That power is like the working [energeia] of his mighty [kratos] strength [ischus] which he exerted in Christ when he raised him from the dead and seated him at his right hand in the heavenly realms...."* You can experience that power today. God's power will make you a new person on the inside.

The powerful act of the resurrection designated Jesus of Nazareth as the Son of God. It authenticated all He did in His life and death. The resurrection of Jesus is the ultimate and final proof of His deity, the assurance to us that the One we believe in is truth.

III. The Good News Is God's Free Gift to Everyone (5)

We are to pass on this good news of Jesus to everyone. Jesus lived, died and rose again, not just for one special race of people, but for every human being. Grace refers to God's gift that is unearned and undeserved. The difference between God's grace and religion is expressed in this statement: "The law [or religion] lays down what a person must do; the gospel lays down what God has done." Which system do you function in? Are you trying to do everything possible to qualify yourself for heaven? Or are you personally receiving the gift of what God has done for you in Christ?

IV. The Good News Calls for Action

We have "the urgent task of passing it on to others who receive it by entering into obedient trust in Jesus." We don't become Christians by being born in America or by having Christian parents. We don't become Christians by going to church. Obedient trust is to turn away from all our attempts at self-righteousness and place our faith in the Lord Jesus Christ alone as our only hope of heaven. Having become a recipient of God's love and forgiveness, we are to pass the great news to others.

V. The Good News Means We Belong

"You are who you are through this gift and call of Jesus Christ." Being a Christian is a personal relationship of belonging to Jesus.

Application

We live in a pluralistic society which means every religion is given equal treatment by the law. Therefore, it is imperative that we know why Jesus and not Buddha, Shinto or

Mohammed, why the Bible and not the New Age. The reason is found in the resurrection.

Jesus rose from the dead, so what you ask? The first 'so what' is the resurrection proves that Jesus is **the** Truth. He is not just one among the many, but **the One** above the many. How do we know Christ is not dead? By the empty tomb.

John Singleton Copley, one of the great legal minds in British history and three times High Chancellor of England, wrote, "I know pretty well what evidence is, and I tell you, such evidence as that for the resurrection has never broken down yet."

The second 'so what' is the resurrection brings a personal triumph over death. This is illustrated by Dr. W. B. Hinson, a former Baptist pastor from Portland, Oregon. One year after he had contracted a disease that finally took his life, he told his congregation: "I remember a year ago, when a man in this city said, 'You have got to go to your death.' I walked out to where I live, five miles out of this city, and I looked across at that mountain that I love [perhaps Mt. Hood or Mt. St. Helens before the volcano] and I looked at the river in which I rejoice [the Columbia River], and I looked at the stately trees that are always God's own poetry to my soul.

"Then in the evening I looked up into the great sky where God was lighting his lamps, and I said: 'I may not see you many more times, but Mountain, I shall be alive when you are gone; and, River, I shall be alive when you cease running toward the sea; and Stars, I shall be alive when you have fallen from your sockets in the great down-pulling of the material universe!" The resurrection of Jesus will enable you also to triumph over death.

After Jesus had risen from the dead, He came alongside a couple of fellows who were walking to a town called Emmaus.

He is here today to come alongside of you to give you forgiveness of sins and eternal life. He will fill the emptiness of your heart if you will turn to Him. He will also come alongside us as believers and give us power and courage to openly share His good news.

If you desire to open your heart to Jesus as your personal Lord and Savior, you believe in your heart that God raised Him from the dead and confess with your mouth that Jesus is Lord, will you also stand as an open testimony that you have placed your faith in Jesus? Then, let someone else know of your trust in Christ.

For your reflection:
- Of the assurances of the resurrection of Jesus, what brings the greatest comfort to you?
- How does the guarantee of your resurrection shape your thinking about death?

2

Romans 1:8-15

Serving God with Our Whole Heart

"The main characteristic of love is unselfishness. Love thinks of the loved one before it thinks of self. The interests of the beloved are paramount. So it was in the life of Paul the apostle. He loved all the believers in the Lord Jesus Christ with a great and tender love, and thus he desired that they might be strengthened by the truth of God. All of his great expression of desire to see them was in order to convey to them the fact that he had something to give that was going to be for their great good."[5]

Scripture: Romans 1:8-15

Main Idea: Paul's whole-hearted service to God included his prayer for the church, and his obligation in preaching the Gospel to the whole world.

Introduction

Queen Mary of England was on a walk one day with some children. They were caught in a down-pour of rain, forcing them to take shelter on the porch of a home. The queen knocked on the door and asked to borrow an umbrella promising to return it the next day. She had deliberately disguised herself with plain clothes and a hat that partly covered her face.

---

5   Donald Grey Barnhouse, *Romans, Vol. I* (Fincastle, Virginia: Scripture Truth Book Company, 1952), 136.

The lady of the house was wary of the stranger and thought she should not loan her best umbrella because she might never see it again. Instead, with apologies, she gave the queen an older one that was broken with several holes in it. The next day a man with gold braid on his uniform and an envelope in his hand, came to the house. "The queen sent me with this letter and also asked me to thank you personally for the loan of your umbrella." Stunned, the woman burst into tears. "Oh, what an opportunity I missed that I did not give her my very best."

In 2 Corinthians 5:10 Paul warned us: *"For we must all appear before the judgment seat of Christ, that each one may receive what is due him for the things done while in the body, whether good or bad."*

Jesus gave the story of the prince who gave his servants a sum of money and told them to *"Put this money to work until I come back"* (Luke 19:13). In the story, some of the servants doubled their money. When the prince returned, he rewarded them for their faithful service. One did nothing. What he had was taken from him and given to another. The lesson simply states we will be held accountable for our service when Christ returns.

Paul declared he was a servant of Christ Jesus in verse 1, and in this paragraph, he enlarges on what that meant to him. The theme is given in verse 9: *"God, whom I serve with my whole heart."* He served God with a whole heart in prayer, in preaching the gospel, and in ministry to the church.

I. Paul Served God with a Whole Heart in Prayer (8-10)

A. He Praised the Roman Christians for Their Faith

Paul's first expression to the believers in Rome was gratitude to God for the wide-spread testimony of their faith in Jesus as Lord and Savior. Note the personal factor in Paul's reference to "my" God. David repeatedly used the personal pronoun when speaking of God; e.g.., "the LORD is my Shepherd, I shall lack nothing." Paul fits into that tradition. How about you? Do you have a personal relationship with God or simply an institutional one? A personal relationship with God is the heart of Christianity. An institutional relationship with God is the cold and dead formality of religion. Jesus did not come for us to participate in a liturgy or to belong to an institution; He came to give us life by His Spirit joined to our spirit in personal intimacy.

Faith is a word that describes how a personal relationship with God is sustained. It is used in the New Testament of the act of the will based on the promises of God and of the personal trust one person has in another. Here, Paul is grateful that the testimony of Roman Christians trusting in Jesus had gone throughout the entire area. "World" simply referred to a wide area, not to a technical understanding of the world as we know it today.

B. Paul's Service Included Consistent Prayer for the Church in Rome

There are three elements of prayer that all of us can utilize to enhance our prayer lives.

1. First, prayer is full of thanksgiving: "I thank my God through Jesus Christ." Did the church in Rome have problems that caused Paul to pray for change? Yes, since they were

human beings, though the problems aren't recorded. As we pray for our church and one another, let's identify those things for which we can give thanks.

2. His prayer was through Jesus Christ. We do not pray through Mary. We do not pray on the basis of our own goodness or personal achievement. The only way to approach God is through Jesus Christ who is the one Mediator between God and man.

3. He prayed for them "at all times." This phrase gives insight to the heart of Paul's ministry and the basis of his success. He was a good writer, but that was not the key. He was a skilled orator even though he told the Corinthians that he did not come to them with persuasive speech. The key to his ministry was the time he spent in prayer.

Church historians may well indict the American church for its absorption with programs. We are entertainment centered. We talk about prayer with spiritual tones, but we do little praying. It is the hardest aspect of my own walk with the Lord. The time demands in today's world are enormous, and we run like fools trying to cram in every possible activity, and prayer is left out. I am deeply grateful for you who consistently and faithfully pray.

Whole-hearted service begins with prayer.

II. Paul Served God with a Whole Heart by Preaching the Gospel

A. He Preached the Gospel of God's Son (9a)

Paul did not primarily preach dogma or philosophy, he presented a person. Verse 4 identified the focus was on Jesus' humanity as the descendant of David, and on the proof of His being the Son of God through of the resurrection. The good news about Jesus is that we can be forgiven our sins and can be made right with a holy God.

B. He Felt Obligated to Preach to Everyone (13-15)

The *"harvest"* Paul looked for was not so much among the believers, but the unbelievers. He was an evangelist, calling people to trust in Christ. He wanted a ministry to the church, as we shall see in a moment, but primarily he desired a ministry to people outside of Christ.

In verse 14, Paul classified people in two groups of pairs. It is probably best to understand both pairs to refer to the entire Gentile population. Gentiles referred to those of the Graeco-Roman culture, *"non-Greeks"* [literally *"barbarians"*] to the rest of humanity. He further described the groups of humanity as educated and uneducated.[6] We have an obligation to declare the grace of God to all groups of society and to all people in the world. That includes the down-and-out and the up-and-out.

Jerry MacAuley was converted during a seven-year hitch in Sing Sing prison. He later began sharing his faith with other men who had been enslaved by sin. He started America's first rescue mission in New York city, where he was the friend of criminals and skid-row bums. Just before his death in 1884, he said to his wife, "I know that soon tuberculosis will take my life, but I want to die on my knees, still praying for the lost. I'd rather have some poor soul that I led to the Lord put one small rose on my grave than to have the wealth of a millionaire." At his funeral an aged, shabbily dressed man appeared. Handing one of the ushers a few flowers, he asked him in a voice trembling with emotion to place them on the coffin. He said apologetically, "I hope Jerry who was my friend will know that they came from old Joe Chappy."

---

6   J. A. Emerton, C. E. B. Cranfield, general editors, *The International Critical Commentary of the Holy Scriptures of the Old and New Testaments, Romans, Vol.* 1 (Edinburgh: T&T Clark Limited, 1975), 84.

Serving God with a whole heart includes compassion for the needy in society—the *"barbarian"* and *"foolish"*. No church can fulfill every need of a community. He was also obligated to the *"wise"*. The debt Paul felt was the obligation God laid on him as his called apostle, set apart for the gospel. Going to Rome was not a matter of personal desire, but fulfilling his duty to God. Likewise, every church has an obligation to take the gospel to the entire world to bring people to Christ.

III. Paul Served God with a Whole Heart in Ministry to the Church (11-12)

A. He Desired to Impart a Spiritual Gift

"Gift" is in the singular form. The apostle was not assuming that he would be the source of providing that church with all the spiritual gifts they needed. But he did have something to give. The result of the spiritual gift was to "make you strong". The same word is used at the close of the letter in 16:25. His benediction stated: "Now to him who is able to *establish* you." Jesus told Peter just prior to the cross that when he turned back, or repented, he was to strengthen the brethren. The word carries the thought of confirmation.

A primary goal of the use of our spiritual gifts is not for personal exhilaration, but for the strengthening of others. Too often spiritual gifts are seen as a blessing to us personally instead of their benefit to others.

B. It Was a Two-Way Experience

Paul almost interrupted himself. Rather than giving the impression that he was the great apostle, the knight in shining armor wanting to come to Rome to be the ultimate answer to the church, he immediately said, "That is, that you and I may be mutually encouraged by each other's faith." While preaching as a one-way street is a biblical part of the church, it's not all of it. The pastor doesn't have it all, nor is he self-sufficient. We share together, and are mutually strengthened.

"Encouraged" is a great New Testament word of coming along side and giving courage to another. That is the ministry of the church to itself. Its result is the strengthening of the believers with an outreach in evangelism to people who do not know God through Christ.

Conclusion

Serving God with our whole heart—what does that mean to you and me? Could we write a letter to a friend or family member and say that we serve God with our whole heart? Is this only for full-time Christian workers? Is it not possible to work full-time in secular employment or as a home-maker and still be serving God with your whole heart? The most effective construction worker, home-maker, truck driver, business person, teacher, lawyer, publisher, health-care giver, is the one whose first objective is to serve God with his or her whole heart.

The great preacher of a past generation, Dr. Harry Ironside told of his experience as a youth. His mother was a widow and he got a job working Saturdays and vacations for a Scottish Christian shoe-maker. Bible verses were posted all over the shop. Every package went out with a gospel tract or a word of testimony. Many came to Christ as a result.

Ironside's job was to pound the leather for the soles of the shoes. A piece of cowhide was cut to size, soaked in water, and pounded until it was hard and dry. It was a tiresome job. One day he noticed a different cobbler wasn't finishing the pounding, but nailed on the soles while they were still wet. When asked why, he replied, "So they come back quicker."

Ironside's Christian boss explained why he did it the hard way. "I do not cobble just for 50 or 75 cents from customers. I do it for the glory of God. In heaven, I expect every shoe returned to me in a pile, and I do not want the Lord to say, 'Dan, that was a poor job. You did not do your best.'"

To serve God with our whole heart begins in prayer, and reaches out to include sharing the gospel with the world. We may not receive a letter from a queen, but we will stand face-to-face with the King of kings and give account for our service to Him. When we get to heaven will we have to face the disappointment of having given to the Lord a broken umbrella, or the joy of knowing we gave Him our best? How will you serve the Lord this week?

For your reflection:
- List ways in which you seek to serve the Lord including your service to others.
- How have the current culture divisions in our country made it hard to share your faith?
- There is an increasing hostility toward biblical Christianity. Where have you personally experienced it and how did you cope with it?
- What do you think is an effective way to share the Gospel in our culture?

3

Romans 1:16-17

God's Power is for Everyone

"The English word 'gospel' (from the Anglo-Saxon *god-spell*, i.e., God-story) is the usual New Testament translation of the Greek *euangelion*. According to Tyndale, the renowned English Reformer and Bible translator, it signified 'good, mery, glad and ioyfull tydinge, that maketh a mannes hert glad, and maketh hym synge, daunce, and leepe for ioye' (*Prologue to New Testament*). While his definition is more experiential than explicative, it has touched that inner quality which brings the word to life. The gospel is the joyous proclamation of God's redemptive activity in Christ Jesus on behalf of man enslaved by sin."[7]

Scripture: Romans 1:16-17

Main Idea: Being made righteous, God's powerful work of salvation, is available to all through faith.

"God's righteousness is that by which we become worthy of His great salvation, or through which alone we are (accounted) righteous before Him…. Only the Gospel reveals the righteousness of God, that is, who is righteous, or how a person becomes righteous before God, namely, alone by faith, which trust the Word of God…. It is called the righteousness of God in contradistinction to man's righteousness which comes from works."[8]

---

7   R. H. Mounce, "Gospel", *Evangelical Dictionary of Theology*, Walter A. Elwell, ed., (Grand Rapids, Michigan: Baker Book House, 1984), 472.
8   Luther, 40-41.

Introduction

The core of Christianity is a personal relationship with God. Christianity addresses the matters of right and wrong, heaven and hell, how God designed life to work, but the central factor is God's personal love for each of us and our knowing Him in personal relationship as our Father. No human being is born into the world with that relationship secured. We are born separated from God. The good news, or gospel, of Jesus Christ is that He came to bring us to God. The gospel is God's powerful act of relationship with humankind. Our Scripture expresses it this way:

> *I am not ashamed of the gospel, because it is the power of God for the salvation of everyone who believes: first for the Jew, then for the Gentile. For in the gospel a righteousness from God is revealed, a righteousness that is by faith from first to last, just as it is written: "The righteous will live by faith."*

All Protestants owe a deep debt to Martin Luther. Through the Reformation he instigated, we have received the legacy of a clear understanding of how a person can gain a right relationship with God. Anyone can know God personally, not through the institution of the church or by doing the religious thing, but through faith in what God did for humanity on the cross. Achieving our salvation is God's powerful work and every human being can experience that power.

Luther was born in a peasant home. Like the poor throughout history, they were mistreated by both politicians and religious authorities. As a young man, he set his sights on a career in law and received his master's degree by the age of 22. However, he was deeply troubled on the inside. The Roman Church demanded submission and obedience with the threats of punishment in purgatory if defied. God was inaccessible, and Christ was portrayed as a dreaded judge.

In quest of inner peace, Luther abandoned his law career and entered the Augustinian monastery in Erfurt. But he did not find peace. Into his life came a mentor, John Von Staupitz the vicar of the monastery, who directed Luther into theological studies. It is not clear when Luther came to an understanding of the gospel during his studies. Through the phrase, "the just shall live by faith," his eyes and heart were opened to understand his sins were forgiven through faith in Jesus alone.

These verses are possibly the most important two verses in the entire Bible. All scholars agree they constitute the theme for Romans. They state that God's powerful work of making sinners right with God is available to everyone.

I. We are to be Proud of the Gospel

"I am not ashamed of the gospel" stands in contrast to the way many Christians act. The original meaning of the word *ashamed* was to disfigure or make ugly. In the middle and passive voice, it refers to feeling shame. In our day, the word *shame* is almost a forgotten word. There is very little sense of moral shame left in people. Yet we Christians often feel embarrassed about our faith. Followers of other religions are open and aggressive in talking about their religion, but we often hide our witness. Many are even embarrassed to offer a prayer of thanksgiving in a restaurant. The word for *gospel* means *good news*. It is the good news of God's love and forgiveness through Jesus. We are not to be ashamed of the good news of Jesus' love and saving grace.

Paul wrote to the Corinthians that the gospel message of a crucified Savior appears weak and foolish to the world. There is something in the very nature of the good news of Jesus that is unimpressive in comparison to the world—especially in

American society. We love the grandiose. We are enamored with glitz. We pay our entertainers enormous amounts of money. In our culture, the simple message of John 3:16 is a laugher.

If we had a more glamorous scheme that required a person do a dramatic thing in order to get to heaven, maybe it would capture our imagination. The common thread of false religions and the cults is the requirement to do something to gain eternal life. Luther found that salvation is by grace through faith plus nothing. That still holds today. A right relationship with God is not the result of human power in doing the religious thing or living a good life, it is the power of God's love to forgive and transform us on the inside.

In today's world, Paul's reasons for not being ashamed of the gospel, or for being proud of it, are all the more important. What *seems* weak is in fact the power of an almighty God. It accomplishes its goal of saving lost people—any and all who believe in the Lord Jesus Christ.

We are to be proud of the good news of Jesus...

A. Because It Is God's Power

The word for power is, *dunamis*, and means more than sheer force. It is effective power, power that accomplishes its objective.

The gospel works in the hearts of believing recipients to transform them from sinners to saints, from under judgment to sons and daughters of God. It brings people into a right relationship to God.

We are to be prouder of the gospel than we are of our flag or our personal heritage. We belong to God and have His powerful message to give. Second, we are to be proud of the gospel...

B. Because It Saves

The word, *salvation*, is a broad word. It includes all of God's work in our lives from before our conversion until we are glorified in his presence. Negatively, we are saved from the wrath of an angry God. Positively, we are restored as human beings to our fullest potential. We are made whole people. The gospel is God's effective power at work and that means the goal will be achieved. The preposition, *unto*, means "movement right up to and into," resulting in the actual achievement of salvation.

The good news is Jesus Himself, it is the gospel of Christ. He is the Savior. Paul is not referring to some system of religion, but the person, the Lord Jesus Christ. Paul declared he was not ashamed of Jesus who is God's effective power to deliver us from judgment for sin, and to transform us from sinners to people who do what is right. The gospel doesn't just start us toward heaven with a big push and then its anybody's guess who will make it. It "embraces the totality of the process toward and into salvation."[9]

Third, we are to be proud of the gospel…

C. Because it is Available to Everyone

"*To everyone who believes*" is inclusive. The only qualifier is the word believe. The word, *everyone*, is critically important. No one is left out. The poor, the wealthy, the educated, the unlearned, the slave, the master, children, youth, adults, senior adults, religious, non-religious, are all included. All who believe are the recipients of God's saving power.

There is a definite priority in saying, "*to the Jew first.*" It was historically true—the Jew was the first to hear the gospel

---

9   James D. G. Dunn, Romans 1-8, David A. Hubbard, Glenn W. Barker, General Editors, *Word Biblical Commentary, Vol. 38* (Dallas, Texas: Word Books, Publisher, 1988), 47.

on the day of Pentecost. It is also a statement of priority reflected in the rest of the letter.

II. The Gospel Reveals How We Are Made Right with God

A. The Gospel Is Something God Made Known That We Did Not Know Before

"For in the gospel a righteousness from God is revealed."

Revealed refers to something God has made known to us that we would not have known unless He told us. The present tense is used meaning something that is on-going. It is NOT used in the sense that God is continuing to reveal new truth, or that the Bible is an incomplete book. Rather, throughout the last 2,000 years, right now and in the future until the last bell tolls, God is working in the hearts of people through the gospel to bring them to Himself.

B. The Gospel Makes Us Right with God Because It Solves the Problem of Sin

The whole point of religion is to bridge the gap between sinful people and God. Through the gospel God's power solves the problem of sin by giving to us the righteousness of God Himself.

Righteousness, or a right standing with God, comes "from God." He is the source of it. A right standing with God is not the product of our religious efforts. Just what is righteousness? I usually think of righteousness in terms of a moral and ethical norm that reflects a holy God. However, James Dunn effectively argued that the Hebrew concept of righteousness was centered in relationship. When applied to God, it referred to His covenant relationship to His people in which He remained faithful to "restore his own and to sustain them within the covenant" (Dunn, 41). This verse speaks of how we can come into a personal relationship with God. God did everything necessary for us to have a personal relationship with Him. Then He told us what He did for us in Christ.

Righteousness carries two concepts. One, a right relationship with God, and two, right behavior. We have a right relationship God, and we are in process of becoming righteous in character now. Both are brought about by God's power.

C. A Right Relationship with God is Experienced Through Faith

"A righteousness that is by faith from first to last, just as it is written: 'The righteous will live by faith.'"

It literally reads "from faith to faith"—from the faithfulness of God to His promises, to the response of faith by us. Faith carries two ideas: 1) believing, or being convinced by the evidence, that the gospel is truth; and, 2) trust in a personal reliance upon Jesus.

The word for faith also is in the present tense. Its significance lies in the true character of faith. American evangelicalism has been enamored with a faulty view of faith that one termed "decision salvation". Faith is not a one-time thing done at some special event. When a person hears of God's love in Christ, there is an initial response. But faith continues to go on trusting in Jesus in a full commitment of our lives to Him. Anything short of that is bogus Christianity.

Conclusion

There was another minister who came two centuries after Martin Luther. He was an Anglican, a don at Oxford University. John Wesley was a preacher's kid, his mother an exceptionally beautiful, pious, and brilliant woman. He was one of 19 children, only nine of whom lived to be adults. His mother home-schooled her children in Latin, Greek, history, literature, and religion. When he entered the university, he continued with the discipline of saying prayers, reading the Bible, and going to church. He was frustrated in his spiritual life with the internal struggle against sin. He read books, visited prisons, assisted the poor and sick. Wesley described his struggle as searching for a right relationship with God by works, not by faith.

Wesley left his post to preach in the new land of America and came to Savannah, Georgia. There he encountered the Moravians who impressed him because they were so sure of their faith. Upon returning to Britain, he attended a home meeting of a group of Moravians on Aldersgate. Someone in the group read from Luther's preface to his commentary on Romans. Wesley's heart was "strangely warmed."

Hear it in his own words: "In the evening I went very unwillingly to a society in Aldersgate street, where one was reading Luther's preface to the *Epistle to the Romans*. About a quarter before nine, while he was describing the change which God works in the heart through faith in Christ, I felt my heart strangely warmed. I felt I did trust in Christ, Christ alone for salvation; and an assurance was given me that He had taken away *my* sins, even *mine*, and saved *me* from the law of sin and death".[10]

Have you come to trust in Christ alone as your Savior? If not, what do you need to do? First, acknowledge the fact of your sin. Second, acknowledge you can't take away your own sin, you need the Savior. Third, state your personal trust in Jesus Christ as your Savior and your desire to walk with Him all your life.

---

10   Hugh T. Kerr and John M. Mulder, *Conversions* (Grand Rapids, Michigan: William B. Eerdmans Publishing Company, 1983), 59.

Later in Romans 10:9-10 Paul wrote: "If you confess with your mouth, 'Jesus is Lord,' and believe in your heart that God raised him from the dead, you will be saved. For it is with your heart that you believe and are justified, and it is with your mouth that you confess and are saved."

For your reflection"
- Why can we be proud of the Gospel?
- To whom does the Gospel apply?
- What makes the Gospel effective?

Do I Have to be GOOD to go to Heaven?

4

Romans 1:18-23

What Happens to People Who Haven't Heard About Jesus?

"God has written, on every human conscience and consciousness, enough of His mighty name to make them accountable at His judgment seat, and given sufficient conception of right and wrong to make them guilty when they disobey the instincts of conscience. And they have disobeyed. The testimony of missionaries in all lands is that they have never found a human soul without this instinct of a guilty conscience, and a sense of wrong, and without some idea of worship, some conception of God, and some method of propitiating the invisible powers for conscious will."[11]

Scripture: Romans 1:18-23

Main Idea: People in remote places or crowded cities who have not heard the gospel of Jesus Christ are lost and subject to the wrath of God.

Introduction

Our granddaughter, Britton, has a stuffed animal, "Bear-Bear" (This was 1996, she is now married and a mother herself and pastor's wife). You must not call it, "Bear". It is "Bear-Bear". Over the years she has carried it with her, talked to it, played imaginative games with it. Even now, "Bear-Bear" has a special place in her life. Its cute and we love it. She

---

11 A. B. Simpson, *Christ in the Bible Series, Vol. XVII* (Harrisburg, Pa: Christian Publications, Inc., n.d.), 49-50.

got this propensity from her mother. Cindy had a stuffed dog named "Fred". Fred was named after a member of a church in which we served when she was little. He went through two total rebuilds over the years. She nearly walked down the isle with Fred on her wedding day. The whole thing is innocent. "Bear-Bear" was manufactured, but has taken on a life and personality given it by Britton.

What is not innocent is humanity's manufacture of gods. Isaiah wrote of the absurdity of gods made of wood, metal or stone.

> *"Is there any God besides me? No, there is no other Rock; I know not one." All who make idols are nothing, and the things they treasure are worthless. Those who would speak up for them are blind; they are ignorant, to their own shame. Who shapes a god and casts an idol, which can profit him nothing? He and his kind will be put to shame; craftsmen are nothing but men. Let them all come together and take their stand; they will be brought down to terror and infamy. The blacksmith takes a tool and works with it in the coals; he shapes an idol with hammers, he forges it with the might of his arm. He gets hungry and loses his strength; he drinks no water and grows faint.*

> *"The carpenter measures with a line and makes an outline with a marker; he roughs it out with chisels and marks it with compasses. He shapes it in the form of man, of man in all his glory, that it may dwell in a shrine. He cut down cedars, or perhaps took a cypress or oak. He let it grow among the trees of the forest, or planted a pine, and the rain made it grow. It is man's fuel for burning; some of it he takes and warms himself, he kindles a fire and bakes bread. But he also fashions a god and worships it; he makes an idol and bows down to it. Half of the wood he burns in the fire; over it he prepares his meal, he roasts his meat and eats his fill. He also warms himself and says, "Ah! I am warm; I see the fire." From the rest he makes a*

> *god, his idol; he bows down to it and worships. He prays to it and says, "Save me; you are my god." They know nothing, they understand nothing; their eyes are plastered over so they cannot see, and their minds closed so they cannot understand. No one stops to think, no one has the knowledge or understanding to say, "Half of it I used for fuel; I even baked bread over its coals, I roasted meat and I ate. Shall I make a detestable thing from what is left? Shall I bow down to a block of wood?" (44:8-18).*

In reality, worshiping idols is virtually the same thing as "Bear-Bear". The worshiper believes the idol hears, can answer prayer, will act in changing his or her life. That's the tragedy and absurdity. Britton has grown out of "Bear-Bear", but the idol worshiper will go to hell in his or her fantasy world.

Most Americans do not worship idols, but a large segment of the population are willing to say its not a big deal. A person can choose to worship anything they wish. It is true anyone can worship whatever they wish, but it is a big deal for not all religions lead to heaven. All, except Jesus Christ lead to hell. That may seem terribly bigoted to some, and it is. At the heart of the discussion is truth—which religions deliver the goods? Will this given system of belief link me up to God and take me to heaven when I die? The Christian takes at face-value the word of Jesus: "I am the way, the truth, and the life, no one comes to the Father except through me." Idolatry, New Age religion, the major religions of the world, all religious systems, are rejections of the worship of the true God through his Son, Jesus Christ.

I have heard people say that it's not *fair* for God to judge those who have not had a chance to hear the gospel. There are at least two things wrong with our judgment of what is "fair". First, we are not in a position to be informing God on this issue. Second, those without Christ and even those without a Bible, are not without a source of knowing the truth. That is why God is angry.

I. God is Angry with Sin and the Promotion of False Religion

To properly understand what God is saying in this passage we need to answer some questions:

A. Who is the Lost Person?

It is anyone who has not heard of Jesus, who doesn't have the Bible, or who has chosen to reject the Bible and its central message.

A German scholar wrote a century ago: The lost person [heathen] is not a follower of a "primeval religion, from which man might gradually [rise] to the knowledge of the true God, but is [one who has fallen] away from the known original revelation of the true God in His works."[12]

Simply, religion has not evolved on an upward plane, it has degenerated. Man has turned his back on the light of true revelation. A person is born lost until he or she submits to the Gospel. The Bible says everyone is lost.

B. What Happens to "Lost" People? (21)

"For although they knew God, they neither glorified him as God nor gave thanks to him, but their thinking became futile and their foolish hearts were darkened."

Futile thinking and darkened, foolish hearts describe people as religious beings. A *foolish heart* is one without understanding. That is fully evident when religion is looked at with objectivity. Included is the peacock pageantry of

---

12   H.A.W. Meyer, quoted by John Murray, *The Epistle to the Romans, The New International Commentary on the New Testament*, F. F. Bruce, General Editor, Vol. I (Grand Rapids, Michigan: Wm B. Eerdmans Publishing Co., 1959), 41.

religion, many of the absurd rituals of religious practices, the arrogant cockiness of secular humanism which deifies man, the bankruptcy of ancestral worship, and the enslaving fear of spirit worship and its witch doctors. People around the world are lost—they don't know who God is nor how to find Him.

God is not angry because people are lost, He is angry because they have rejected His saving love on their behalf. He is angry because we have "suppressed the truth by our wickedness." He is angry because He has made Himself known and we have rejected that self-disclosure in favor of creating idols and every kind of religious system to escape the true, living, almighty God. God has made His existence "plain" to us. His "invisible qualities—his eternal power and divine nature"—are clearly seen in creation. The immensity of the universe, the power of nature in the storms that bring massive destruction, the beauty of the desert flower and delicate rose, the variety of animal life all testify to the power of God and His design in creation. He is angry with a jealous love because we have rejected His true love in pursuit of false lovers who will abuse and trash us. He is angry because we are determined to follow behaviors that will ultimately destroy us.

Though the founding fathers of our country based their thinking upon the existence of God, we have turned away from that supposition in favor of a pluralism that makes all religions equal. We have rejected the primacy of the spiritual core of the human being. The result: we are ethically bankrupt.

Apologist and evangelist, Ravi Zacharias, wrote in *Can Man Live Without God*:

> "Time and again it [has been proven] that it is not possible to establish a reasonable and coherent ethical theory *without first establishing the tēlos, i.e. the purpose and destiny of human life.* Even Kant concluded that without

a *telos* it all got wrongheaded. If life itself is purposeless, ethics falls into disarray. As Dostoevsky said, if God is dead everything is justifiable.

"This, may I suggest, is North America's predicament. This is the albatross around our educators' necks. This is the goad that keeps stabbing away at us as we bleed one another. We continue to talk of values and ethics; we persist in establishing moral boundaries for others while erasing the lines that are drawn for life itself. If my happiness is a right and the ultimate goal of life, why worry about anyone else's claims to happiness? And if I *must* worry about someone else's happiness, whose—and why his or hers, and not another's? If life is pointless, why should ethics serve any purpose except my own? If I am merely the product of matter and at the mercy of material determinism, why should I subject myself to anyone else's moral convictions?"[13]

II. The Lost Person Has Rejected God

Their rejection is seen in a refusal to accept God's self-disclosure.

A. People Refuse to Accept God's Self-Disclosure

Paul argues that God has spoken very plainly to all humanity in creation. Anyone who is alive, whether they have a Bible and can read it or not, can "read" creation. Creation says there is an eternal creative power who is God. The question must be asked: "Why is there something instead of nothing?"

Tertullian, an early church father wrote: "It was not the pen of Moses that initiated the knowledge of the Creator.... The vast majority of mankind, though they had never heard

---

13   Ravi Zacharias, *Can Man Live Without God?* (Nashville, Tenn.: Harper Collins, 1994), 30-40)

the name of Moses—to say nothing of his book—know the God of Moses none-the-less." Murray Eden, an MIT scientist, some years ago used a computer to calculate the possibility of whether there could be so much complexity in the universe within any acceptable amount of time on the basis of chance. His conclusion was zero possibility.

God has made His existence plain, clearly perceivable, but we have rejected that knowledge. Our thinking is futile, and our hearts are without understanding and darkened because we have chosen to turn out the lights of truth. As a result, God is angry with sophisticated Americans and primitive third world people in the bush because of their rejection of His self-disclosure. The rejection of God is also seen in...

B. People Prefer Their Own gods to <u>the</u> God

James Dunn comments:

> "By closing the eye of understanding which has the capacity to receive and recognize God's self-revelation, they shut off the light of the mind and left it fumbling with inane trifles and relatively worthless side issues. Their whole intellectual and emotional life ('heart') by thus demonstrating this foolishness became clouded and less capable of receiving or responding to that light. In other words, by withholding the appropriate recognition of God they became less (not more) able to function as rational beings; failure to recognize their own creatureliness brought with it a decreasing ability to function as a human being."[14]

Paul lists three things in a descending spiral to spiritual bankruptcy that mankind has done to evoke the anger of God:

---

[14] Dunn, 71.

1. They refused to glorify God as God. We do not want to face the fact that God is God and He made us, not the other way around.

2. They were unthankful. It is a slur upon God when we gripe about how He runs things. Adam and Eve were no longer satisfied with the pleasantries of Eden. They lusted for more. The road to sensuality leads to greater thirst, not satisfaction.

Paul wrote to the Ephesians: "They live blindfold in a world of illusion, and are cut off from the life of God through ignorance and insensitiveness. They have stifled their consciences and then surrendered themselves to sensuality, practicing any form of impurity which lust can suggest" (4:18ff Philipps' paraphrase).

3. While claiming to be wise, they acted like fools. Notice another descending scale in objects of worship:

They exchanged the glory of the immortal God for images made like mortal man, then images of birds, of animals, and finally of reptiles. This is the best humans can do unaided by God's revelation.

Paul took a statement from Psalm 106:20. Israel rejected the LORD who had dramatically and powerfully brought them out of Egypt. In God's place, they made the golden calf and declared it had done the miracles.

Daniel told of Babylon's Nebuchadnezzar who had erected a nine-story golden image of himself and demanded all to bow before it in worship. In the Revelation, the worship of the image and the beast are brought together at the end time in the person of the antichrist and the false prophet.

Paul directly attacked the intellectual community of the Greeks. In their pride and multiplicity of gods they had not found God. They had idols, myths, sensual worship, but failed to find God in it all.

- Zeus was the god of the sky and was worshiped at Olympia where the Pan-Hellenic games were held in his honor.
- Hera was the goddess of marriage.
- Athena was the maiden goddess of war and the arts.
- Apollo was the protector of the crops and the flocks. He was the god of music and prophecy.
- Artemis was the queen of the wild creatures and the mother of life in plants and animals.

"How long, O men, will you turn my glory into shame? How long will you love delusions and seek false gods?" asked the psalmist (4:2).

Egyptian gods included the crocodile, beetle, and frog. That's the best they could come up with. Pretty ignorant for smart people. After all, they built the Pyramids. Have we done any better than the ancients? What is your god?

Application

We're back to "Bear-Bear". It's innocent enough for a two-year-old little girl to carry around her stuffed bear. It's really okay for us older folks to bring our stuffed animals to church, too. But it makes God angry when people worship man-made idols, birds, animals, or reptiles. It angers Him when we turn our back on His clear self-disclosure in creation.

Because it is so easy to see God and to know Him, because we have stubbornly chosen to reject the light of His truth, "men are without excuse." Isaiah warned: "But those who trust in idols, who say to images, 'You are our gods,' will be turned back in utter shame" (42:17). Idolatry is not just the worship of idols. It is accepting non-gods in whatever form as deities and objects of worship. The end-result of the anger of God is eternal separation from Him in hell.

The end-result of His love for us is that all who 'read' His self-disclosure in creation, in the Bible, and most completely in Jesus Christ, will be forgiven and will receive eternal life. Jesus came to save lost people. One of the two major reasons this church exists is to share that good news.

What do you and I need to do to receive God's gift of eternal life?
- Acknowledge the fact of our lostness and sin.
- Make a personal commitment to trust Jesus and to become His follower.

Eternal life is God's gift to sinful people and turns away His wrath. Will you receive Jesus who is that life?

For your refection:
- Culture's correctness is that it is arrogant and discriminatory for Christians to claim their God is the only true God. What is your response?
- Why do you think God is justified to be angry with unbelieving humanity?
- As creatures with free will, why should a person be condemned for exercising that right?

5

Romans 1:24-32

Why Do Good People Do Bad Things?

"'Hear ye! Hear ye! Court is now in session!' Paul could have used those awesome words at this point in his letter, because Romans 1:18 is the door that leads us into God's courtroom. The theme of Romans is the righteousness of God, but Paul had to begin with the unrighteousness of man. Until man knows he is a sinner, he cannot appreciate the gracious salvation God offers in Jesus Christ. Paul followed the basic Bible pattern: first Law and condemnation; then grace and salvation."[15]

Scripture: Romans 1:24-32

Main Idea: Sinful behaviors are a result of shutting God out of life. Sin retrogresses until a depraved mind calls evil, good, and good, evil.

Introduction

This week (1996) we were sickened by two news stories, each with its own horror. One was the horror of Dunblane by the Highlands of Ireland. Thomas Hamilton, 43, known to the kids as "Mr. Creepy", boldly walked into a kindergarten class and opened fire killing 16 little children and their teacher and wounding 12 others. Two of three doctors threw-up when they walked into the gym.

---

15 Warren W. Wiersbe, *Be Right: A practical guide to discover how to be right with God, yourself, others* (Wheaton, Illinois: Victor Books, 1978)21.

The other horror was the cold-blooded murder of Kathleen Weinstein, a special-ed teacher and mother, by a 17-year-old who simply wanted her Toyota Camry. Though she reasoned with him calmly and gave every opportunity out, he took her life.

How would these two men describe themselves? Would they call themselves bad people? I think probably not. They most likely thought of themselves as ordinary people with some problems or frustrations, but not as evil people.

Why do good people do bad things? I have talked with a lot of different people over the course of my life, and I have yet to find someone who thinks he or she is a bad person. Yet every day we are hit with the ugly news of horrible things people do to other people.

George Washington said in his "Farewell Address:"

"Of all the dispositions and habits which lead to political prosperity, religion and morality are indispensable supports. In vain would that man claim the tribute of patriotism, who should labor to subvert these great pillars.... Whatever may be conceded to the influence of refined education...reason and experience both forbid us to expect that national morality can prevail in exclusion of religious principle."

Contrast that with a description of existential thought that has dominated our society's standards and behaviors in the last 50 years.

"Existence precedes essence. The subjective overrides the objective. What I feel is more important than what is. What I do determines what I am. 'I do what I do because it feels good, and I will continue to do it even if it doesn't feel good to you.'"[16]

---

16   Ravi Zacharias sermon: "Why I am Not an Atheist"

WHY DO GOOD PEOPLE DO BAD THINGS?

While we have seen a moral plunge in our country, we have simply backed up to where humanity has been throughout the ages. Paul stated that God is angry with people because we have wickedly suppressed the truth. Not wanting to glorify God as God and being unthankful, our thinking became futile and our foolish hearts were darkened. The result—a list of sinful behaviors.

If you have wondered why we are in the moral morass and confusion we're in, this passage will help you find an answer. The dynamic prophet, John the Baptist, said to his generation, "The ax is already at the root of the trees, and every tree that does not produce good fruit will be cut down and thrown into the fire" (Matthew 5:10). Let's take this metaphor of a tree to identify the roots of the tree of sin and the fruit those roots produce as found in Romans 1:24-32.

I. The Roots of the Tree of Sin (25)

The first root that produces sin is....

A. Exchanging the Truth for a Lie

"They exchanged the truth of God for a lie, and worshipped and served created things rather than the Creator—who is forever praised. Amen."

The truth is there is one God, the Almighty, the Creator, the God of Abraham, Isaac and Jacob, the Father of our Lord Jesus Christ. When people turn away from that God, they overtly or inadvertently turn to a lie as their god and the end result is the fostering of sinful behaviors.

The second root that produces our sin is. . .

B. Worshipping the Creature Rather Than the Creator

Human beings are by creation religious beings. When we rejected the living God, we were forced to replace God with non-existent gods fashioned in form like humans, birds, animals and reptiles.

Ideas and the actions that flow from them have consequences. Paul argued that when mankind chose to reject God, God acted in return. Just because a philosopher or theologian states God has died, or that He doesn't exist does not cause God to go into a panic. However, such thoughts and actions do have a consequence. God let people go to follow their sinful drives to their final consequence. As the roots produce a tree, so these ideas of rejecting God and replacing Him with the creature have consequences.

II. The Fruit of the Tree of Sin (26-32)

The first category of fruit is...

A. Sexual Sins (25,26-27)

"Therefore, God gave them over in the sinful desires of their hearts to sexual impurity for the degrading of their bodies with one another.... Because of this, God gave them over to shameful lusts. Even their women exchanged natural relations for unnatural ones. In the same way, the men also abandoned natural relations with women and were inflamed with lust for one another. Men committed indecent acts with other men, and received in themselves the due penalty for their perversion."

1. The emphasis is on God's action. The phrase, "God gave them over" occurs also in verses 25, 26, and 28. It does not mean that God compels people to sin, rather He stops holding us back. The only power that keeps us from going our full distance into degradation is the preventive power of a loving God. When we close out God, God lets us pursue our sin until it literally destroys us physically and spiritually, the final end being hell.

Malcolm Muggeridge stated, "If God is dead, somebody is going to have to take his place. Either megalomania or erotomania, the drive for power or the drive for pleasure, the clenched fist or the phallus, Hitler or Hugh Heffner."[17] We have obviously opted for erotomania, though we spend billions on power to assure us that no outsider will rob us of our headlong run for a hedonistic orgasm. The phrase, "sinful desire," represents a person who accepts no higher criterion for value than his or her own desires for pleasure.

We have slammed the door on the God of the Bible, and have chosen to bow at the shrine of sensualism. We have exchanged the truth for a lie. The erotic world tells our youth that sex will give you worth because you are proving you are desirable. The truth is that sex outside of marriage undermines a healthy self-esteem. Sex is unique because of the level of intimacy built into the experience. The Bible says the two become one flesh. In reality a person is giving part of themselves away in sex which means some people have scattered themselves all over the globe and wonder why they can't find themselves.

2. It is not without reason that the first category of sin listed is sexual. First, because it is the most powerful pleasure the human being experiences, it dominates our desires. Second, it is the primary metaphor God used to communicate the sacred intimacy of His love for us. A futile mind takes the most holy and makes it the most defiled, and that's how human beings have behaved throughout the centuries.

3. There cannot be any doubt that these two verses denounce homosexual relations. No honest exegesis could come to any other conclusion. Sexual lust, like any other lust, will degenerate into perversions when it is considered the

---

17   Quoted by Ravi Zacharias, *A Shattered Visage: The Real Face of Atheism* (Brentwood, Tennessee: Wolgemuth & Hyatt, Publishers, Inc., 1990), 25.

means of fulfillment and happiness. God has created us with an internal guidance system directed to Him. We will only find satisfaction in God. When we knock out our guidance system, we are plainly lost.

Though the Greco/Roman world knew nothing about AIDS, they were very familiar with homosexuality. It was celebrated and praised, especially the relationship of an adult male and a young boy. Paul spoke of their receiving "in themselves the due penalty for their perversion." The word for "receiving" has a prefix that indicates the deservedness of the punishment.[18]

In terse and direct language, theologian Harold O. J. Brown wrote: "Whatever else the AIDS epidemic has done, it has brought most public discourse on sexual matters down into what Sorokin called the social sewers. The prevailing assumption in all this health-related discussion is that human beings have no more control over their sexual behavior than dogs...in heat." [19]

Dr. Ed Payne (MD), commenting on the fact that three-fourths of all cases of AIDS traceable to sodomy and/or drug abuse. "The 'fueling' of the epidemic is dependent upon the behaviors that spread it. There is no AIDS epidemic. There is only an epidemic of the behaviors that are deadly within themselves."[20]

Andres Tapia wrote in Christianity Today that in the past two years (written 1996) AIDS among 14- to 23- year-olds has gone up 72%. One out of 500 college students is HIV positive. Some 6,000 teenagers contract an STD each day, with one in seven teens infected. There are over 30 different STDs today

---

18   C. E. B. Cranfield, *The Epistle to the Romans: a critical and exegetical commentary* (Edinburgh: T. & T. Clark Limited, 1987), 127.
19   Harold O. J. Brown, *Religion & Society Report*, April 1992.
20   Ed Payne, *Biblical Reflections on Modern Medicine*, May 1995.

compared to only four twenty years ago. The attitude of our society is illustrated by a vote on the HIV/AIDS Advisory Council of the Board of Education in New York City. In one of the first meetings this statement was overwhelmingly defeated, "Children should not be having sex."[21] These are old stats, but sexual promiscuity continues in our culture and around the world in most others.

The second category of sinful fruit is a wide variety of behaviors...

B. A Variety of Sinful Behaviors (28-32)

Verses 29-31 contain a list of 21 sinful attitudes and behaviors. Paul begins with a repetition of the basic sin involved: "they did not think it worthwhile t retain the knowledge of God." "Worthwhile" means to approve by testing. Because of our desires to pursue our own agenda of pleasure, we have decided to not take God seriously. We want heaven, because that sounds like a good place to go when we die. The polls say Americans believe in Jesus, His death and resurrection. About 40% go to church each week. But our religious activities have very little influence on our moral values and behaviors. People commit fornication and adultery during the week and go to church on Sunday, and don't see the problem.

That is what Paul calls a reprobate or depraved mind. A depraved mind is a mind abandoned or rejected by God and therefore not fit for anything worthy of His esteem. It is one that is rejected as worthless. A depraved mind calls evil, good, and good, evil. A depraved mind has nothing to do with intelligence or education, but moral degeneracy.

---

21   Andres Tapia, "Abstinence: the Radical Choice for Sex Ed," *Christianity Today*, Feb. 8, 1992, 24-29.

This list can be grammatically divided into three groups. The phrase "filled with" describes the entire list, not just the first sin. Group 1 includes "every kind of wickedness"—a generic term that would include all sins that follow—"evil, greed and adultery." Cranfield described "greed" as "the ruthless self-assertion of the 'man who will pursue his own interests with complete disregard for the rights of others.'"[22] The next group is "envy, murder, strife, deceit and malice." Then follow "gossips, slanderers, God-haters, insolent, arrogant and boastful; they invent ways of doing evil; they disobey parents." Kids, look at the sins that surround being disobedient. Is God serious about your attitude and behavior toward your parents? Then he wraps it up saying, "they are senseless, faithless, heartless, ruthless."

The last verse is the ultimate depravity. Knowing it brings God's judgment, these people cheer others on in their sin. Our degenerate talk shows abundantly illustrate this is where our culture is at this moment.

Conclusion

The magazines and newscasts have all raised the question: How could the horrors of repeated terrorist attacks throughout Europe, the East and our country take place? Why do ordinarily good people do evil things? Social scientists and psychologists will propose a variety of reasons, but the Bible is very clear that every human being is born with a love of evil. Evil is nurtured and grows exponentially when God is put into the back seat and trivialized.

The nation is awakening to an alarming growth of vicious crimes committed by youth. They have no remorse, no regrets, no conscience. There is a generation of Menendez-type people. The Menendez brothers brutally murdered their father

---

22 Cranfield, 130.

and mother and demonstrated no regret. A movie has been produced on the sordid story. Young mothers abandon their babies in dumpsters, people install alarm systems in their cars and homes, and many are afraid to venture outside, even in daylight.

In the face of a barrage of threatening news in our 24/7 news cycle, the believer can take refuge in the same God as David who repeatedly declared Him to be a tower of safety. That is true even when believers are slaughtered or burned to death as in Nero's time or ours.

God's answer to the sinful heart is forgiveness and heart transformation. Jesus came, lived, died and rose again to make us new creations. If anyone is in Christ, he is a new creation. Through Jesus we are born again and receive new life. He can change the worst of sinners, and has done so from Paul down to contemporary society. He can change your heart, too. You may see yourself as a good person, but we are all sinners who need to be forgiven. Until we are changed by God, we are capable of the worst of crimes if the situation is right.

Good people do bad things because we shut God out. Inside, we have a love of sin. Sin is a powerful, driving, controlling force in human behavior. That is why we need a Savior. Christians do sinful things because they refuse to look at sin and its causes and bring it to the cross to be crucified with Christ.

The good news is God loves us as sinners. Jesus came to bring forgiveness and to release us from rage and its behaviors. He came to change us on the inside which means it's okay to face our sins and bring them to Him. He is NOT angry with people who bring their sins to Him—no matter how bad those are. He is only angry with us when we slam the door on Him and say He is not the answer to the human need. He is angry and will judge in damnation all who will not face their sins and come to Him for salvation.

Will you come to Jesus to be cleansed of your sin? He is waiting with open arms to welcome you into His love and acceptance.

For your reflection:
- What is the relationship of the lostness of humanity to the missions' movement of the last 150 years?
- Why is God fair in limiting the options of salvation to Jesus as the only way to God?

6

Romans 2:1-11

Which Way Does the Finger Point?

"Paul's style is that appropriate to the type of composition which the ancients called diatribe, in which questions or objections are put into the mouth of an imagined critic in order to be answered or demolished. One can almost envisage him has he dictates his letter, suddenly picking out the complacent individual who has been enjoying the exposure of those sins he 'has no mind to', and telling him that he is no better than anyone else."[23]

Scripture: Romans 2:1-11

Main Idea: Our judgment of others is an exposure of our own sin, a rejection of God's kindness, and will assure God's judgment unless we turn from our sin and do good.

Introduction

My little 5'4" mother used to point her finger at me and say, "Now Roy, you be a good boy." She also was very good at using that finger to reprimand me when I was bad.

The basic thrust of the first chapter is to establish the justice of God's anger against humanity's sin. Paul's goal is to prove that everyone in the world needs a Savior. Some of the sins listed often capture the headlines of attention, but there are others we can too easily pass over: greed, envy,

---

23   F. F. Bruce, *Romans, Tyndale New Testament Commentaries*, revised edition (Grand Rapids, Michigan: Wm B. Eerdmans Publishing Co., 1989), 81-82.

strife, deceit, malice, gossip, slander, insolence, arrogance and boastfulness, parental disobedience, senseless, faithless, heartless, applauding sin.

Many of us would quickly denounce these and the grosser sins in the list, and we feel we are not touched by the list. Paul says to us, "No way! You are without excuse, you, whoever you are."

Is there anyone who has never, and I do mean never, said, "You, he, she, they should not have...?" I seriously doubt it.

It is the religious, self-righteously smug, whom Paul addresses in this passage. The style of writing is polemical in which an imaginary person has responded to his statements in chapter one saying, "Those categories are not pertinent to me." Who is this imaginary debater? Some scholars think it is Paul himself recalling his self-righteous life as a Pharisee, sharing the inner thoughts he had before he came to Christ.[24] Let's look at his argument.

I. Judging Others (Pointing the Finger) Is Self-Judgment (3 Fingers Pointing Back) (1-3)

A. To Judge Another is an Exposé of Our Own Sin

Who is the "you" at the beginning of the verse? It is the religious who feel their good works remove them from God's wrath. It is the self-righteous who see the sins of everyone else, but not of themselves. Specifically, Paul is addressing the Jew who felt that their special place as a descendant of Abraham removed them from the judgment of God. Those people felt they were saved by virtue of being a Jew. That is the same thing as people in America who feel they must be okay with God because they are Americans or have Christian parents. We all want to plead a special case situation to exempt

---

24   Dunn, 91.

our sinful behavior from the wrath of God. We feel we don't deserve to go to hell.

Worse, our culture has embraced humanism which denies the sinfulness of humanity. We are basically good. The cause of evil is the system or one's environment. If that is so, guess who created the negative environment. I can guarantee us it wasn't a bunch of Redwood trees or the massive waterfalls of Yosemite. Sinful people, with twisted, evil hearts do sinful things. The problem with Larry Don McQuay (USA Today 4/5/96, convicted child molester) is not a deprived environment of some sort, but an evil heart controlled by lust. That cannot be removed by surgery. Theodore Kaczynski's (Unabomber) problem is not lack of a decent family, brains or an education. He has an evil, callused heart. Goethe said to Eckermann in a conversation: "Man is a darkened being, he knows little of the world, and least of himself. I know not myself, and God forbid that I should."[25] The Bible describes us as sinners who need a Savior to change our hearts.

Our Scripture states the good moral person has no case, no excuse, no 'out' from the wrath of God. The very act of pointing one's finger against another's wrong actions, results in three pointing back at ourselves. There are no special cases with God. It is clear-cut. To judge another is an expose of our own failures and sin.

B. Therefore, we are Without Excuse Before God

When God points the finger of judgment, it is based upon truth. What God defines as sin is sin. When God says a person has lied, he or she is a liar. It is truth, it fits the facts of the universe as God has established it, not as we would like to make it.

---

25   Donald Grey Barnhouse: *Romans* Vol I, Part 2 (Fincastle, Virginia: Scripture Truth Book Company,1953), 14.

If we are capable of judging accurately, we can be sure God will accurately judge us. It is true, that most of the time when someone points the finger at someone or something and says it is wrong, it probably is wrong. If sinful humans can judge right and wrong accurately, we can be sure when God judges us based upon truth, it will be accurate.

The late Francis Schaeffer said if a new-born baby were equipped with a tape recorder that activated every time a moral statement was made, the lifetime recording would serve as the basis of God's judging that person. God says: "On the basis of your own words, have you kept these moral standards?" Everyone would be condemned by their own words. Schaeffer wrote: "No person in all the world has kept the moral standards with which he has tried to bind others.... The whole world will stand totally condemned before God in utter justice, because they will be judged not upon what they have known, but upon what they have known and have not kept."[26] The second point of his argument is...

II. Self-Justification (Rejecting the 3 Fingers Pointing Back) Shows Contempt for the Kindness of God (4)

A. God Responds to Our Sin with Kindness

Three powerful words describe God's attitude and action toward sinners: "kindness, tolerance, and patience."

- "Kindness" is the pure goodness of God that has no hidden ill motives.

- "Tolerance" means God has called a truce to the expression of His just anger against sin. It is not a carte blanche to go on sinning because lightning hasn't struck.

---

26   Frances A Schaeffer, *How Should We Then Live? : The rise and decline of western thought and culture* (London : Marshall Morgan & Scott, 1980), 113.

- "Patience" refers to a person who has power to avenge himself and doesn't.

In the record-breaking Broadway musical, *Les Misérables*, the central figure, Jean Valjean, has the opportunity to avenge himself of the bitter treatment he received of Inspector Javert. When Javert is discovered by the students of the French revolution to be a spy, he is turned over to Valjean for execution. Instead of executing him, Valjean fakes a shooting and allows Javert to escape. Finally, haunted by the kindness of Valjean, the inspector cannot cope with his own judgmental spirit contrasted with the former thief's kindness. He commits suicide by jumping into the Seine River.

God has every right to proceed with His wrath, and one day He will. But now we experience His kindness and patience.

Contempt for the kindness of God is a refusal to accept the fact of one's sin and the need of a Savior. It denies there are three fingers pointing back, or that those sins are not enough to damn one's soul in hell. Our determination to make ourselves look good and not in need of a Savior is the supreme expression of the arrogance and sinful heart of the human being.

B. His Kindness is Designed to Lead Us to Repentance

The reason God has not acted in judgment is not to give us a false sense of security, but to give us time to respond to Him in repentance.

Repentance means to have a change of mind. To the Jew, it was a change of mind about his condition before God. Being a descendant of Abraham was not enough. To you, it may mean a change of mind in assuming that because you have attended church all your life, or that God has answered a prayer for you, or that you are a highly moral person, you are a Christian.

The word for "lead" means to compel, to put pressure on. God's kindness in delaying His wrath is His way of putting pressure on us to push us to repent of our sin and believe on the Lord Jesus Christ.

Misinterpreting God's kindness can lead to a callousness toward God that produces a stubborn and rebellious heart. The third point of Paul's argument:

III. The Crucial Issue is Our Response to God's Finger Pointing at Us (5-11)

A. Persisting in Sin Increases the Reservoir of God's Wrath Against Us (5-6)

Not only do we show contempt for God's kindness when we refuse to repent of our sin, we actually store up wrath like bank deposits. Paul charges that we have hard and impenitent hearts. The ancient Hebrew people demonstrated that quality repeatedly. Pharaoh brought disaster upon himself, his nation and people because of his hardened heart. Humanity hasn't changed over the centuries. We may have more technical knowledge but our hearts are just as stubborn and impenitent as people were 3500 years ago.

The principle of verse 6 is given in Psalm 62:12: "God 'will give to each person according to what he has done.'" It is individual— "each". It is universal— "each person". It is fairly based on their own behavioral record— "according to what he has done."

The "day of God's wrath" is nothing to be casual about. Are you ready to risk eternity? The prophet Zephaniah wrote extensively about God's wrath.

> *(1:15) "That day will be a day of wrath, a day of distress and anguish, a day of trouble and ruin, a day of darkness and gloom, a day of clouds and blackness... (1:18). Neither their silver nor their gold will be able to save them on the day of the Lord's wrath. In the fire of his jealousy the whole world will be consumed, for he will make a sudden end of all who live in the earth... (2:2). Before the appointed time arrives and that day sweeps on like chaff, before the fierce anger of the LORD comes upon you, before the day of the Lord's wrath comes upon you (3:8). "Therefore, wait for me," declares the LORD, "for the day I will stand up to testify. I have decided to assemble the nations, to gather the kingdoms and to pour out my wrath on them—all my fierce anger. The whole world will be consumed by the fire of my jealous anger."*

B. A Perfect Life Free of Sin Will Give Eternal Life (7)

There are two ways of interpreting this verse, neither of which supports being saved by works which would violate the whole argument of the book of Romans.

First, the "doing good" refers to the good of believing the gospel and seeking its "glory, honor and immortality." Faith in Jesus Christ as Savior, and a life lived under His authority and control are the ultimate "good works".

Second, the "doing good" refers to a salvation by works that no one can fulfill. The standard of how good one must be is the very perfection of God: "Be perfect as your Father in heaven is perfect."

Believing on Jesus alone for salvation—the ultimate of good works—will bring salvation. Living an absolutely perfect life will do the same, but Jesus is the only One who has ever done so.

C. The Contrasts of Response (8-10)

To clarify the reality of God's wrath and judgment and sin, Paul stated:

"For those who are self-seeking and who reject the truth and follow evil, there will be wrath and anger. There will be trouble and distress for every human being who does evil: first for the Jew, then for the Gentile."

Note again the personal "every" and the universal "every human being." First, the Jew, or in today's terms, the religious person. Then, the rest of humanity.

He then follows the contrasting result that those who do the good—believing on the Lord Jesus Christ as Savior and obeying Him as Lord—will receive "glory, honor and peace."

Conclusion

As a final wrap-up statement, Paul wrote, "God does not show favoritism." It doesn't matter if one is a Jew (the called and chosen people), or a Gentile, if one is wealthy or poor, educated or uneducated, sophisticated or primitive. If you want to get to heaven you must either be morally perfect, or you must have a Savior.

We have all pointed our finger at someone else in moral judgment. In doing so, three fingers point back to convict us of our moral failure. We can be sure of God's accurate judgment based upon truth. Unless we have a Savior, we're sunk.

For your reflection:
- Name an occasion when you were critical of another person and it reflected a weakness you have struggled with.
- Why do we tend to be judgmental of others when we don't like that to happen to us?
- Does this study encourage or discourage you? Why?

Do I Have to be GOOD to go to Heaven?

7

Romans 2:12-29

The Religion of the Heart

The Scriptures the ancient Hebrew possessed was what we know as the Old Testament. Dominant were the first five books of Moses they knew as the Torah. Outlined in Exodus 20 are the Ten Commandments. One who has read or listened to those Scriptures knows what is right and wrong and what God expects. What about a person who doesn't have the Bible? Paul affirms that in both cases humanity stands guilty as sinners before God. In the first instance knowing right and wrong, we still choose the wrong. In the second case, Paul argues: "1. A man will be judged by what he had the opportunity to know…. God is fair…. A man will be judged by his fidelity to the highest that it was possible for him to know…. 2. Those who did not know the written Law had an unwritten law within their hearts."[27] It is that moral code that a person without the Bible's morality is guilty of breaking. We do what we inwardly understand is wrong.

Scripture: Romans 2:12-29

Main idea: Whether we have a religious code (the Bible, the Law of Moses) or nothing, we are guilty before God. True religion is a heart changed by the Holy Spirit.

Introduction

George Eliot in Adam Bede, set the scene for our Scripture:

---

[27] William Barclay, *The Letter to the Romans* (Philadelphia: The Westminster Press, 1957),39-40.

"Religious doctrines had taken no hold on Hetty's mind; she was one of those numerous people who have had godfathers and godmothers, learned their catechism, been confirmed, and gone to church every Sunday and yet, for any practical result of strength in life or trust in death, have never appropriated a single Christian idea or Christian feeling."

In our Scripture, Paul makes two primary statements: (1) Whether we have a religious code (the Bible, the Law of Moses, or another source) or nothing, we are guilty before God. (2) True religion is a heart changed by the Holy Spirit, not what nation we are born in or what religious practices we observe.

For our purposes, there are two narrow biblical references that we will look at in a broader religious framework. Where Paul refers to the Jew, I am referring to the religious person. The Jewish community revolved around religion. Such could still be said about the United States if the repeated Gallup polls are reliable. The majority of people believe in God, and believe the right things about Jesus—at least intellectually. On any given day, just under 40% of the population would say they attended religious services within the last week.

The second reference is to circumcision. Today circumcision is simply a medical procedure. In the time of Paul, it was a highly charged religious ritual through which people laid claim to the privileges of belonging to God. We will refer to this in the broader category of religious ritual which people believe give them privilege with God and through which they will ultimately be saved. Such ritual would include church attendance, baptism, communion, church membership, and church contributions. Paul states...

I. Everyone Will be Condemned When God Judges Our Secrets (12-24)

A. The Person Without a Religious Code Will be Judged by Their Own Conscience (12-16)

The conscience is that pesky little fellow sitting on our shoulder and screaming—he doesn't whisper, he screams—in your ear: "You did wrong!" Where did he come from? Some hold that the conscience is only a product of our cultural formulations of right and wrong.

There is more to it than that for an examination of cultural codes reveals the presence of universally accepted standards of right and wrong. Murder, for example, is not only condemned in the Ten Commandments, but in the ancient literature of Egypt and Scandinavia. Conscience is the voice of God to convict of sin. It is cultivated and shaped by culture.

C. S. Lewis wrote of the "Law of Human Nature" in the opening paragraphs of Mere Christianity:

> Everyone has heard people quarreling. Sometimes it sounds funny and sometimes it sounds merely unpleasant; but however it sounds, I believe we can learn something very important from listening to the kinds of things they say. They say things like this: "How'd you like it if anyone did the same to you?"—"That's my seat, I was there first"—"Leave him alone, he isn't doing you any harm"—"Why should you shove in first?"—"Give me a bit of your orange, I gave you a bit of mine—. Come on, you promised." People say things like that every day, educated people as well as uneducated, and children as well as grown-ups.
>
> "Now what interests me about all these remarks is that the man who makes them is not merely saying that the other man's behaviour does not happen to please him. He is

appealing to some kind of standard of behaviour which he expects the other man to know about."[28]

You might identify with the game wardens who on opening day put a sign by the highway: "Check-Station 1000 Yards Ahead." At 500 yards, there was a convenient side road. Lawful hunters went straight ahead. The over-limit and doubtful ducked down the side road. The Check-Station was located down the side road.

The question is often asked, are the people who have never heard of Christ lost? In Paul's day, the question would be framed: How can God condemn the Gentile who has not heard of Moses nor His law? Paul's answer is simply, the person who has a moral code such as the Law of Moses—or we who have the Bible—will be judged by that law. The person who doesn't have such a code will be judged by his or her own conscience for we have all failed to adhere to our own pronouncements of right and wrong.

> *Verse 15 reads: "Since they show that the requirements of the law are written on their hearts, their consciences also bearing witness, and their thoughts now accusing, now even defending them."* Or as The Message reads: *"They show that God's law is not something alien, imposed on us from without, but woven into the very fabric of our creation."*

King Richard III was a bloody man. At the end of Shakespeare's play, he speaks of his conscience.

> **"O coward conscience, how dost thou afflict me....**
>
> **My conscience hath a thousand several tongues,**
>
> **And every tongue brings in a several tale,**
>
> **And every tale condemns me for a villain."**

---

28 C. S. Lewis, *Mere Christianity* (New York: Harpers, 1952), 17.

Religious and possessing a code or without one, humankind is guilty before a holy God. You and I don't fit the classification of being without a code. We have both the law of Moses and the Sermon on the Mount. What about us?

B. The Person with a Religious Code will be Judged by that Code (17-24)

The Bible states that a violation of one law makes one guilty of the whole (Jas 2:10). The old law said to not murder, Jesus said hate is the same as murder. The old law said to not commit adultery, Jesus said if you look on a woman and lust for her you are an adulterer. The old law said to love your neighbor, Jesus said we are to love our enemies.

John Murray commented: "The more enhanced the privilege the more heinous become the sins exposed." If the Jew was privileged as a possessor of the law of Moses, we in the United States in the early 21st century have been much more privileged. We have Moses, Jesus, the Puritans, our own Constitution, the Scriptures engraved on virtually every Federal building in the country, and over 300,000 churches. Our sins scream the louder at us. That's the code that will judge us and damn us.

Many kids have grown up in Sunday school, VBS, AWANA, home Bible studies, and multiple-activity youth programs. They can quote John 3:16 and rattle off the Apostles' Creed as if in a coma. We know church and code, but not Christ. We have religion, but our hearts are dead. Religion and code don't change one's behavior or daily life.

At Westmont College, I was privileged to sing in the school quartet. Our bass was phenomenal. Any day, any time of day, he could belt out a low B-flat. In brass instrument terms, that's the pedal note. It is low—very low. He grew up in a Swedish Baptist home and attended Seattle Christian School.

In his testimony, he would quote from Psalm 16:11, You will show me the path of life, in Your presence is fullness of joy. "I have found fullness of joy in Jesus Christ," he would say. Yet he was finally expelled from Westmont and ended up singing in a rock group, The Diamonds. A few years ago, he died as his private plane crashed into Mt. Shasta. Knowing the truth, saying the right things, but was his heart unchanged by the Holy Spirit? Only the Lord can answer that question. I assume I will see him in heaven where he will stand before Jesus and account for his choices.

Not only are we judged by an exacting code, our religious ritual is helpless to save us. Don't assume if you have been brought up in a Christian home and church that you will get into heaven. Have you allowed Jesus to change your heart?

II. Religious Ritual is of Value only if Accompanied by a Perfect Life (25-29)

A. Religious Ritual is Inadequate to Bring Salvation (25-27)

By Paul's time, circumcision had become the essential element of Jewishness. If a male was circumcised, he was in the covenant. But Paul, in line with Old Testament teaching, said the outward, the physical alone, will not make us right with God. Circumcision has value only if a person keeps the whole of the law's requirements.

True circumcision is of the heart, not of the flesh. Religion is not ritual, it is a personal and intimate relationship with God. It is a matter of the heart.

B. The Truly Religious Person Has a Changed Heart (28-29)

At the end of his recitation of the law, Moses prophesied: "The LORD your God will circumcise your hearts…so that you may love him with all your heart and with all your soul, and live" (Deut. 30:6). Jesus came to make it happen.

Jeremiah denounced Israel and said they were as the surrounding nations for their hearts were not circumcised.

True religion is not in codes or ritual, it is a heart that is changed by the Holy Spirit, not by a written code. Such a person truly worships God.

Conclusion

Several news reports this past week [4/15-19/96] focused on the breakdown in the Naval Academy. Midshipmen of this prestigious school have been in a lockdown of confinement to their campus. Theft, rape, and other like activities in violation of the institution's code of ethics, have resulted in administration and faculty emphasizing the school's ethical code. But, as one prof in the institution expressed, having a code and explaining it, will not result in significant change. When asked by a reporter if it reflected the larger issues of the society, the admiral in charge said he thought so.

If we think that having a code will change the heart, we are missing a primary lesson of the ancient Hebrew people. They had the law of Moses. It was the highest expression of ethics and morality ever given. They said they agreed with it and would follow it. However, until the heart is changed through the power of God the Holy Spirit Himself coming to live inside the heart, codes won't work. They certainly won't get us into heaven, and they won't change the heart which produces our sins.

I assume some people are like George Eliot's Heddy. All the truth they have heard has not penetrated into their heart. You can trust in having the right code, in believing the right things, in doing religious rituals. But unless your heart has been changed by the Holy Spirit, you are without salvation. You will not go to heaven.

For your reflection:
- What is meant by religious code?
- What is the essence of true religion?
- Why did Paul use the term "Jew" and this message refers to the same term as the religious person?
- What is the meaning behind circumcision?
- What is the place of ritual (formal or informal) in the church?

8

Romans 3:1-20

The Conclusion: We Are All Guilty

"This passage contains a four-fold classification of man's sin. First, negatively the things that are lacking; second, positively, the sins of the heart; third, the sins of the tongue, and, fourth, the sins of the life. Under these four categories the world has been found utterly and irretrievable guilty and lost."[29]

Scripture: Romans 3:1-20

Main Idea: the bottom line—whether a person is religious or not, he or she stands guilty in the presence of a holy God and needs a Savior.

Introduction

The heart of the Bible is John 3:16: *"God so loved the world that he gave his one and only Son, that whoever believes in him shall not perish but have eternal life."* That verse is predicated upon a basic assumption: We are all sinners who need a Savior. What is also true, we have interesting ways of sliding around our sins, like a slippery running back, Emmitt Smith of the Dallas Cowboys, who slid through would-be tacklers.

Some reports from actual police records illustrate the point. "I was taking my canary to the hospital, it got loose in the car and few out the window. The next thing I saw was

---

[29]   Simpson, 69.

his rear end and there was a crash." That's simple enough, we can all relate to that. Here's another: "I approached the intersection, a stop sign suddenly appeared in a place where no stop sign had ever appeared before. I was unable to stop in time to avoid the accident." Or, "To avoid hitting the bumper of the car in front, I hit the pedestrian." "An invisible car came out of nowhere, struck my vehicle, and vanished." "I told the police that I was not injured, but upon removing my hat, I found that I had a fractured skull." One last one: "When I saw I could not avoid a collision, I stepped on the gas and crashed into the other car."

The first three chapters of Romans builds a careful argument that all people—religious and non-religious, those who have a religious or moral code and those who do not—are guilty of sin before God and therefore need a Savior.

Our study now brings us to chapter 3 in which Paul wraps up his argument in powerful illustration of man's sinful nature and behavior.

Chapter 2 conclusively proved that the Jew--or religious person as we are referring to the term--cannot be saved by doing religious things. The reason is simply that the religious person is a sinner and therefore under God's judgment. If that is so, a natural question to ask is, why be religious?

> *"So, what difference does it make who's a Jew and who isn't, who has been trained in God's ways and who hasn't? As it turns out, it makes a lot of difference—but not the difference so many have assumed. First, there's the matter of being put in charge of writing down and caring for God's revelation, these Holy Scriptures. So, what if, in the course of doing that, some of those Jews abandoned their post? God didn't abandon them. Do you think their faithlessness cancels out his faithfulness? Not on your life! Depend on it: God keeps his word even when the whole world is*

lying through its teeth. Scripture says the same: "Your words stand fast and true; rejection doesn't faze you" (The Message, 1-3).

I. If Being Religious Doesn't Save a Person, Why Be Religious? (1-8)

Two reasons are given.

A. Because God's Promises Are Valid Even If People Do Not Believe (1-3)

Two thoughts dominate these verses. One is: "They have been entrusted with the very words of God." Here we cannot speak in the generality of the religious person, as such, but specifically of the Hebrew, the Jew of the Old Testament. Their advantage over the Gentile world was they had received the Word of God, His promises. Even when people misuse and abuse the Bible, they at least have the truth of God's promises.

The second point is the faithfulness of God. God gave to Israel His promise and He was faithful to that promise even when they were unfaithful. These two points are very important to Paul's argument.

> *"Not at all! Let God be true, and every man a liar. As it is written: 'So that you may be proved right when you speak and prevail when you judge.' But if our unrighteousness brings out God's righteousness more clearly, what shall we say? That God is unjust in bringing his wrath on us? (I am using a human argument.) Certainly not! If that were so, how could God judge the world? Someone might argue, 'If my falsehood enhances God's truthfulness and so increases his glory, why am I still condemned as a sinner?' Why not say—as we are being slanderously reported as saying and as some claim that we say— 'Let us do evil that good may result'? Their condemnation is deserved" (4-8).*

The flow of thought is that God will be true to his word even if all men are liars, if they are unfaithful to their commitments. One key phrase is "God's faithfulness." Another is "God's righteousness" which speaks of His love, mercy and grace—i.e., His saving actions—toward His people Judah and Israel. Because God is righteous He will act in judgment of sin even to people who possess His promises. The second reason there is value in being religious is…

B. Because God will Judge Sin even if People Abuse His Grace (4-6)

Paul goes to Psalm 51:4 for a supporting proof of the judgment of sin. That psalm is the penitent prayer of David after his adultery with Bathsheba is exposed by Nathan the prophet. What occurred in that incident? David sent his troops to war. One warm, sultry evening, he went to his own peep show. What is wrong with a stroll upon one's own roof in the evening? Nothing. Except he saw his neighbor's wife bathing. Instead of doing the right thing and turning from that, he watched her bathe until his heart was racing and lust was surging through his body.

Out of his lust came overt adultery and the conception of a child. In today's world, they could have quietly murdered the baby in abortion and no one would have ever known. But, that wasn't available to them. God took the life of the illicit child. David's mourned and repented of his sin:

> *"I know my transgressions, and my sin is always before me. Against you, you only have I sinned and done what is evil in your sight, so that you are proved right when you speak and justified when you judge."*

David made no attempts to get out of judgment because he was a Jew or a deeply religious person. He understood God will judge the sin of people who have received the promises of His goodness as well as those who do not have God's Word. Because he was religious, his sin drove him to genuine repentance and to God's forgiving grace. More than any other Old Testament writer, David used the word, *hesed*, which is often translated as unfailing love. It is the equivalent of the word, grace in the New Testament. It is found throughout David's psalms.

This section is almost a digression of thought and is a rather complicated passage. To get back to the primary flow of his thought Paul raised a second question: "What shall we conclude then?" Is the religious person any better off than the non-religious? Does the person who goes to church and reads his Bible any different before God because he or she does those things? The answer is no.

II. How Bad is Man's Status as a Sinner? (9-19)

A. Paul's List

The general condition and attitude of humanity toward God is recited from the Old Testament, the literature of the smug religious community. *"There's nobody living right, not even one, nobody who knows the score, nobody alert for God. They've all taken the wrong turn; they've all wandered down blind alleys. No one's living right; I can't find a single one."*

Then follows a recitation of specific sins:

1. Sins of the tongue: *"Their throats are gaping graves, their tongues slick as mud slides. Every word they speak is tinged with poison. They open their mouths and pollute the air."*

2. Sins of personal violence: *"Their feet are swift to shed blood; ruin and misery mark their ways, and the way of peace they do not know."*

3. Sins of insolence: *"There is no fear of God before their eyes."*

B. A Look at Some of Our Sins Today

Things are getting so bad on the streets of New York City, that if you want to see a Jehovah's Witness, you have to go to their house.

Alexander Solzhenitsyn stated when he received the Templeton Prize in Religion in London:

> "Through decades of gradual erosion, the meaning of life in the West has ceased to be seen as anything more lofty than the 'pursuit of happiness'.... The concepts of good and evil have been ridiculed for several centuries.... It has become embarrassing to appeal to eternal concepts.... The West is ineluctably [cannot be escaped or eluded] slipping toward the abyss...losing more and more of its religious essence as it thoughtlessly yields up its younger generation to atheism."[30]

Where do we begin our list? Murder? From the James City, Virginia Daily Press a few years ago, an article that a girl who said she loves what Freddy Krueger does in the Nightmare on Elm Street movies was charged with attempted murder. She tried to murder a 13-year-old boy with a jump rope—her fourth such assault. "It feels good to try and strangle—it is fun to kill." That may not be the norm but it sure illustrates the power of sin on the heart and its impact on society.

At the end of 1980, 1 in every 450 US residents were incarcerated; by the end of 1994, that figure grew to 1 in every 175. Are we violent? What is scary is the overall crime rate dropped in 1994, but the youth crime rate has sky-rocketed. The homicide rate for youths 14 to 17 jumped 16% between 1990 and 1994, while it declined 25% for those over 25.[31]

Or drug addiction. Jack Kelley wrote in *USA Today* (5/10/90) it is estimated 2.2 million are addicted to cocaine in

---
30   http://www.roca.org/OA/36/36h.htm (accessed 08.17.17).
31   *Time*, "Law and Order,"01/15/96, 48-56.

the US. A survey indicated one addict for every 100 people. Among the statistics is 1 out of every 5 people arrested for any crime is a hard-core cocaine addict, and homeless people are 5 times more likely than average to be cocaine addicts.

And morality. Two of the hottest spots on the internet are Playboy and Hustler. The USA Today (9/12/89) reported high school guys who had a game to see how many children they could father during a school year. "It's a prescription for long-term poverty" for teen mothers, said Jack Levine of the Florida Center for Children and Youth.

Another *USA Today* (11/30/90) front page featured the stories of women who had been raped while college students. We as evangelical Christians might dismiss the problem on university campuses as part of the world's system, but one story was a New York girl who had gone to a Christian college in Tennessee and was gang raped along with her roommate.

Paul lived in the Roman world. Phillip Myers in *Rome, Its Rise and Fall*, observed: "Almost from the beginning, the Roman stage was gross, and immorality was one of the main agencies to which must be attributed the undermining of the originally sound moral life of Roman society. So absorbed did the people become in the indecent representations of the stage that they lost all thought and care of the affairs of real life." Madonna illustrates our replication of Roman life. A cartoon this last week portrayed her as saying, "Of course I'll raise her in a normal home and normal environment and she will be a normal child."

The story is of a little girl who asked her father to pick a flower for her. He bent over and broke off the stem. "Now put it back," she said. The father asked, "How can you explain that it cannot be done? How can one make clear to students that there are some things which when once broken, once mutilated, can never be replaced or mended?"

Billy Graham said it succinctly: "Most of us follow our conscience as we follow a wheelbarrow. We push it in front of us in the direction we want it to go."

III. The Conclusion (19-20)

A. The Whole World is Held Accountable to God

"This makes it clear, doesn't it, that whatever is written in these Scriptures is not what God says about others but to us to whom these Scriptures were addressed in the first place! And it's clear enough, isn't it, that we're sinners, every one of us, in the same sinking boat with everybody else? Our involvement with God's revelation doesn't put us right with God. What it does is force us to face our complicity in everyone else's sin."

The law, or the religious code whether formal as in the Ten Commandments, or informal, as in a personal moral code, serves the primary purpose of pointing to our moral failure. So, the Jew who had the Law of Moses, and the Gentile who had essentially the same moral code in the form of his conscience, stand guilty before God and need a Savior.

B. No One is Declared Righteous in God's Sight

These verses gives the theological underpinning to the whole argument. Nobody can escape the conclusion for "no one will be declared righteous"—period. No, not period, an exclamation point!

Conclusion

If everyone is guilty, is there hope? Yes. But our hope is not in our religious acts or goodness. *"No one will be declared righteous in his sight by observing the law."* The technical idea of "observing the law" is not so much trying to keep the moral code to achieve righteousness or heaven, but rather doing the religious thing to be identified with the people of God. To the Jewish people of that day, that was circumcision. To us it may be being baptized, receiving communion, attending church services. Those things won't get us accepted before God.

If you haven't received Jesus as your personal Savior, you will have to stand accountable for your sins before a holy God.

This is where the good news comes in. Back in the first chapter Paul gave us the good news. Let's review it.

"I am not ashamed of the gospel, because it is the power of God for the salvation of everyone who believes.... For in the gospel a righteousness that is by faith is revealed, a righteousness that is by faith from first to last..." (1:16).

Everyone is guilty. Everyone who believes the gospel receives a gift of right relationship with God. And the gospel? It is Jesus himself, not a moral code, not a church institution. Jesus paid the penalty of our sin to allow a holy God to forgive us and receive us as His children.

While the conclusion is we are all guilty, the end does not have to be condemnation. It can be salvation, if we will believe on the Lord Jesus Christ.

Those of us who have experienced God's magnificent grace in forgiveness have a responsibility to get the good news of forgiveness out to those who don't know about it. Do we really believe that lost people go to hell? What about all those nice people around us with whom we associate and work? They're really nice people—some of them anyway. Are they lost? Is hell really their destination? What impact does that have in our thinking and behavior? May God give us courage to speak the name of Jesus when appropriate and not be ashamed to identify as His beloved children.

For your reflection:

- Since this was written and the statistics are dated, what evidence to you see of moral decline in our culture?

- Why has the church become marginalized as a moral voice?

- How can the move to atheism and agnosticism be countered by the Gospel?

9

Romans 3:21-31

There's Only One Way, and It's Free

Scripture: Romans 3:21-31

Main idea: God has provided the way sinful mankind to come into a right relationship with him, through Christ's atoning sacrifice, by faith, apart from keeping a religious or ethical code.

Introduction

One of the great movers and shakers in Christian history, and certainly in religious history in the US, was George Whitefield. His evangelistic ministry in early America is truly legendary. When 16 years old, he became deeply convicted of his sin. He tried everything to become acceptable to God. His experience is common to many in our country today. He wrote,

> I fasted for 36 hours twice a week. I prayed formal prayers several times a day and almost starved myself to death during Lent, but only felt more miserable. Then by God's grace I met Charles Wesley, who put a book in my hand that showed me from the Scriptures that I must be "born again" or be eternally lost.

After the long searching and tortuous religious activity, Whitefield understood that salvation came only by trusting in Jesus Christ, His death in payment for our sin, and His resurrection of victory over sin and the grave. The church is powerless to give salvation, doing religious things can't take away sin, and our attempts at keeping a religious or ethical code will not take us to heaven.

In the opening two and a half chapters, Paul established the conclusion that everyone—the religious person and the non-religious—is a sinner, guilty before God, and under His wrath.

We are looking at Romans 3:21-31. In this passage we have the answer to this desperate state. Because each of us is a sinner, since being religious and doing the religious thing will not save us, then what will? Is there any hope for us? What is the answer to the greatest problem any person faces—how can I be forgiven; how can I have eternal life? Paul answers these questions. It is a very full passage, but I hope we can successfully work our way through in understandable terms. There are five points.

I. God Has Provided a Way to a Right Relationship with Him Apart from Keeping a Religious or Ethical Code (21)

"But in our time, something new has been added. What Moses and the prophets witnessed to all those years has happened. The God-setting-things-right that we read about [i.e., in the Old Testament Scriptures] has become Jesus-setting-things-right for us" (The Message)

The phrase, "God-setting-things-right", or "righteousness from God" refers to God's saving activity. Emphasis is placed on the initiation of God. He is the One who acts in rescuing us from sin. Our action is only a response to what He initiated—a point that is critical to understand. We have defined "righteousness of God" as having a right relationship with God.

God's way is totally apart from doing the religious thing. We cannot come into a right relationship with God by doing religious or good things. Many, many people are misled by the perception that "I'm doing the best I can, what more does God want?" The point is, while there is nothing we can do that will put us in a right relationship with God, there is something which God Himself has done. An important insight of grammar is in the phrase, "has been made known." It is in the perfect tense meaning God accomplished something in a decisive act of the past that is still in effect today. The decisive act was Jesus' death on the cross in full payment of our sins. He died once for all time and that death still applies to us today.[32]

Further, Paul stated that it was testified to in the Law (the books of Moses or Torah) and the Prophets (the last third of the Old Testament). God's way to a right relationship was misunderstood by most Old Testament people, but it was not because God had kept it hidden during that time.

God has provided a way to a right relationship with Him apart from keeping a religious or ethical code.

II. The Way is Faith in Jesus Christ (22)

"Jesus-setting-things-right for us. And not only for us, but for everyone who believes in Him."

The question is, if we can't become right with God by being religious or doing good, how then do we gain a right relationship with God? The answer: "everyone who believes in Him," or "through faith in Jesus Christ to all who believe."

There are two parts to faith. One is to understand with the mind. A person must know some things to become a Christian. It is not an emotional feeling, it is not believing in any religious system—having faith in faith. Faith requires a mental understanding of our sin, our need of a Savior, who is Jesus, and what He did to become our Savior. The second part

---

32   Dunn, 176

is an act of trust, of commitment, of surrendering our hearts and total lives to Him.

To make sure the readers would understand his point, Paul wrote of faith in redundant fashion: "through faith in Jesus Christ to all who believe." Not to some, the religious person, the good person, but to all. All are sinners, and all who believe in Jesus Christ will be brought into a right relationship with God.

It is not just faith. It is faith in Jesus Christ. Some think that all they have to do is believe—Charlie Brown style. Faith in faith, or faith in Allah, or Buddha, or a New Age channel, or some philosophy will not bring a person into a right relationship with God. It must be faith in Jesus Christ.

God has provided a way to a right relationship with Him apart from keeping a religious or ethical code. The way is faith in Jesus Christ.

III. Everyone Has Sinned and Needs a Savior (23)

"Since we've compiled this long and sorry record as sinners (both us and them) and proved that we are utterly incapable of living the glorious lives God wills for us, God did it for us."

Salvation must be available to all for all are sinners—the religious person who does all the right religious things or good things, and the non-religious person alike. There is no distinction between the two. In falling short of the glory of God, Paul alluded to Adam's failure in the garden of Eden when he sinned in breaking God's restriction. The wonderful hope of the believer is the day when we will be restored to that original plan and share in the full glory of God (1 Corinthians 11:7).

God has provided a way to a right relationship with Him apart from keeping a religious or ethical code. The way is faith in Jesus Christ. Everyone has sinned and needs a Savior.

IV. All Who Believe are Made Right with God as a Free Gift (24-26)

"Out of sheer generosity he put us in right standing with himself. A pure gift. He got us out of the mess we're in and restored us to where he always wanted us to be. And he did it by means of Jesus Christ. God sacrificed Jesus on the altar of the world to clear that world of sin. Having faith in him sets us in the clear. God decided on this course of action in full view of the public—to set the world in the clear with himself through the sacrifice of Jesus, finally taking care of the sins he had so patiently endured. This is not only clear, but it's now—this is current history! God sets things right. He also makes it possible for us to live in his rightness."

In the NIV, there are several key words that require definition. First, "right standing or justified" (24), comes out of the court of law, and refers to how God, as our judge, treats the sinner. He treats us as though we are not sinners. It is not acquittal where a person is declared not guilty. It is more than a pardon. We are guilty, but we are treated as though we had never committed our sins. We are exonerated.

God does two things in justification. First, he wipes our record clean of all our sins. In the OT He promised He would not remember our sins. It is like the delete function on a computer. God has a perfect record of every sin in thought, motive, or action. He wipes the disk clean of all record, and no utility can find it—it is gone.

Second, He gives us the righteousness of Jesus. Jesus never sinned. All of His good works are credited to our account. Now, which way do you want to try to get to heaven—doing your own good or religious thing, or accepting the free gift of Christ's forgiveness and righteousness?

We are justified freely—it is free. We do not deserve it, and we cannot earn being right with God. He gives it to us in grace. The person who is depending upon religious or good works to become acceptable to God must wait until he or she stands before the judgment seat of God. In Christ, God declares us righteous the very moment we believe in Jesus Christ.

How can He do so?

Because Jesus redeemed us by being an atoning sacrifice; as such He satisfied the demands of God's holy nature. As the word "justified" came out of the court room, so the word "redemption" came out of the slave market. It means to be bought out of slavery. The price of our redemption was the very blood of Christ.

One last reason God can offer a right relationship with Him as a free gift: God presented Jesus as the "sacrifice of atonement." Paul referred to the court in justification, to the slave-market in redemption, and here to the Old Testament altar of sacrifice.

The allusion is to the OT ritual of worship and the Day of Atonement—Yom Kippur. Once a year the priest killed the sacrificial lamb, removed his priestly garments and wore simple white linen. He then took blood from the sacrifice and entered into the Holy of Holies—a small room in which rested the Ark of the Covenant. The lid of that ark was called the mercy seat, or the cover of atonement. There the priest sprinkled blood to provide atonement for the people's sins. Paul said Jesus became that sacrifice of atonement for us.

All of this action is God's, not humankind's. This is the "righteousness of God", the way sinners can have a right relationship with a holy God. God does not merely put our sins away symbolically. They are really done away with, gone, completely, totally, finally, eternally G O N E, gone. In an identical reference, **Hebrews 8:12** quotes **Jeremiah 31:34** saying: "I will remember their sins no more." And with our sins being gone, we avoid the wrath of God against sin.

J. Vernon McGee told the story of the young boy in Texas who wanted to join the church. The deacons asked him, "How did you come to Christ?" He answered: "God did His part, and I did my part." They thought he didn't really understand, so they asked: "What was God's part, and what was your part?" He said, "God's part was the saving, and my part was the sinning. I ran from Him as fast as my sinful heart and rebellious legs could take me. He took out after me until he ran me down." That's the way it is with every one of us.

There is a special word for time in verse 26, *kairos*: time that is pregnant with significance, the time of opportunity "whose decisions and actions will determine the future".[33] This is your time of opportunity to trust in Christ alone as your Savior.

God has provided a way to a right relationship with Him apart from keeping a religious or ethical code. The way is faith in Jesus Christ. Everyone has sinned and needs a Savior. All who believe are made right with God as a free gift.

V. As a Result, Boasting is Excluded (27-31)

"So where does that leave our proud Jewish [religious] insider claims and counterclaims? Canceled? Yes, canceled. What we've learned is this: God does not respond to what we do; we respond to what God does.

---

[33] Dunn, 174.

> *We've finally figured it out. Our lives get in step with God and all others by letting him set the pace, not by proudly or anxiously trying to run the parade."*

All other systems of salvation are based upon what man does, and they only accommodate the expression of one of our primary problems, pride. We can't brag about how good we have been, how much money we have given, how often we have gone to church, the offices we have held, the volunteer work we have done. That's out the window. The only boasting is in Jesus.

Verse 28 says it again: "What we've learned is this: God does not respond to what *we* do; we respond to what *God* does." It absolutely cuts the legs out from under the person who says: "I do the best I can, what more does God want from me?" We are brought into a right relationship with God by what Jesus did as our redeemer and sacrifice of atonement by faith—alone. Martin Luther added the word "alone" to his translation and took a lot of heat for it, but he was dead on target. It is by faith alone, absolutely apart from doing the religious thing or keeping an ethical code.

Conclusion

Just before President Dwight D. Eisenhower died, Billy Graham was invited to visit him at the Walter Reed Hospital, in Washington, DC. He was told he could only stay 30 minutes. Greeted with that big Eisenhower grin, they conversed for a time. Graham told what happened.

> When the 30 minutes were up, he asked me to stay longer and said to me, "Billy, I want you to tell me again how can I be sure my sins were forgiven and that I am going to heaven, because nothing else matters now."
>
> I took my New Testament and read him Scriptures. I pointed out that we are not going to heaven because of

our good works, or because of money we've given to the church. We are going to heaven totally and completely on the basis of the merits of what Christ did on the cross. Therefore, he could rest in the comfort that Jesus paid it all.

After prayer, Ike said, "Thank you, I'm ready."

Are you ready? Don't think you can wait until you're on your death-bed to get this matter settled. Your life may end with suddenness and without warning. Now is the time. This is the moment for you to believe in Jesus Christ and come into a right relationship with God.

I suggest the following possible steps to take:

1. You can pray right now where you are. Make the prayer your personal prayer to God. "Lord Jesus, I confess I am a sinner and come to you as my personal Savior. Forgive my sins and come into my heart to change me. I receive You as my gift of eternal life."

2. As soon as appropriate, tell a personal friend who is a Christian of your trust in Christ.

3. Find a church that teaches the Bible and offers salvation only through Jesus Christ.

Do I Have to be GOOD to go to Heaven?

10

Romans 4:1-15

Did Abraham Get a Paycheck?

"Abraham's acceptance with God was clearly not based on his works, good as they were.... For Abraham's good works, his obedience to the divine commandments, were the frit of his unquestioning faith in God; had he not first believed the promises of God he would never have set out for the promised land or conducted his life there in the light of what he knew of God's will. No; when God gave Abraham a promise...he simply took God at his word, and acted accordingly."[34]

Scripture: Romans 4:1-15

Main Idea: a right relationship with God is a gift given to the believer, not a paycheck because of work rendered.

Introduction

One of my most satisfying and proud moments was when I landed my first job. I had mowed lawns, done odd jobs around the house and in the neighborhood, but this was different. It was a real job. I had gone to the backyard of a lady's house who was a distributor for the Long Beach *Press-Telegram*, and had gotten a paper-route. Then came time to do the collection task. I didn't get my pay until I had collected enough money to pay for the papers I had delivered. The rest was my pay—including the money I got in December as Christmas tips! And, I really earned all that money—at least I thought so.

---

[34] Bruce, 105.

Many people have that same kind of view of heaven or eternal life. They assume heaven is a paycheck for all the good and religious things they have done in their lives.

So far in our study of Romans, we have found that we are all guilty and under the wrath of God, whether we are religious or not, a good person or a debauched sinner. Because we are sinners, we cannot save ourselves. Instead, we need a Savior. Our Savior is Jesus Christ who became our Redeemer by paying the price to purchase us from sin. He did this by being a sacrifice of atonement for us. We cannot earn salvation (it is not a paycheck), nor do we deserve it. It is a free gift received by faith alone, totally apart from keeping a moral code or doing religious things. In fact, being religious doesn't contribute a thing to one's salvation.

A powerful illustration is Adolf Hitler. W.W. II theologian, Helmut Thielecke, wrote of him:

"Hitler knew how to dissemble. One had to look very closely at his terrible book *Mein Kampf* to see the cloven hoof beneath the angel's luminous robes.

"He made free use of the Christian vocabulary, talked about the blessing of the Almighty and the Christian confessions which would become the pillars of the new state; he rang bells and pulled out all the organ stops. He assumed the earnestness of a man who is utterly weighed down by historic responsibility. He handed out pious stories to the press, especially the church papers.

"It was reported, for example, that he showed his tattered Bible to some deaconesses and declared that he drew the strength for his great work from the Word of God. He was able to introduce a pietistic timbre into his voice which caused many religious people to welcome him as a man sent from God. And a skilled propaganda machine saw to it that despite all the atrocities which were already happening and despite the rabid invasions of the Nazis in the churches, the rumor got around that the good Führer knew nothing about these things."[35]

Being religious did not contribute a thing to Hitler's gaining a right relationship with God or to changing his heart. Having made the bold statement that the righteousness from God is by faith apart from the law, or doing the religious thing, Paul now seeks to support his thesis from the Scriptures.

I. The Scriptural record is that Abraham gained a right relationship with God by faith (1-3)

Having stated his thesis, Paul brought his primary witness to the stand. Enter Abraham, the father of the Jews. If Paul can establish that the testimony of Scripture supports Abraham's being made right with God by faith, apart from doing the religious thing, he has won his argument.

"What then shall we say that Abraham, our forefather, discovered in this matter? If, in fact, Abraham was justified by works, he had something to boast about—but not before God. What does the Scripture say? 'Abraham believed God, and it was credited to him as righteousness.'"

The supporting text used is Genesis 15:6. Paul referred to this same passage in the earlier writing of Galatians. Now he more fully explains this Scripture. Abraham's dilemma (at this stage in his life he is still called Abram in the Old Testament) was how could God work out His earlier promise to him that he would father a large nation? He had no children, and by custom, without an heir, his estate would be passed on to one of his servants. That didn't seem to fit properly.

God promised him in Genesis 15 that a son coming from his own body would be his heir. Verse 6 states:

---

[35] Source a former illustration service I no longer have.

"Abram believed the LORD, and he credited it to him as righteousness." Then followed the further promise of giving him the land we now know as Israel. Those to whom Paul wrote understood that 'righteous' did not mean acceptable to God, but as accepted by God—"righteousness as the status which God accorded to his covenant people and in which he sustained them."[36] What was at issue was how membership in that special community was attained.

The key word, "credited", came from the financial field. It means to credit to our account. "The concept implies an activity of the reason which, starting with ascertainable facts, draws a conclusion"[37]. God's logical conclusion was Abraham was "righteous", not because he was a good man, nor because he did the religious thing, but because he believed God's promise to him.

In our previous discussion I mentioned that the word justified came from the court of law and referred to God's treating sinners as if they are righteous. He is able to do this because Christ paid the price of redemption, a word from the slave market meaning to purchase by paying a price. Our gaining a right relationship with God (being justified) is a gift, but it wasn't without price. Jesus paid a tremendous price of blood to provide the gift. When He paid the price He also became the sacrifice of atonement to satisfy the holy nature of God.

Because of these things, God can offer eternal life as a free gift to be received by faith in Jesus Christ. In this latest allusion, Paul turned to the financial field to convey the idea

---

36   James D. G. Dunn, *Word Biblical Commentary* Vol 38 (Dallas, TX: Word Books, Pub, 1988), 203.
37   Gerhard Kittel; Gerhard Friedrich; Geoffrey William Bromiley, *Theological Dictionary of the New Testament* Vol III (Grand Rapids, Michigan: W. B. Eerdmans, 1993), 822.

that God writes across the account of the believer, righteous, not because he or she is religious, but because that person believes God's promises in Christ.

"Credited" occurs eleven times in this fourth chapter. In every instance it refers to God making us righteous as a result of faith not of works.

II. A Paycheck is the Obligation Paid when Earned through Work and cannot be Considered a Gift (4-8)

The church staff is paid on the first working day following the 15th and the last day of the month. When I get paid, I take my check and deposit it. I'd like to think it was not a gift of charity, but that I really earned the money and am worth something to this church. Someone gave me a cartoon that I hung in my office. The pastor is at the door shaking hands: "In spite of what everyone says, Pastor, I really enjoy your sermons." My paycheck is not a gift, but an obligation. So it was with Abraham. Had he done certain good works or religious things that obligated God to make him righteous, it would have been a paycheck. Abraham did not get a paycheck, he got a gift.

Verse 5 is remarkable. God flung the galaxies and the stars into space; He created the fish, birds, and animals, and gave us the seasons of the year. But much more than these, He "justifies the wicked". The great, holy God treats the wicked as though they were without sin.

Jesus told a parable about the Pharisee who stood and prayed bragging about all the religious things he had done, what a great guy he was. Off in the corner the sinner couldn't even lift his head said, *"Be merciful to me a sinner."* He went home justified, but the Pharisee was left standing in his sin.

In Exodus 23:7, God told Moses and Israel, "*I will not acquit the guilty.*" Now He justifies the wicked. Why the change? It is because Jesus paid the price of redemption and became the sacrifice of atonement.

A second Scriptural support cited by Paul was David. The quotation in verses 7-8 is taken from Psalm 32. The only link between Abraham and Paul's argument is the common word, credited. It occurs in the second verse, "*Blessed is the man whose sin the LORD will never credit against him.*" The blessed person is the one whose sins are forgiven. When God forgives our sins, He removes them from us. Then, in their place, He credits to us the actual righteousness of Jesus, and we stand in His presence without sin.

That is the greatest gift we could possibly hope for. Forgiven, made righteous, not by works but by faith in Jesus Christ—that's good news.

III. Abraham was Declared Righteous before he Participated in Religious Ritual (9-12)

The ritual was circumcision. In Paul's day circumcision was the foremost indicator that a male was a Jew religiously and so sharing in the covenant blessings. A Gentile male who became a Jewish proselyte had to be circumcised. Abraham, as father of the Jewish race, was the first to be circumcised. Paul's question—was Abraham circumcised before or after he was put into a right relationship with God? The answer—after. Abraham was circumcised 14 years after it was recorded in Genesis 15:6 that "*Abraham believed the LORD, and he credited it to him as righteousness.*" He was circumcised later in Genesis 17 as a sign of the previous covenant, or promise, which Abraham had believed.

The conclusion, Abraham was not only the father of his fleshly descendants, but also of all who believe God's promise.

In direct parallel, one does not gain a right relationship with God (or is made righteous) by baptism, receiving communion, or joining a church. Those are all appropriate religious activities and belong to the church in this day. They come after being justified by faith in Jesus Christ. Works follow faith, not precede it.

IV. The Promise Abraham would be Heir of the World came as a Result of a Right Relationship with God through Faith (13-15)

In the same way, long before there was any Law of Moses, which came 430 years later, Abraham was the recipient of the promise of God regarding his world-wide family and the possession of Canaan as his land.

The Law, or trying to keep a moral code, only brings God's wrath because of our failures. Therefore, it cannot save us. The law, or ethical code, simply proves to us we need a Savior.

Conclusion

A beggar stopped a lawyer on the street in a large southern city and asked him for a quarter. Taking a long, hard look into the man's unshaven face, the attorney asked, "Don't I know you from somewhere?" "You should. I'm your former classmate. Remember, second floor, old Main Hall?" "Why, Sam, of course I know you!" Without further question the lawyer wrote a check for $100. "Here, take this and get a new start. I don't care what's happened in the past, it's the future that counts." And with that he hurried on.

Tears welled up in the man's eyes as he walked to a nearby bank. Stopping at the door, he saw the well-dressed tellers through the glass and the spotlessly clean interior. Then he looked at his filthy rags. "They won't take this from me. They'll swear that I forged it," he muttered as he turned away.

The next day the two men met again. "Why Sam, what did you do with my check? Gamble it away? Drink it up?" "No," said the beggar as he pulled it out of his dirty shirt pocket and told why he hadn't cashed it. "Listen, friend. What makes that check good is not your clothes or appearance, but my signature. Go cash it."

There is a check but it's not a paycheck. God wrote it as a gift to beggars whose sins make them dirty. It is signed in blood by His Son, Jesus, made payable to the believer—forgiven, eternal life, it reads. All we have to do is take it to heaven's window and cash it.

For your reflection:
- The illustration of Abraham gets to the core issue of faith versus some kind of human activity to gain merit with God. When asked the question, "why should God let you into His heaven," what would some people answer?
- How can you help someone understand there is nothing a person can do to guarantee they would go to heaven?
- Why won't going to church and doing good things result in a person going to heaven?
- How good does a person have to be in order to enter heaven?
- What is God's one requirement for people to receive His gift of eternal life?

11

Romans 4:16-25

Hope When Everything Seems Hopeless

"Abraham had such a faith. Our text tells us, indeed, that he was strong in faith. I have tried to analyze what strength of faith really means. After eliminating all of the counterfeits—credulity, superstition, presumption, and the like, we come to the simplicity of understanding that strength of faith is the reality of believing with all your heart and action upon that belief."[38]

Scripture: Romans 4:16-25

Main idea: Our faith, which is based on God's promise and verified by the resurrection, gives us hope when all else is hopeless.

Introduction

The late Charles Colson was one of the foremost apologist for Christianity in the 20th century. His brilliance landed him a top position in Richard Nixon's government and gave him razor-sharp insight into our society. "This century," he wrote a few years ago, "has not been a good century for human dignity." Why? "100 million of us have died because of state action: war, genocide, induced famine, inhuman prison conditions and the like. Private action—abortion, euthanasia, withheld treatment—has taken millions more lives."

---

[38] Barnhouse, vol. II, 354.

Frederick Nietzsche was a son of a Lutheran minister. He was grandson of Lutheran pastors on both sides of his parentage, a syphilitic who became an insane philosopher. He had a profound effect on Hitler, Stalin, and Mussolini—three devils of the 20th century. He wrote:

"I call Christianity the one great curse, the one enormous and inner-most perversion, the one great instinct of revenge, for which no means are too venomous, too underhand, too underground, and too petty."[39]

Nietzche shaped the philosophical mind-set of the death of God. In the *Gay Science* he wrote:

Have you not heard of the man who lit a lamp on a bright morning and went to the marketplace crying ceaselessly, "I seek God; I seek God."

There were many among those standing there who didn't believe in God, so he made them laugh.

"Is God lost?" one of them said.

"Has He gone astray like a child?" said another.

"Or is He hiding? Has He gone on board ship and emigrated?"

"So they laughed, and they shouted at one another. The man sprang into their midst and looked daggers at them. "Where is God?" he cried. "I will tell you. We have killed Him, you and I."

"We are all His killers, but how can we have done that? How could we swallow up the sea? Who gave us the sponge to wipe away the horizon? What will we do as the earth is set loose from its sun?"

---

39   Ravi Zacharias, *A Shattered Visage: The Real Face of Atheism* (Brentwood, Tennessee: Wolgemuth & Hyatt, Publishers, 1990), 18.

Colson commented: "When Nietzsche spoke of the 'death of God,' God's actual existence was beside the point. The point was that people would learn to live, to educate themselves, to build families and societies in complete oblivion to God. From here it looks like he wasn't far off."[40]

The reason I use these references is that a Christian is properly called a believer. We are not believers in faith, or simply any idea. We believe in Jesus of Nazareth as the Lord and Christ. That faith is firmly welded to the Bible as a book of truth given by God, and not human fable.

Regardless of who you are, what your academic credentials are or aren't, the wealth you have accumulated or haven't accumulated, you believe a list of assumptions that control your decisions and behavior. Those assumptions are embraced in faith. Nietzsche's faith began with the assumption that God is dead, that is, He is irrelevant to life.

In contrast, the Christian's assumptions begin with the existence of an infinite personal God who has spoken in clear terms in a book called the Bible. In that book, God has given promises of what He will do for those who trust Him.

In a nutshell, Paul argued that Abraham, the father of Judaism, did not gain a right relationship with God, was not "declared fit before God," [*The Message*] by doing religious ritual or sticking to a moral code called the Ten Commandments. God credited Abraham as righteous, or declared him fit before God, because he believed God's promise to him. Paul adamantly held that in the same way we are declared fit before God by believing in Christ Jesus who died for our sins and rose from the dead. "Credited as righteous," or "declared fit before God," is a key phrase from the accounting field. It refers to entering something in a ledger.

---

[40]   Charles Colson, *World Vision*, Dec/Jan, 88, 4-5.

In this case, God takes away the debits of our sins, and credits to our assets the righteousness of Jesus himself. This makes us right with God.

The reliability of our faith is the integrity of God who gave the promise and who proved its truthfulness by the resurrection of Jesus from the dead. In spite of the failures of the church throughout history, millions of people from all walks of life have found trusting in Jesus really works in daily life. There are two primary points in this passage. One, faith's assurance is the power and integrity of God who has given the promise. Two, faith generates hope when everything seems hopeless

I. Faith's Assurance is the Power and Integrity of God Who Has Given the Promise (16-17)

The fulfillment of God's promise depends entirely on trusting God and His way, then simply embracing Him and what He does. The promise Abraham believed is stated in Genesis 15:5 where God said his offspring would be as numerous as the stars in the heavens and the sands of the seashore. Abraham did not have any children and was getting on the old side—he was over 75 years old. Yet he believed God's promise of a son. This promise was a gift Abraham did not earn. God gave it to him through grace. Let's summarize these two verses:

A. A Right Relationship with God is a Gift Anyone Can Receive by Faith

The title one commentator gave to this section is: "Abraham's faith was nothing other than unquestioning trust in God's power"[41].

---

41   James D. G. Dunn, *Word Biblical Commentary, Vol 38, Romans 1-8* (Dallas, Texas: Word Books, Publisher, 1988) 236.

The good news is that not only was Abraham declared fit before God through faith, but all who believe God's promise are also declared fit before God and are therefore the sons of Abraham.

B. Behind the Promise is God Who Does the Impossible.

The God Abraham believed was "the God who gives life to the dead and with a word makes something out of nothing." This is a reference to Abraham's fathering a son at the age of 99 and Sarah bearing Isaac when she was 90. Genesis 18:11 reads: "Abraham and Sarah were already old and well advanced in years, and Sarah was past the age of childbearing." When she heard the prophecy of her bearing a son she laughed. Isaac means, "he laughs". In creating the world, God made something out of nothing. In giving Abraham and Sarah a son, He made something out of nothing.

The inference is to a more dramatic demonstration of God's power than an old woman having a child. Paul spoke of the resurrection of Christ. God gave life to the corpse of Jesus in the same way He enabled Abraham and Sarah to have Isaac. The same power of God takes us in the hopelessness of sin, forgives us, and credits to our account the righteousness of Jesus Himself. That power is available to anyone through faith. We are nothing. He makes non-children, children of the living God. How wonderful is that?

II. Faith Generates Hope When Everything Seems Hopeless (18-21)

A. Faith Faces the Facts but Chooses to See God (18-19)

Abraham wasn't stupid, nor was he an airhead. He faced the fact that he was too old, *"his body was as good as dead,"* and *"that Sarah's womb was also dead."* When God said he was going to father a son, Abraham did not allow science to control his attitude or actions. He faced the facts as he knew them, the impossibility of becoming parents at their age. Faith caused him to go with the promise of God. When everything was hopeless, Abraham believed anyway, deciding to live, not on the basis of what he saw he couldn't do, but on what God said He would do. *"Against all hope, Abraham in hope believed and so became the father of many nations."*

You may hold a worldview that denies the supernatural. You question the existence of God, not understanding how there can be a heaven or hell, or how a person can rise again from the dead. Some of you may even feel that you are personally beyond hope. You despair of life. Raise the questions but also to hear the promise of God— *"believe on the Lord Jesus Christ and you will be saved."* Behind that promise is a God who gives life to the dead and makes something out of nothing.

B. Faith Strengthens a Person to Keep Going (20a)

"Yet he did not waver through unbelief regarding the promise of God, but was strengthened in his faith." Can you imagine this century old fellow going over to Walmart and buying a bunch of diapers, a baby crib, blankets and all? "For your great grand kids, huh, Pops?" the clerk asks. "No, my ninety-year-old wife is going to have a baby." "Oh, is she pregnant?" "Nope, not yet."

All Abraham "had to hang on to was the bare word of God; but that was enough.... The strength of Abraham's faith was precisely that it was unsupported by anything else; it was not something that Abraham could do. It was trust, simple trust, nothing but trust"[42]. With confidence, you can know you

---

42   Dunn, 238.

are going to heaven precisely because you accept it as a gift of God's grace and not a result of your good works.

Faith in God's promises will likewise keep you going every day. God has promised peace when you're anxious, to answer prayer, to help you in temptation, to pick you up when you fall, and to provide for your needs. Jesus promised He is coming back again to take you to a magnificent home He has specifically prepared for you. The time will come when God says, "That's it! It's over." With those promises, we can make it.

C. Faith Praises God Before Anything Happens (20b-21)

Abraham gave glory to God. Though Sarah laughed to herself at the prophecy, she laughed aloud when she got pregnant. Abraham must have told everyone he met what was going to happen and praised God for His gracious gift. How could Abraham do that? Paul stated he was "fully persuaded that God had power to do what He had promised." The key to faith is God's power and integrity. We do not believe a God who is inconsistent or weak, but the immense God of creation in whom everything exists. As A. W. Tozer wrote, "Grant me God and that settles it." Faith takes the promises of God regarding the future and acts as though they have already happened.

D. Faith Results in a Right Relationship with God Because of What Jesus Accomplished (22-25)

Abraham's vital, living, and dynamic faith resulted in God giving him righteousness. The good news is this is not a history lesson.

"The words 'it was credited to him' were written not for him alone, but also for us, to whom God will credit righteousness—for us who believe in Him who raised Jesus our

Lord from the dead. He was delivered over to death for our sins and was raised for our justification."

You can have the audacity to claim today, "I know for certain I am going to heaven because God has made me fit for His home." When does that happen? The moment you join the church, are baptized, give money to charity, or clean up your life? Never in a thousand years! We can't force God to give us a paycheck because we do religious or moral activities. A right standing with God is credited to us the moment we believe in Jesus as Lord and Savior.

Conclusion

In April 1990, an Associated Press article read:

"It's Maundy Thursday, 1990, and thousands of Filipinos are re-enacting the last agony of Jesus. Barefoot, over the hot stone streets in scorching sun, they are dragging heavy wooden crosses, flogging their bare backs bloody with glass-studded whips, grizzly Lenten rituals in which at least a dozen people will be nailed to crosses, seeking redemption through pain and suffering. It is tradition, so in a Moslem shrine in Bangladesh, a woman worshipper offering prayers extended her arms toward one of the crocodiles which live there; it bit off her hand and swallowed it."

It's that kind of religious nonsense that caused Nietzsche to turn in anger and hostility against Christianity and religion. That isn't the Bible. It isn't good news. It isn't good religion. Yet that is what many people think Christianity is. There is no hope nor assurance in religious works. How do you think people are going to get the right picture of how to know God? You and I have to be the conduit of God's Word to lost people.

Writers H.G. Wells and George Bernard Shaw were brilliant men, yet they rejected the Bible. They placed their trust in their own systems of belief, which were based on humanistic rationale. They did not find lasting inner peace and slowly lost confidence in their assumptions. Wells' final literary work has been aptly called "a scream of despair." Shortly before Shaw died in 1950, he wrote, "The science to which I pinned my faith is bankrupt. Its counsels, which should have established the millennium, have led directly to the suicide of Europe. I believed them once. In their name, I helped to destroy the faith of millions. And now they look at me and witness the great tragedy of an atheist who has lost his faith."

This passage is primarily about Abraham as an illustration of how a person is made right before God. It also speaks about hope when everything around us seems hopeless. What in your life is the hopeless situation? How can Abraham's experience be helpful to you as you face a bleak future? God's call of Abraham to begin a people through whom the Savior would come was unique to him. You and I aren't in that position. He also was given a specific promise about fathering a son through whom the Savior would come. That doesn't fit us either.

The heart of this magnificent story is a trustworthy God. Regardless of the hopelessness of any problem, God will be true to Himself and to you. You can trust Him. He will always be there for you. There may be some promises in the Bible that directly address your situation. Claim them. Make them personal. The primary issue involved in your hopeless situation is not your impotence but God's power. The core of this passage is that "Abraham's faith was nothing other than unquestioning trust in God's power." We can have the same faith Abraham had because we worship the same God.

He did not waver through unbelief regarding the promise of God, but was strengthened in his faith and gave glory to

God, being fully persuaded that God had power to do what He had promised.

For your reflection:
- What description does Hebrews 11:6 give of faith? How does the rest of the chapter support the description?
- Romans 10:17 states the origin, basis and development of faith. Taking this verse literally, how can you grow in your faith?
- Why do you feel the concept of works, doing good or religious things, persists in people's minds as the way a person can go heaven?
- How good does a person have to be to earn heaven? Jesus answered that in Matthew 5:48. Does that support the idea that a person can be good enough to earn heaven?
-

12

Romans 5:1-5

Peace in Spite of Pain

"Justification means more than the removal of guilt. Justification does not leave a man morally neutral; it is to be made righteous, to have the righteousness of Christ added.... This it is to be justified; not simply to be absolved from guilt but literally to be made righteous by Jesus Christ, to be seen by God in the righteousness of Jesus Christ. When the Father looks at the justified man, he sees him clothed in the perfection of the son of God."[43]

Scripture: Romans 5:1-5

Main Idea: faith brings peace with God and purpose to adversities and suffering.

Introduction

In early December 1983 while Jerry Levin was bureau chief at Cable News Network's Chicago's bureau, CNN's president asked him to transfer to Beirut, Lebanon, to run the company's troubled bureau there and to serve as a correspondent. Three weeks later he was in Beirut, a country brutalized by war. He worked seven days a week for the next eleven weeks covering the war that had devastated that country. It was probably the most dangerous assignment in the world. On March 7, 1984, he was kidnapped by terrorists and held hostage for eleven and a half weeks.

---

43   Richard C. Halverson, *Prologue to Prison: Paul's Epistle to the Romans* (Los Angeles, California: Cowman Publishing Company, Inc., 1964), 113.

Charles Colson tells the story of what happened: "In his captivity, Jerry Levin discovered ultimate freedom: After struggling for weeks with the question of whether or not God is real, the former atheist made his decision. He says, 'I approached and then crossed a kind of spiritual Rubicon, a diminishing point in time, a shrinking thousandth, then millionth of a second, on one side of which I did not believe and then on the other side I did.'

"For his wife, Lucille, or 'Sis,' Jerry's imprisonment provided a challenge not only to rely on her faith in the God who could use the evil intentions of Jerry's captors for good, but also to fight for her husband's release. After months of waiting for news, she traveled to Syria. There she met with officials to determine what could be done to free Jerry; she also worked in a rehabilitation hospital for children wounded in Middle East hostilities. Her actions demonstrated the integrity of her message of reconciliation.

"The Levins' message today is still one of reconciliation: of the God who draws men and women to himself, and of the forgiveness and restoration so desperately needed in a world fractured by hostility."[44]

John Keats wrote:

"The weariness, the fever, and the fret,

Here where men sit and hear each other groan."

We groan any time adversity comes to us: we get sick and groan (Sandra would describe me as a groaner). We lose our job or don't get a raise, are misunderstood by someone, go through interpersonal conflicts, financial losses, or the death of a friend or loved one—and we groan.

---

44   Charles Colson, *World*, 7/1/89.

Having established that a person gains a right relationship with God only by faith in Jesus Christ as redeemer and the atoning sacrifice for our sins, Paul then spelled out the ramifications of such a faith. His first statement is of the personal benefit received of having peace with God, and the power to look at adversity from a distinctly different viewpoint.

"Therefore, since we have been justified through faith, we have peace with God through our Lord Jesus Christ, through whom we have gained access by faith into this grace in which we now stand. And we rejoice in the hope of the glory of God. Not only so, but we also rejoice in our sufferings, because we know that suffering produces perseverance; perseverance, character; and character, hope. And hope does not disappoint us, because God has poured out his love into our hearts by the Holy Spirit, whom he has given us."

I. Faith Results in Peace with God (1-2a)

A. Peace with God is Based Upon Justification by Faith (1)

For review, "justify" is a word that comes from the court of law and means that God treats sinners as righteous, not as their sins deserve. He erases our sins from the debit column and puts in the credit column the very righteousness of Jesus. We experience that only through faith, not by following religious rituals or keeping a moral code.

The basis of our faith is God's R.O.P. In the dairy business, a "record of performance" is kept on each cow. The cow's milk is weighed and the butterfat content is measured. After a few years, a cow establishes a R.O.P.—record of performance. A buyer is interested not only in the cow but her offspring. He is pretty sure that if the cow was a good producer, the heifer born to her will be also. The buyer has faith in the cow, and puts the money where his faith is.

By examining biblical and Christian history the Christian can establish God's R.O.P. The Old Testament is a record of His performance in fulfilling His promises to His people. Everything we have is ours only through the Lord Jesus Christ. It is not ours through the church, our personal good works, or performing religious ritual. We enjoy God's blessings through faith.

The result of that faith is peace, not primarily personal peace, but peace with God. Out of peace with God comes peace in interpersonal relations. The angel's statement to the shepherds at the nativity has been misunderstood because of a poor translation. It is not peace on earth, good will toward men, but peace to men on whom His favor rests. It is not the good will of men but the saving action of God which brings peace to people.

Peace with God controls how we respond under the pressures of adversity. A person who becomes a Christian to escape the pressures of life is under a delusion. Jesus promised that "in this world you will have trouble. But take heart! I have overcome the world." What the Christian does have is a sense of purpose in it all and an inner power to cope through the Holy Spirit.

B. Peace with God Gives Us Access into Grace (2a)

"Access" refers to being ushered into the presence of royalty. Imagine if you had access into a powerful and rich monarch, any time for anything. Through Jesus we have access into the throne room of the almighty God. Hebrews 4:16 states we can come boldly before His throne to make our requests. How? Our consciences have been made clean through the blood of Christ. Jesus paid the price for our sin. He spanned the gap between sinful humanity and a holy God. He tore the veil that shrouded God from humanity.

In that grace, we stand. There is a confident strength in Paul's statement. A person can stand in the presence of God because it is a gift, not a paycheck she or he has earned.

II. Faith Produces Joy (2b-5)

A. The Christian Rejoices in the Glory of God (2b)

At the root of the word for "rejoice" is the idea of boasting. Rather than boasting in our religious activities, or keeping some moral code, or in being a Jew or an American, we boast in God's glory. God's glory is the praise He receives for providing our salvation. He gets all the credit, all the glory from the believer. Every Sunday we sing hymns and songs of praise to God for who He is and what He has done for sinful humanity.

B. The Christian Rejoices in Suffering (3-5)

L. E. Maxwell, founder of Prairie Bible Institute in Three Hills, Alberta, Canada, wrote *Crowded to Christ* in 1950. In the first chapter he stated if pain, poverty, affliction, wars, plagues, famines, disease, destruction, death, endless tyranny, unpitied tears, broken hearts crowd people to Christ, they are of great value. I have known many people who never gave God the time of day until their lives collapsed around them.

Rod Foster, known as "The Rocket" in the world of basketball was a UCLA great and played in the NBA. He was raised in a Christian home, but UCLA was 3,000 miles from home. He said: "I stopped going to church. I just got wrapped up by the peer pressure. It got even worse in the NBA. The three years I played in the NBA were just wild and carefree. I was partying at clubs every night. I was more concerned about what we were going to do after the ballgame, instead of focusing on the ballgame itself."

While four-wheeling in the desert, his Jeep began to fishtail. Foster instinctively put out his left foot and it snapped just above the ankle in a compound fracture. "I can remember lying in the desert thinking: 'This didn't happen.' But a second later, I thought: 'This happened for a reason.'" The reason became clear during recovery.

Three months after the accident he went to a party in L.A. It was shortly after the cocaine deaths of Len Bias and Don Rogers. He had known Rogers and it shocked him to realize that a young guy could die. After watching a film, "Faces of Death," he drove home haunted by the question, "If I were to die right now, what would happen to me? Where would I go?"

He called a Christian friend that night and asked him to take him to church. At the end of that service he went forward to place his trust in Christ as Savior and Lord.

One of the products of faith in Christ is a different perspective on adversity and suffering. The Christian can boast in adversity knowing that God is working out His plan of redemption. Adversity, or suffering, is to be under pressure and go through pain, like crushing grapes. Paul knew the pressures of adversity:

> *"It seems to me that God has put us apostles on display.... We have been made a spectacle.... We are fools for Christ.... We are weak ... dishonored. To this very hour, we go hungry and thirsty, we are in rags, we are brutally treated, we are homeless. We work hard with our own hands. When we are cursed, we bless; when we are persecuted, we endure it; when we are slandered, we answer kindly. Up to this moment we have become the scum of the earth, the refuse of the world" (1 Cor. 4:9-13).*

Our Scripture gives three distinctive perspectives on suffering's value:

1. Adversity produces perseverance. "Perseverance" means to overcome the trials and tribulations of life, not to passively stick it out. It is standing with our face to the storm. When Beethoven was confronted with his deafness, he said, "I will take life by the throat." The Christian perseveres in submission to and dependence upon Christ.

2. Perseverance produces character. The special meaning of character refers to something proven through testing. The person who has persevered through suffering can testify to God's faithfulness to His promises. We know God more than theoretically; we have experienced Him in the tough times. In addition, Peter says we are purified like gold that goes through fire. God uses adversity to clean up our lives. Sterling silver is free of alloy, and God's work in us this side of heaven is to use suffering to clean us up in preparation for the future.

3. Proven character produces hope and hope will not disappoint us. If we never hurt, if all of our personal needs are perfectly fulfilled, then we would not have a longing for the future where God has promised a perfect environment and a totally fulfilled existence. We go through life with a degree of emptiness, of a longing that one day Christ will fully satisfy. That is not escapism, its realism.

We know our hope will not disappoint us because we have experienced the love of God by the inside work of the Holy Spirit. That love is more than intellectual. It is love that touches the heart, the soul, in a powerful way, and changes our lives.

Conclusion

C. S. Lewis said, "God whispers to us in our pleasures, speaks to us in our work, but shouts to us in our pains." In 1975 Gallop conducted a survey and found a significant relationship between changes in faith and what was termed "periods of transition and crisis." The crises most often mentioned were long periods of loneliness, a conscious decision to leave one's present church or faith community, undergoing professional counseling or therapy for emotional difficulty, the birth of a child (for both fathers and mothers), divorce, and being born again. Your situation may fit into one of these or be in a different category, but you are going through a personal crisis of some sort. The value of faith in the Lord Jesus Christ is first the peace we have with God. Second, it is gaining a new perspective on suffering. There is purpose to the seemingly random events of life. God who loves us is working in the suffering to develop a maturity and hope.

Paul Brand was a world-renowned hand surgeon and leprosy specialist—the disease that takes away the ability to feel pain. In the opening chapter in his book, *Pain: the Gift Nobody Wants*, he wrote:

> "Few experiences in life are more universal than pain, which flows like lava beneath the crust of daily life. I know well the typical attitude toward pain, especially in Western societies. J. K. Huysmans calls it "the useless, unjust, incomprehensible, inept abomination that is physical pain." Neurologist Russell Martin adds, "Pain is greedy, boorish, meanly debilitating. It is cruel and calamitous and often constant, and, as its Latin root *poena* implies, it is the corporeal punishment each of us ultimately suffers for being alive."

> "I have heard similar complaints from patients. My own encounters with pain, though, as well as the specter of painlessness, have produced in me an attitude of wonder and appreciation. I do not desire, and cannot even imagine, a life without pain. For that reason, I accept the challenge of trying to restore balance to how we think about pain.

"For good or for ill, the human species has among its privileges the preeminence of pain. We have the unique ability to step outside ourselves and self-reflect, by reading a book about pain, for example, or by summoning up the memory of a terrifying ordeal. Some pains—the pain of grief or emotional trauma—have no physical stimulus whatever. They are states of mind, concocted by the alchemy of the brain. These feats of consciousness make it possible for suffering to loiter in the mind long after the body's need for it has passed. Yet they also give us the potential to attain an outlook that will change the very landscape of the pain experience. We can learn to cope, and even to triumph."[45]

Helen Lesheid offered these coping tools in *Discipleship Journal:* (1) Maintain as normal a schedule as possible. (2) Plan happy experiences for yourself. (3) Be grateful for the small blessings of life. (4) Seek out people who can encourage you.[46]

The Christian's hope pays off when suffering comes. Without hope, life is little more than random meaninglessness. Robert Marston interviewed twelve people about the relationship of their spiritual beliefs to suffering. Six were atheists or agnostics, six were active church members. The Christian interviewees all shared vivid accounts of how God had helped them in their time of need. The non-believers had similar experiences of escaping from difficult circumstances but attributed their deliverance to luck or their own skill. The difference between the two groups was not just a matter of labels.

The Christians who experienced the presence of God all indicated that it resulted in a changed outlook and an ability

---

[45] Paul Brand, Philipp Yancy, *Pain: the Gift Nobody Wants* (London: Marshall Pickering, 1994), 12-13.
[46] Helen Lesheid, *Discipleship Journal*, Nov/Dec 1990 [Issue 60], 16-19.

to cope with their particular challenges more successfully. Although members of both groups went through similar emotions (fear, joy, anxiety), the Christians found a great sense of peace based upon their belief in the purposefulness of their existence. The atheists did not have this peace, particularly when facing death. Marston concluded that because God had definitely intervened in the Christians' lives they have internal strength for facing future trials. Non-believers simply do not have any comparable resource [47].

I would add a fifth to Helen Lesheid's coping skills: deliberately, audibly, thank God that He is faithful, victorious, and lovingly working out His plan. Boasting in Him brings peace when in pain.

For your reflection:
- What are the benefits of justification in Halverson's opening quotation?
- How has your experience of suffering and its result correspond to Paul's outline of benefits in verses 3-5.
- Compare this passage with James 1:2-7

---

[47] Robert Marston, "Experiencing the Presence of God During Times of Need: a case study" (*Journal of Pastoral Care*, Fall 1990), 258-264.

13

Romans 5:6-11

Life for the Powerless

"There is no passage of the New Testament which has had such an influence on theology as this passage; and there is no passage which is more difficult for a modern mind to understand.... If we were to put the thought of this passage into one sentence...it would be this: 'By the sin of Adam all men became sinners and were alienated from God; by the righteousness of Jesus Christ all men become righteous and are restored to a right relationship with God.'"[48]

Scripture: Romans 5:6-11

Main Idea: God's love, proved by Jesus' death for us, justified, reconciled, delivered us from wrath, and gave us life.

Introduction

A Spanish lad in Vigo, a coastal city in northwest Spain, was asked one day by an Englishman why he had become a Christian. "It was all because of the odd sparrow," the boy replied. "I do not understand," said the Englishman.

"Well, Senõr, it is this way. A man gave me a Testament and I read in one Gospel that two sparrows were sold for a farthing. And again in Luke, I saw, 'Are not five sparrows sold for two farthings...?' And I said to myself that Nuestro Senõr Jesus Christ knew well our custom of selling birds. As you know, sir, we trap birds, and get one chico for two, but for two

---
[48] William Barclay, *The Letter to the Romans* (Philadelphia: The Westminster Press,1957), 77.

chicos we throw in an extra sparrow. That extra sparrow is only a make-weight, and of no account at all.

"Now, I think to myself that I am so insignificant, so poor and so small that no one would think of counting me. I'm like the fifth sparrow. And yet Nuestro Senõr says, 'Not one of them is forgotten before God.' I have never heard anything like it, Sir. No one but He could ever have thought of not forgetting me."

In Romans 5:1-5 Paul identifies the first two practical expressions of believing in Jesus Christ. They are peace with God, and a perspective on adversity that allows us to accept the power and love of God in those times of hurt. We rejoice in sufferings because they produce perseverance; "perseverance, character; and character, hope. And hope does not disappoint us, because God has poured out His love into our hearts by the Holy Spirit, whom He has given us."

Next, He assures us that God's love is unique because He loved us when we were powerless, ungodly, sinners, enemies.

I. God Loves Us (6-8)

> *"You see, at just the right time, when we were still powerless, Christ died for the ungodly. Very rarely will anyone die for a righteous man, though for a good man someone might possibly dare to die. But God demonstrates his own love for us in this: While we were still sinners, Christ died for us."*

The evidence of the depth of God's love is who and what we were when He demonstrated His love for us. It was at the "right time." God's timing is always perfect. We often wonder about His alertness to our hurts and problems, but He never misses. Hebrews 4:16: "Let us then [because Jesus sympathizes with our weaknesses] approach the throne of grace with confidence so that we may receive mercy and find grace to help us in our time of need." As in Romans, the word for "time" has reference to critically right time, the opportune time.

His love is proved by who and what we were when He loved us enough to die for us.

A. He Loves Sinners

There is a crescendo of description of our condition. First, we are powerless, weak (6). Second, we are ungodly (7), living as though God didn't matter. Third, we are sinners (8) guilty of breaking His laws. Fourth, we are enemies (10) who hate God.

God loves us in that condition. Lucy and Snoopy were talking together. She shouts, "There are times when you really bug me! I must admit, however, there are times when I feel like giving you a hug." In a nonchalant manner Snoopy responds, "That's the way I am, Lucy, huggable and buggable." In this Scripture, there aren't any 'huggable' qualities to us.

God knows us accurately in every detail of thought, motive and act, and yet He loves us. He doesn't call on us to do some great moral or religious acts to make us lovable. There isn't anything we can do. He doesn't love us because of our beauty or huggableness, He loves us because that is what He is. It is His nature to love the sinner.

The word "demonstrates" is in the present tense indicating an on-going activity. He didn't just love us 2,000 years ago when Jesus died and rose again, He still loves us. He died once, but His love is on-going and the value of His death and resurrection applies to us now.

How did God love us? Aggressively. He came seeking us. Jesus used the comparison to a shepherd who left the ninety-nine-safe sheep and went out into the night and cold to find the one that was lost. Finding it, He put it on His shoulders, carried it back home and nursed it to health.

A story in the *Sunshine Magazine* told of a professor of psychology who had no children of his own. Whenever he saw a neighbor scolding a child for some wrongdoing, he would say, "You should love your boy, not punish him."

One hot summer afternoon the prof was doing some repair work on a concrete driveway leading to his garage. Tired after several hours of work, he laid down the trowel, wiped the perspiration from his forehead, and started toward the house. Just then out of the corner of his eye he caught a little boy putting his foot into the fresh cement. He rushed over, grabbed him, and was about to spank him. A neighbor watching the scene, leaned out the window and yelled, "Watch it, Professor! Don't you remember? You must 'love' the child!" The prof yelled back furiously, "I do love him in the abstract but not in the concrete!"

B. His Love Took Him to Death

"While we were still sinners, Christ died for us [for the sake of, or benefit of]."

Paul wrote that it might be possible for some to die for a good person, but no one is going to die for an evil person, and especially one who is an enemy.

After the U.S.S. Pueblo was captured by the North Koreans off the Korean coast in the Sea of Japan on January 23, 1968, the 82 surviving crew members were thrown into brutal captivity. In one instance, 13 of the men were required to sit in a rigid manner around a table for hours. After several hours the door was violently flung open and a Korean guard brutally beat the man in the first chair with the butt of his rifle. The next day as each man sat at his assigned place, the door was thrown open and the man in the first chair was harshly beaten again. On the third day, same scene and the same man was beaten.

Knowing his colleague could not survive, a young sailor took his place. When the door was flung open the guard automatically beat the new victim senseless. For weeks, each day a new man stepped forward to sit in that horrible chair knowing full well what would happen. At last the guards gave up in exasperation. They couldn't defeat that kind of love.

In far greater measure, God demonstrated His love for us in paying our debt of sin. As I applied this to my life, I thought, "I'm a fairly decent person. Some might even call me a good man. However, I don't know of anyone who would deliberately choose to give their life that I might live. As a sinner in rebellion against God, Christ died for me." That's how much God loves us.

II. In Love He Saved Us (9-10)

> *"Since we have now been justified by his blood, how much more shall we be saved from God's wrath through him! For if, when we were God's enemies, we were reconciled to him through the death of his Son, how much more, having been reconciled, shall we be saved through his life!"*

Three wonderful things God achieved for us in His saving love:

A. We Are Justified Through His Blood

Because Jesus paid the legal debt of our sin in giving His blood through death on the cross, God now treats us as though we had no sin.

B. We are Saved from Wrath

In the first chapter, God is emphatically angry with our sin. Now through Christ, we are delivered from that wrath. God's attributes of love and justice are never in conflict. Some refer to the kindness and severity of God. It is not either/or with God; it is both/and. A. W. Tozer wrote: "Justice embodies the idea of moral equity, and iniquity is the exact opposite; it is in-equity, the absence of equality from human thoughts and acts. Judgment is the application of equity to moral situations and may be favorable or unfavorable according to whether the one under examination has been equitable or inequitable in heart and conduct."[49] God's wrath focuses on ungodliness, or behavior that defies and deliberately violates God's law. The purpose of the Ten Commandments, or the Law, is to express the essential nature of who God is as the ultimate moral being. Sin violates God and brings His just wrath in judgment. Is it personal? Yes, because in love God established boundaries for the joy, health and life of His creation. Because every person has sinned and is therefore under God's wrath, Jesus, in love, took the penalty Himself, and through His blood delivered those who placed their faith in Him from God's judgment.

C. We are Reconciled to God

Once enemies we are now made friends of God. We must realize that we were the enemies, not God. We needed to be reconciled to God, not He to us.

The phrase, "how much more," appears in vv. 9-10. It is used to emphasize the total package of what is included in God's saving actions to us. He justifies us, delivers us from wrath, reconciles us to Himself, and gives us His eternal life.

III. In Response, to God's Love and Salvation, we are to Rejoice in Him (11)

> *"Not only is this so, but we also rejoice in God through our Lord Jesus Christ, through whom we have now received reconciliation."*

---

[49] A. W. Tozer, *The Knowledge of The Holy* (New York: Harper and row Publishers, 1961), 93.

A. We Rejoice in God through Christ

Again, Paul's emphasis is the contrast of the boasting of a religious person bragging about all the things he or she has done, versus a believer bragging about all the things Jesus has done on her or his behalf.

B. How We Can Express our Rejoicing

We are to rejoice in God through our Lord Jesus Christ. We are not told how. Rejoicing in God is an act of worship. The word for "rejoice" is in the present tense indicating something that we are to do continuously.[50] Our hymns and choruses of praise rejoice in God's power and love as found in our salvation.

Another way to rejoice in God is to tell others of His love and salvation. The woman of Samaria who experienced the power of Jesus' forgiving love did not keep it a secret. She didn't have a defined presentation of the Gospel to give, she simply told everyone in the town of Sychar of her encounter with Jesus. Because of the depth of skepticism about religion in our day, how we live our lives before unbelievers is as important as going through a Gospel presentation. They need to see the reality of the change God has accomplished in our lives.

Conclusion

Perhaps you have seen or read the dramatic story of "Damien". It is the moving story of a Belgian Priest, Damien DeVeuster, who gave his life to care for lepers on the island of Molokai, Hawaii. He died in 1889 at the age of 49. At that time, Molokai was a place where lepers were banned to literally rot and die. A leper was considered an unclean person and isolated from society.

---

50   Dunn,261.

Damien felt God's call to be a witness to the ends of the earth, including Molokai. He went to his bishop and asked permission to move to the island to be with the people and do what he could to help them. The bishop loved the young priest and felt he had great potential and so tried to argue him out of throwing away his life in a place of desolation. Damien persisted and was allowed to go.

He said that in the early weeks he was often dreadfully sick at his stomach as he moved among the people and saw the horror of their living conditions. It was all he could do to force himself to stay in spite of his strong intention. But he went to work. First, he found a source of fresh water in a nearby mountain and devised a system of getting it to the colony. From this came a sanitation system. He showed the lepers how to build little houses to replace the flimsy shacks and hovels in which they had been living. He built a clinic and, although he had little medical knowledge, he dressed their sores and gave them some comfort.

Damien helped them build a small chapel where he preached on Sunday. The lepers became accustomed to seeing him go into the pulpit every Sunday, cross himself, and begin the sermon with these words: "You lepers know that God the Father loves you." And then he would preach a sermon of hope, full of life and joy.

Several years went by until one Sunday morning he went into the pulpit, crossed himself and said, "We lepers know that God the Father loves us." It was the first indication that Damien had contracted leprosy. He continued to pour out his love in ministry until he died among the lepers he learned to love through Christ.

Jesus came to give life to powerless, ungodly, sinful enemies. You might be like the Spanish boy who thought he didn't count, or like a leper. God loves you now. He not only paid the price of your sin, He became sin so that you might stand clean before a holy God.

"God demonstrates His own love for us in this: While we were still sinners, Christ died for us."

For your reflection:
- Describe your inner thoughts and feelings when you think about God's love.
- What is your favorite way of rejoicing in Jesus and His saving grace?
- What does it mean that you are reconciled to God?
- Some have scorned Christianity as a bloody religion. Why do we rejoice in the fact of Jesus' blood?

Do I Have to be GOOD to go to Heaven?

14

Romans 5:12-21

Lives in Contrast: Adam and Jesus

"Here then is the problem of sin. Adam, by the fall, introduced to his race, as yet unborn, the deadly virus of sin. We are not sinners because we sin' we sin because we are sinners. And because we sinned in Adam, death is imputed to us. Therefore, we die, some younger, some older, but sooner or later we die."[51]

Scripture: Romans 5:12-21

Main Idea: Every person is in one of two cycles; the first cycle leads to death; the second cycle leads to life. It all depends upon a person's association with Adam or Christ.

Introduction

"With few dissenting exceptions, 96 hours and 96 zillion column inches of sentiment washed over the falls about how all this proved the need for 'safe sex' before someone finally said that Magic Johnson's sex life was, simply, wrong" wrote Daniel Henninger in an editorial of the *Wall Street Journal* (December, 1991).

Entitled "The Joy of What?" the essay condemned sex scandals involving public figures and rejected the moral relativism spawned by the sexual revolution. The writer,

---

51   John Phillips, Exploring Romans: the Gospel According to Paul (Chicago: Moody Monthly, 1969)96.

who is deputy editor of the paper, lamented that just about everybody—including churches—were afraid to speak out about the old-fashioned idea of sin. In the case of Magic Johnson, a lot was said about his experience proving the need for "safe sex" before hardly anyone ever suggested that his lifestyle was just plain wrong. Henninger, a Catholic, said that priests and ministers have less credibility than therapists these days, but it is time for people in positions of responsibility to let people know that some of the things they are doing are morally wrong. The editorial was later reprinted as a full-page ad in the business section of the *New York Times*.[52]

Some people want to blame God for the bad things in the world and ignore the reality that God isn't the one guilty of sin. People do sinful things and most of the time their sins damage other people. We don't want to face the fact of sin and our accountability for sinful behavior. Why people sin is a fundamental question and the Bible is the only book with a valid answer.

The world was locked in shock by the downing of TWA Flight 800 (July 17, 1996) now defined as a terrorist act. We have heard the stories of a husband and father whose beautiful wife and two daughters were on that flight; of the 16 high school French students and five chaperones from Montoursville, PA, who were on their way to France to visit the country first-hand and try out their language skills for real. Did God do that, or did evil people plan and carry-out their murderous designs? Since then are the travesties of multiple terrorist acts of destruction including the twin towers on September 11, 2001.

Mark Twain and Charles Dudley Warner wrote in *The Guilded Age*: "You can buy now and then a Senator or a

---

52   "An editorial on sin." *National & International Religion Report*, Jan 27, 1992, 2.

Representative; but they do not know it is wrong, and so they are not ashamed of it." John Noonan wrote a book bluntly titled, *Bribes*. He illustrated a gallery of public figures including Francis Bacon, Thomas á Becket, and presidents Monroe, Garfield, Johnson, and Nixon. Whitewater ground on for years before forcing President Nixon to resign. The Clintons have been involved in one scandal after another. Why do men in public trust sell themselves in bribery?

An evangelical pastor in Michigan was arrested a few years ago, for robbing five banks to raise money for sex with prostitutes. The papers said he "robbed banks to satisfy an insatiable desire for sex." How can a pastor who fully understood the Gospel and Christian life principles become so debased?

We have been horrified by the human carnage in Serbia in the late nineties. Then there is Rwanda's massacre of tens of thousands. Do we remember the bloodshed under communist Romania's Nicolae Ceausescu? Amnesty International exposed Saddam Hussein's gross brutalities in Kuwait. How can people be so debased? How can a woman sell a baby to get drugs? How can a spouse walk out on a mate to take a fling with someone else? Why the seething racial hatred gurgling like molten lava that erupts easily and quickly in violence? Is God to blame?

In a very complex passage, Paul addresses the heart of the human problem. The world analyzes the problem through psychological, political, and sociological perspectives. The Bible goes to the heart and addresses the spiritual roots of sin.

This passage contrasts the lives and results of two men: Adam and Jesus. Every person is in one of two cause and effect cycles: Cycle one is sin-condemnation-death. Cycle two is the gift of righteousness-justification-life. We are born into cycle one as children of Adam. No choice, no options. It's the fact of human existence since Adam. We get into cycle two through faith in Jesus Christ. Only those who believe in Him are in that cycle.

These verses are a conclusion to the first five chapters. Paul now addresses humanity as a whole, the cause of sin, and its antidote in Christ. This is a difficult passage which leaves many unanswered questions and ambiguities. We will only seek to understand the clear statements.

I. The Result of the Life of Adam: Sin-Condemnation-Death (12-14)

A. Everyone Belongs to this Cycle Because We Belong to Adam

"You know the story of how Adam landed us in the dilemma we're in—first sin, then death, and no one exempt from either sin or death."

Without stating how sin came, Paul simply says it came into the world through one man. Adam is not named until v. 14, and Eve is omitted as the person responsible for the curse. Man was God's first creation and bore the accountability for his actions. Adam's act was a deliberate disobedience of God's law—don't eat of the fruit of the tree of the knowledge of good and evil. 1 John 3 defines sin as disobedience. Seduced by Satan, Adam ate, and sin entered the world.

The proof of our identity with Adam is our own personal deliberate disobedience to God. We, too, have been seduced and have broken God's law. Whether we have a Bible or not, are cultured or primitive, all have sinned.

B. We Belong to Adam through Sin (13-14).

That sin disturbed relations with God in everything and everyone, but the extent of the disturbance was not clear until

God spelled it out in detail to Moses. Death, this huge abyss separating us from God, dominated the landscape from Adam to Moses. Even those who didn't sin precisely as Adam did by disobeying a specific command of God still had to experience this termination of life, this separation from God. But Adam, who got us into this also pointed ahead to the One who would get us out of it.

There is a break in thought at the end of verse 12. Typical of Paul, he interrupts the continuity of his statement to clarify what he just said. He doesn't continue his thought again until verse 18. The comments of verses 13-17 are a clarification of verse 12 in which he stated everyone has sinned and that is why everyone dies.

The proof that all are sinners is that all die. Before Moses and the law, people died. People without the Bible or religion, die. People died who had no knowledge of Old Testament law. The only reason people die is because the cycle of sin produces death, and we are all sinners. Sin is personified here as a power that drives people to disobedience and therefore to death. However, even innocent babies and small children who do not have the capacity of understanding right and wrong die. Why? Because the sin of Adam is imputed to all humans. I do not accept the concept that unless an infant is baptized by a clergyman before death they will be separated from God. The love of God imputes to the child the righteousness of Christ in the same way as the sin of Adam was imputed resulting in the child's death.[53]

Adam is an epochal figure whose choices have affected all human beings. He singularly brought sin into the world. Because of sin's power, every human being has the disease. There is no inoculation. There is a cure. The cure

---

53 See John Phillips and Martin Luther for a more complete discussion, or a Reformed theologian of your choice.

distinguishes the New Testament from the Old Testament. Sin's effect and power were countered by Jesus Christ.

In verse 12, sin is presented as a power that brings death. In verses 13-14, sin is an act for which every human is accountable. Original sin means we are all under the power of sin, but we are not accountable, or guilty, for Adam's act of sin. This is a primary difference between Protestant and Roman Catholic theology. A priest must baptize an infant shortly after birth for it is actually under judgment for Adam's sin. This passage does not teach that. It does teach that because of the power of sin, everyone sins and so is guilty for their own sinful actions.

One last point. A person with a moral code, or the one we call a religious person, is all the more in need of God's salvation because defining right and wrong emphasizes a person's guilt rather than removing it.

II. The Result of the Life of Jesus: the Gift of Righteousness-Justification-Life (15-17)

A. Righteousness is a Gift of Grace through Christ (15-16)

Yet the rescuing gift is not exactly parallel to the death-dealing sin. If one man's sin put crowds of people at the dead-end abyss of separation from God, just think what God's gift poured through one man, Jesus Christ, will do! There's no comparison between that death-dealing sin and this generous, life-giving gift. The verdict on that one sin was the death sentence; the verdict on the many sins that followed was this wonderful life sentence.

Several contrasts highlight a celebration of God's grace in this paragraph. Dunn wrote that "it is language of fervent worship rather than of cold theological reflection."[54] As sin is

---
54   Dunn, 293.

personified in its power, so grace is described in terms of divine power to liberate. The first contrast: if there was power in sin because of one man's sin, there is greater power in overcoming sin in the grace of God. The second contrast: judgment and condemnation came by one man's sin, whereas the gift of God is a "wonderful life sentence."

B. Grace Makes Us Winners in Life through Christ (17)

"If death got the upper hand through one man's wrongdoing, can you imagine the breathtaking recovery life makes, sovereign life, in those who grasp with both hands this wildly extravagant life-gift, this grand setting-everything-right, that the one-man Jesus Christ provides?" (The Message)

A third contrast. One man's sin brought death. One man, Jesus Christ, brought an abundance of grace and God's "wildly extravagant life-gift." Obviously, it is spiritual life, not just physical. We don't have just a trickle of life, it is "wildly extravagant." That is both right now in our present life and will also be ours in heaven.

The next paragraph brings us to conclusion.

III. Which Cycle we're in Depends upon Whether We Are Attached to Adam or to Christ (18-21)

A. The Cycles Are Products of the Two Men (18-19)

Paul's original thought is picked up again. Let's read it without the break in thought.

"You know the story of how Adam landed us in the dilemma we're in—first sin, then death, and no one exempt from either sin or death.... Here it is in a nutshell: Just as one person did it wrong and got us in all this trouble with sin and death, another person did it right and got us out of it. But more than just getting us out of trouble, he got us

into life! One man said no to God and put many people in the wrong; one man said yes to God and put many in the right."

One man brought death to all—every human being. So one man brought justification to all—the basis of receiving is faith in Jesus Christ. Through the disobedience of one man, Adam, the world was made sinners. Through the obedience of one man, Jesus Christ, all who believe are made right with God.

B. The Moral Code Brought Death; Grace Brought Life (20-21)

All that passing laws against sin did was produce more lawbreakers. But sin didn't, and doesn't, have a chance in competition with the aggressive forgiveness we call grace. When it's sin versus grace, grace wins hands down. All sin can do is threaten us with death, and that's the end of it. Grace, because God is putting everything together again through the Messiah, invites us into life—a life that goes on and on and on, without end.

Rather than the religious person taking comfort in having a moral code, as the Jew who had the law of God, they are brought to judgment because their sin of disobedience is more sharply evident. As sin has reigned in death in human history, so grace will reign through the righteousness of Christ to bring us eternal life.

Conclusion

Paul has systematically outlined in these five chapters that the primary condition of all humanity is sin. We are born separated from God as children of Adam and prove our ancestry by our own personal, deliberate acts of sin. How can sinners come into a right relationship with God? Negatively, we cannot be made right with God by going to church, being religious, or trying to live up to some list of right and wrong. The good news is that God, in love and grace, has provided the way to Himself. It is a gift that is undeserved and unearned. A gift can only be received, and God's gift can only be received by faith. The first matter for each of us is to know whether we are in Adam still, or if we have moved over into Christ.

I can understand and better live with some degree of sanity if I know that most of the evil in the world is the result of sinful people doing sinful acts against God and other people. That isn't going to change, and it isn't any worse now than it has been historically. Humanity's record is wretched.

But why do people, who have moved from Adam to Christ, who have received God's gift of forgiveness and eternal life, do sinful things? The next eleven chapters provide a theological discussion of what goes on inside when Christians sin and the resources God has provided to enable us to live this wildly extravagant life of victory.

Why do evil things happen to good people who belong to God as well as to good people who are separated from God? God has promised to be with His children. He does protect us. We will find out in eternity how many times He directly intervened to keep us from tragedy. He hasn't said we will escape the sting of all evil or bad things. Christians, too, find themselves on the receiving end of a bomb on an airplane, or some stray bullet. We also have hope. When believers die they go immediately into God's presence. The sinner goes into an eternity of total separation from God and all that is good in hell.

In addition, God has promised to walk with us and in us by His Holy Spirit to provide the inside strength to cope with life's disappointments and pain. We aren't left to struggle alone.

Ultimate victory and reigning in life are assured in heaven. We will be victorious. Between now and then, we will know valleys and mountains, plains and desert, failures, victories, joys, sorrows. Jesus is victorious over every expression of sin we face. The more we know Him and walk in His life and power, the more that "wildly extravagant life" we have in Him will be ours in experience.

There is a gruesome but spiritually graphic event in Judges 1:1-7. After Joshua's death, Judah attacked the little country of Bezek. Their king's name was Adoni-Bezek, meaning, Lord-lightning. He might have been a fast runner, because when he saw he was getting whipped, he ran. They chased him down and cut off his thumbs and big toes. He then could no longer hold a sword or run. That is what Jesus has done to Satan. He has defanged the snake. He has crippled the lord of hell.

For your reflection:
- What is sin, and why do people sin?
- This sermon summarizes the passage with two cycles: what are they and what is your understanding of their meaning?

15

Romans 6:1-11, Part 1

The Way to Life is Through Death: a Lesson from the Phoenix

"If sin in the human heart is the basic problem in history from which all other problems issue…then what greater gift could God give than a full and final solution to the problem of sin? This is precisely what God has done in His Son Jesus Christ, which is why Christmas, rightly understood, is eternally significant…. Everything the Apostle Paul is saying to us now can be summed up in the word 'believe.' The theme of his epistle is, The just shall live by faith…. The words that we now read in Romans 6, 7 and 8 are really a commentary on the one word, 'believe.' How does one believe? What does it mean to believe? How are the benefits or the fruits of belief appropriated? This is what he is talking about."[55]

Scripture: Romans 6:1-11, Part 1

Main idea: God broke the sin/death syndrome on the cross by crucifying the old way of life with Christ. By that act, the believer has been released to the life of victory over sin and death.

Introduction

The legend of the phoenix comes out of ancient Egyptian mythology. Every 500 years, so the legend goes, the phoenix came to Egypt from Arabia. It was said to have looked like an eagle with red and gold feathers, and there was only one alive at a time on earth. At the end of its 500-year life-span the bird

---
[55] Halverson, 131.

would build a nest of herbs, fan its wings and set the nest on fire, burning itself to death. Out of the ashes of the burned carcass came a new bird. Variations of the myth have been told by different writers. The expression, "rising phoenix-like from the ashes" is used today when something is rebuilt where it had been destroyed.

In a similar vein, Jesus said a kernel of wheat must first fall into the ground and die before it can germinate to produce a crop of wheat seeds (John 12:24). The principle is that life comes out of death. Resurrection follows, not precedes, the cross.

The theme of Romans was given in 1:17: *"For in the gospel a righteousness from God* [how to gain a right relationship with God] *is revealed, a righteousness that is by faith from first* [God's faithfulness] *to last* [our faith in the promises of a faithful God]." That theme was traced in the wrath of God against sin, and the impossibility of gaining a right relationship with God by doing the religious thing or by trying to keep a moral code. Because of Adam a syndrome of sin/condemnation/death fell on all humanity. A counter-syndrome of grace/ righteousness/life was instituted by Christ. The climactic statement summarizing the first section is given in Romans is 5:20-21. Just as sin reigned in producing death in the human race, so grace reigns through righteousness to bring life through Jesus Christ our Lord.

The next three chapters explain to us how the sin/death syndrome he outlined in chapter 5 has been broken so that the believer can experience the new syndrome of righteousness and life in Jesus Christ. It is one thing to be made legally right before God (justification), it is quite another to be set free from sin's power in our lives now (sanctification). It is wonderful to be reconciled to God by the death of Christ. It is much more wonderful to experience His saving life enabling us to be victorious over sin.

As though interrupted by a student asking a question, Paul enters into a dialogue with a straw inquirer at the opening of chapter 6. The dialogue might be expressed this way.

Student: "God's grace forgives every sin."

Paul: "Right."

S: "This is the most wonderful news a person can receive."

P: "You've got that right."

S: "If God's grace in forgiveness glorifies Him, doesn't it make sense that to bring more glory to God, we ought to sin more so that His grace can be in greater display?"

P: "What a horrible idea. It is impossible to be dead to sin and continue to live in it. Maybe you missed a basic point: when you were baptized into Christ, you were baptized into His death."

To understand the dialogue, Dunn[56] points out we must understand something of the mind-set of the Jew who saw the law as a gift of grace as an answer to sin. Paul repudiated that point of view by saying the law does not and cannot provide an answer to the power of sin, rather it actually facilitates sin's expression. For example, we all know the inner reaction when we are told, "no." The natural response is, "I will too!" It's the inner rebellion against the law that is the power of sin in the human heart. The law doesn't change that, it exposes it.

The factors that broke the sin/death syndrome were the historic death and resurrection of Christ and God's act of including the believer personally in those events.

---

56   James D. G. Dunn. *Word Biblical Commentary, Volume 38, Romans 1-8* (Dallas, Texas: Word Books, Publisher, 1988), 301-33 for a full discussion of this passage.

I. God's Saving Actions Were Centered in Two Historical Events

A. Jesus Died on a Cross

Christianity is not merely a compilation of doctrinal and moral statements and legendary stories. The events of the Old Testament are historical events of real people. The New Testament centers in the life of a real man, Jesus of Nazareth. Theology is rooted in His death on the cross and His resurrection.

B. Jesus Rose from the Dead and Ascended into Heaven

In 1 Corinthians 15, the great resurrection chapter of the Bible, Paul stated the good news he preached was that Jesus died, was buried, and rose from the dead. The resurrection is the single most powerful validation of the claims of Christianity. But it is more than that, it has a direct relationship to our daily victory over sin.

This is Paul's focus in Romans 6. These historical events have relevance today because...

II. God United the Believer with Christ on the Cross

A. The Meaning of "United"

Throughout this section there are key phrases that communicate the integration of the believer with Christ and His death and resurrection:

Verse 3: *"baptized into Christ Jesus"*; *"into His death"*;

Verse 4: *"buried with Him"*;

Verse 5: *"united with Him"* (2 times)—the primary phrase communicating this unique integration of the believer with Christ;

Verse 6: *"crucified with Him"*;

Verse 8: *"died with Christ"*; *"live with Him"*;

Verse 11: *"in Christ Jesus"*.

These phrases point out that God united the believer with Christ. When a person is baptized into Christ the historical events of Christ's life become the believer's. In union with Christ, the believer has within him or her the personal life of Jesus Himself as a power of righteousness.

The word for "united" (NIV), or "planted together" (KJV), is more aligned with the biological world than the botanical. It was used medically of broken bones fusing together. Literally, it means to "make to grow together, unite (a wound)." We have been fused with Christ in His death and resurrection. In John 14, Jesus spoke of our union with Him on a parallel to His union with the Father. *"I am in the Father, you are in me and I am in you."*

B. The Metaphor of Baptism Conveys the Meaning of Our Crucifixion

The imagery of immersion in water illustrates death and burial. Water baptism is much more than a mere testimony of faith in Christ. It goes deeper to state a union with Christ in His death that severed the sin/death cycle, that voided the power of the world-system, and released the Christian to live a new life.

Dunn wrote on this concept:

"Jesus is the only one who, having reached the end of this age of Adam, broke through the road-end barrier of death into the age beyond; who, having died Adam's death as an act of obedience, rose to a new life beyond. Christ's death and resurrection thus provide the doorway—for Paul the only doorway—through death to life, from this age under the power of sin to the new age free from sin. To make the transition from old age to new age, from sin through death to life, one must as it were, be carried through by Christ, and one must identify oneself unreservedly with the historical event of Christ's death in all its degradation and suffering, as sacrificial offering and act of obedience. Only those who make themselves one with his death can hope to experience the life which is his life in the new age beyond."[57]

Because of our fusion with Christ we have power to live a new life. The word for "new" is also used by Paul in 2 Corinthians 5:17 where he stated that anyone who is in Christ is a new creation (cf. Gal 6:15). The life we have in Christ's resurrection empowers us to live by new values and to establish new patterns of behavior. The old dog can learn new tricks by dying and being raised a different dog. The new life is Jesus Himself.

III. What God Achieved through our Union with Christ

A. Union with Christ In Death Crucified the "Old Self"

1. The "old self", "old man", or "old way of life," refers to our status and condition before we came to faith in Christ. The "body of sin" is a reference to the what the Bible calls the world-system under the control of Satan as the god of this age. Before we became believers, we functioned in this system and were under its control. Ephesians 2:1-3 describes humanity without Christ as following *"the ways of this world and the ruler of the kingdom of the air, the spirit who is now at work in those who are disobedient. All of us also lived among them at one time, gratifying the cravings of our sinful nature and following its desires and thoughts."*

---

57   Dunn, 329.

2. While the "old way of life" is not to be confused with "the flesh", there is a link between the two. The flesh, or selfishness, is that part of us that enjoys sin, lives self-centeredly and selfishly, and moves away from God. Its behaviors are outlined in Galatians 5. The flesh lived out its desires with only modest resistance and control before we came to Christ. The variation of behavior among unbelievers is quite wide, from a highly moral and probably religious life to a sadistic, evil, morally perverted life. In the first case, it is a life of self-righteousness; in the second, a life controlled by lusts.

When a person becomes a Christian, his or her connection to the old way of life is severed by crucifixion, but the flesh, or self-centeredness, lives on into the new life and creates its problems. Understanding these chapters is basic to gaining victory over the flesh and its sinful behaviors.

B. Union with Christ in Resurrection Guarantees Life

If we died with Christ we will also live with Him through His resurrection life being given to us. When He died, it was once for all. Now His resurrection life is on-going to eternity.

Conclusion

The phoenix lesson is that we will know the power of Jesus' resurrection life in direct proportion to our willingness to go through death to sin. The new life of Christ comes out of the ashes of our crucifixion with Christ. Conclusion: we are to "count" ourselves "dead to sin but alive to God in Christ Jesus."

For your reflection:

- In his commentary quoted at the beginning of the sermon, Simpson expressed that sins are the actions people take in disobedience to God. Those are completely forgiven in justification. Sin (singular) refers to a deeper condition in the heart of a person expressed by Paul in the terms of "old self", "old man" or the "sinful nature." This latter is the subject of sanctification. How did God deal with that problem in Christ?

- What does union with Christ mean? When does this union take place in a person's life?

- The word "count" is the equivalent of faith. How is a person to count her or himself dead with Christ and raised to new life?

16

Romans 6:1-11, Part 2,

God Is Still Changing Me

"[Paul] speaks of sin, the state and character of evil from which all our acts spring, as the miasma exhales from a fetid marsh, as the water flows from an unclean fountain. Justification deals with our sins, but sanctification deals with our sin. God can forgive sins, but sin He can never forgive nor tolerate. It must be destroyed and removed, and the very idea of continuing in sin is met at the threshold by the solemn 'God forbid,' which requires from every follower of Christ that 'holiness without which no man shall see the Lord.'

"But how is this deliverance from sin to be brought about? The answer involves three points.... First, we are sanctified, not by the improvement of the old nature, but by its death and the resurrection life of the Lord Jesus Christ, instead. Second, we are sanctified, not by our old master, the law, or by any efforts or struggles of our own, but by the free gift and grace of the Lord Jesus Christ, and through union with Christ alone. Third, we are sanctified by the indwelling life and power of the Holy Spirit in us and filling our spirit, soul and body with the life of Jesus Christ."[58]

> **Scripture:** Romans 6:1-11, part 2
>
> **Main Idea:** God's way of changing behavior is to change us on the inside. He achieved this by putting to death the old way of life and selfishness and giving to us His own resurrection life.

---

[58] Simpson, 133-134.

Introduction

Recently, while weeding our flower-beds, it dawned on me that I had to put ten times the energy into trying to get the good plants to grow, but none into getting weeds to grow. My energy goes mostly into pulling persistent, pesky weeds. Nasty little spurge is an incredible plant. When you pull them, it seems like 39,562 seeds fall to the ground. Some weeds camouflage themselves, others grow tall and big as if in defiance of any attempt to stop them.

While thinking on that and with an increasing back-ache, I transferred my thoughts to my life. I don't have to work at bad personal characteristics—they just seem to have a way of happening. The qualities I want in my life come slowly and with enormous effort. Those weeds of sins, like weeds in the garden, function naturally. I was born with a bias toward certain behaviors, while other people face different tendencies. Some of those natural characteristics develop into weeds that function just like weeds in a garden. There have been times when I have wondered, can I change, can I get a grip on some of these behaviors?

The Bible teaches that the very reason Jesus came was to address this problem. The weed of human behavior is rooted in sin. Sin not only has separated us from God with the threat of an eternal hell hanging over us, it also messes up our lives day after day. How does God propose to do something about it? Jesus came bring us forgiveness and take away the threat of an eternity separated from God. He also came to make inside change possible so that our behavior changes.

What do we do with weeds? The Bible refers to behavioral and attitudinal weeds as the "flesh" or "selfishness." It further tells us that the environment that energizes this flesh is the "body of sin" or world system. Jesus died on the cross to provide forgiveness before a holy God. He also set us free from the control of the flesh in our personal lives.

For some time, we have traced Paul's very careful argument about how a person comes into a right relationship with God. It is NOT by turning religious or doing religious ritual. Nor can we know God by trying to be good, following some list of do's and don'ts. We come into a right relationship with God only by the simple act of faith in Jesus Christ as Savior and Lord. After we come to know God and His forgiveness, we face the enormous issue of stuff on the inside that we know is not right. It seems that sometimes we are almost driven to some wrong behaviors and other times we simply enjoy doing what we know is wrong. What do we do about it?

Our Scripture is a presentation of God's view of where behavior originates and what He did to change us. There are many theories of human behavior that you hear on radio, TV and in the classroom. None of them deal with the reality that on the inside the human being is sinful. That is a basic assumption in the Bible.

If you are not familiar with the Bible, we will use some terms that may sound peculiar to you. I'll do my best to explain what we mean. In attempting to translate the thought into English, scholars have used different phrases. The "old way of life," or "sinful nature," or "old man" all refer to the same thing—a person's life before coming to Christ. I will use the phrase, "old way of life." It simply means what we are when born as human beings. Is it bad to be a human? Only if you wish you were born frog or lion or some other animal. The down-side to being a human is we were born as children of

Adam and as such ended up under Adam's curse of sin. That was not our choice. It is part of being a human.

Because we are Adam's children we make sinful choices. To solve this part of the problem of sin, God brought an end to our attachment to Adam. How? When Jesus died on the cross because of sin, He put us there with Jesus to die to our old way of life.

One writer [John Stott: *Men Made New*] compared it to two volumes of our personal spiritual biography. Volume one is our life from birth to when we trusted Christ as Savior. At that point, we were "*crucified with Christ*." That brought the first volume to an end in death. Volume two began with our new birth—the result of our trusting in Christ as Savior—and will never end, not even when we die physically. The cross of Christ severed our connection to the old life to release us from the controlling power of sin and bring us under God's liberating power.

I. God Ended Our Old Way of Life When Jesus Was Crucified (5-6)

A. Jesus Died 2,000 Years Ago, But His Death Works for Me Today (5)

"Could it be any clearer? Our old way of life was nailed to the Cross with Christ, a decisive end to that sin-miserable life—no longer at sin's every beck and call! What we believe is this: If we get included in Christ's sin-conquering death, we also get included in his life-saving resurrection" (The Message).

Please be patient with a little grammar lesson because it is very important. The verb tenses in this verse are important. The verb "*was*" is actually in the perfect tense. That is an action completed in the past with the effect of the action carrying into the present. God crucified the old way of life on

Jesus' cross two thousand years ago, and that past action is still valid in the believer today.

The second tense is future. We will also be included in Jesus' resurrection. Our fusion with Christ in death is historical, final, completed. Our fusion with Christ in His resurrection is primarily future, though we experience it in part now. That explains the frustrating mix we face in our lives in this life. We deeply desire to experience the full power of Jesus' resurrection life to free us from the controlling power of sin, but we experience it only partially. There is a mix of life and death, of victory and defeat. We anticipate the day when we will know victory over sin in an absolute sense.

B. The Old Way of Life Ended When Christ Was Crucified (6-10)

"Could it be any clearer? Our old way of life was nailed to the Cross with Christ, a decisive end to that sin-miserable life—no longer at sin's every beck and call! What we believe is this: If we get included in Christ's sin-conquering death, we also get included in his life-saving resurrection. ⁹We know that when Jesus was raised from the dead it was a signal of the end of death-as-the-end. Never again will death have the last word. When Jesus died, he took sin down with Him, but alive he brings God down to us. With one stroke, God took sin down and brought his own life and power to make us new on the inside" (The Message).

II. The Crucifixion of the Old Way of Life Left Sin Powerless

A. Sin is Systematic in Its Power

The old way of life refers to a person's life before becoming a believer. There is also a world-system under the control of Satan. That world system of sin has manipulative and controlling power over people under its influence the same way a dictator can control his subjects. We shouldn't be that surprised by the control a Saddam Hussein, Stalin, or Hitler has over his subjects. We were all subject to the same control as unbelievers, only the dictator was unseen. That is why people become substance abusers, why some are sexually addicted, why anger, greed, pride, and dozens of other sins control us.

God made the human being to be under His control—the good, benevolent control of a loving God. When we rejected Him, we came under the control of an evil dictator. There is no choice in the matter—its either/or. A person is either under the control of God through Jesus Christ, or under the control of Satan. It is important to know there is a big difference in existence under the world-system and demonization. Demonic control is a separate discussion.

B. There Is a Carry Over from the Old Way of Life to the New Way of Life

The difficulty in understanding this passage is the tendency to confuse what the Bible here terms the *"sinful nature,"* or the *"old way of life,"* and references in other places where the Bible speaks of the *"flesh"*—or as *The Message* expresses it, *selfishness*. The selfishness of the old way life carries over to the new life. While we are now in volume two of our biography, the old life has intruded into the new life to give us all kinds of grief.

What is the flesh or selfishness? There is a list of behaviors of the flesh listed in Galatians 5:19-21: *"It is obvious what kind of life develops out of trying to get your own way all the time: repetitive, loveless, cheap sex; a stinking accumulation of mental and emotional garbage; frenzied and joyless grabs for happiness; trinket gods; magic-show religion; paranoid loneliness; cutthroat competition; all-consuming-yet-never-satisfied wants; a brutal temper; an impotence to love or be loved; divided homes and divided lives; small-minded and lopsided pursuits; the vicious habit of depersonalizing everyone into a rival; uncontrolled and uncontrollable addictions; ugly parodies of community.*" This long list describes many of our behaviors.

The flesh includes being driven and controlled by our fears, seeking to satisfy our needs on our own instead of in Jesus. The chief characteristic of self, wrote A. W. Tozer, is possessiveness—demanding to have our needs met. He lists the self-sins as: self-righteousness, self-pity, self-sufficiency, self-admiration, self-love. "They are not something we do, they are something we *are*, and therein lies both their subtlety and their power."[59]

Selfishness results in walking out on a marriage because a person no longer "loves" a mate. It refuses to look at sin on the inside and call sin what it is. It causes a person to be bound by habits. Selfishness convinces us we are too busy to serve God, or that we do not have the talent to do so. It finds acceptable excuses for not obeying God's Word. Selfishness lacks desire for God or knowing His Word. It is often angry toward God and the church. We face our selfishness the rest of our lives. Unless we put God's methods to work we will never experience God's wildly extravagant life.

III. A Personal Journey

A. My Early Understanding

My search to get answers on how to cope with inside dynamics that led me into sin began when I was in high school. My pastor invited me to speak one Sunday night during my senior year in high school. I was the church choir director and song leader at the time. My sermon was on Romans 7 because

---

59   A. W. Tozer, *The Pursuit of God* (Harrisburg, PA: Christian Publications, 1982), 45ff.

of the inner struggles I experienced as a student. I desperately wanted to become more like Jesus Christ.

Early in my ministry experience, I heard some tapes by Major Ian Thomas on *The Saving Life of Christ*, and read Watchman Nee's book, *The Normal Christian Life*. Both had a profound effect on me and provided foundational understanding of the inside dynamics of Christian living.

I was confronted with my sexual drives and selfish ambition. I had attempted to duck out on the ministry, but the Lord kept me. Like a good coach He kept reminding me of these principles. Verse 11 states:

> *"That means you must not give sin a vote in the way you conduct your lives. Don't give it the time of day. Don't even run little errands that are connected with that old way of life. Throw yourselves wholeheartedly and full-time—remember, you've been raised from the dead!—into God's way of doing things. Sin can't tell you how to live. After all, you're not living under that old tyranny any longer. You're living in the freedom of God."*

We can't give sin a vote. How do we put this into practice? The starting point is prayer in which we bring a specific behavior to the Lord and ask Him to win the battle. We literally place that sin on the cross and ask Jesus to crucify it. It also means some self-talk, in the same way athletes pump themselves up after having done poorly. Life is a mixed bag of success and failure. We have watched Olympic athletes have good events mixed with failures. In and through Christ we can and we will win. We may end standing like Kerri Strug (U.S.A. Olympic champion gymnast) on one leg with enormous pain, but with arms raised in victory.

B. God's Most Recent Probing

Several years ago I read Dr. Larry Crabb's book, *Inside Out*. While reading the book, and in subsequent months, God unmasked more of the "flesh" in my life. Crabb states the two primary needs we have are for security and significance, the former being primarily the female's need and the latter the male's need. My itch for significance had found expression in my drive for two doctoral degrees. I had successfully rationalized that I needed it for improving my ministry skills when I made the decisions to get the education. It was true and valid. What I did not face was the motive of seeking significance in the degree itself.

Since then, I have looked at the messages I received as a child and adult. These messages shaped decisions and stimulated behaviors that have caused hurt in my family and marriage. Those messages included: "Roy is okay if he works hard, gets good grades, is successful, does things well, and obtains a good education."

I translated those messages to mean my church had to increase numerically, I had to be a model in my personal life and ministry, and to preach good sermons. If you were good you would be invited to speak in camps and conferences, and get the invitation to the larger churches. In my clergy circles a successful person became a denominational leader. I was elected to different positions including national leadership on the denomination's board. Predictably, reaching those attainments did not bring the sense of significance for which I longed because that can only be found in Christ.

All that stuff resulted in a very demanding schedule. That was okay, though, because the real man of God is one who "burns out for the Lord." A dedicated servant dies with his boots on, they said.

Conclusion

I share that with you to tell you I'm still in the middle of the change-process with you. Weeds are weeds. They must be faced and rooted out by placing them on the cross in death. There is no other way.

The following quote from A. W. Tozer will sound strange in this day of narcissistic self-centeredness:

> "Christianity deals with my 'I,' and it deals with it by an intolerant and final destruction. God pronounces a stern condemnation upon it and flatly disapproves of it and fully rejects it and says that this 'I,' this rebellious 'I,' this anti-God 'I,' is filled with sin, the essence of rebellion and disobedience and unbelief. This 'I' God will have nothing to do with.
>
> "There are two kinds of religion. Within the framework of Christianity there are two positions. One is that the Lord came in order to help me, to help my 'I' and to take out the complexes and the twists that I got into because my mother scolded me when I was a baby.
>
> "The other position is that Jesus Christ came to bring an end to this self. We ought not to educate and polish it but rather to put an end to it—not to cultivate it and give it a love for Bach and Beethoven and Leonardo da Vinci but to bring an end to it....
>
> "What does man actually find when he looks in his own heart? He finds he is nothing, that he knows nothing, that he has nothing, and that he can do nothing."[60]

---

[60] A. W. Tozer, "I Have Been Crucified," *The Alliance Witness*, 12/6/72.

God changes behavior by changing us on the inside. If we want to grow, to enter a life that is not manipulated by sin, we must go through the cross. After the cross is the wildly extravagant life of God's victorious power in us.

For your reflection:
- What are the "spurge" issues you battle?
- What activities are the most helpful in your growth in Christ (Bible reading and meditation, prayer, solitude, church attendance), or _____.
- What is meant by the term "old way of life"?
- Name one point in the closing quote of Tozer that you want to think about more.

Do I Have to be GOOD to go to Heaven?

17

Romans 6:1-11, Part 3

I'm Confused: Am I Dead or Alive?

'Know ye not my brethren, that so many of us as were baptized into Jesus Christ were baptized into his death? Therefore, we are buried with him by baptism into death' (Rom. 6:3-4, KJV). What does being baptized into His death mean? It has to do with our dying as He did. We do this by our baptism, for baptism is the cross. What the cross is to Christ, baptism is to us. Christ died in the flesh, we have died to sin. Both are deaths, and both are real.

"But if it is real, what is our part, what must we contribute? Paul goes on to say, 'As Christ was raised up from the dead by the glory of the Father, even so we also should walk in newness of life' (Rom.1 6:4 KJV). Here Paul tells of the importance of the resurrection.

"Do you believe that Christ was raised from the dead? Believe the same of yourself. Just as his death is yours, so also is his resurrection; if you have shared in the one, you shall share in the other. As of now the sin is done away with.

"Paul sets before us a demand: to bring about a newness of life by a changing of habits. For when the fornicator becomes chaste, when the covetous person becomes merciful, when the harsh become subdued, a resurrection has taken place, a prelude to the final resurrection which is to come.

"How is it a resurrection? It is a resurrection because sin has been mortified, and righteousness has risen in its place; the old life has passed away and new, angelic life is now being lived."[61]

Scripture: Romans 6:1-11, part 3

Main Idea: Romans 6 is a discussion of what happens when a person *becomes* a Christian, not how a person is to live the Christian life. If that is not understood or accepted, many confusing ideas can emerge from the passage.

Introduction

I struggled for many years seeking to understand this passage of Scripture. If the "old man," the "old self," or as we have referred to it the "old way of life," was my sinful nature and was historically crucified with Christ, why was it so alive in me? It didn't make sense. I could honestly say to God, "Its not working." My view of the Scriptures as the inerrant Word of God could not allow me to settle for that. Where was the problem?

My mother was an early teacher in the Child Evangelism movement in southern California. I was raised on Bible flannelgraph stories. One story was of Ipse and Newman. Ipse represented my old sinful nature and Newman was my new nature as a Christian, the person of Jesus living inside my heart. Ipse was a burly, mean looking, hairy-chested weight-lifter type. Newman was young, athletic, clean-cut, kind of like ripped young athletes. They were in a constant wrestling match with the hoped-for end of Newman winning the match.

I was given another picture about the Christian life. The two natures are comparable to two dogs—like a pit bull versus

---

[61] John Chrysostom (345-407), "Dead to Sin", *Devotional Classics*, edited by Richard J. Foster & James Bryan Smith (HarperSanFrancisco, 1993), 326-327.

a Collie—both after the same piece of meat. I'm the meat and whoever I say "Sic 'em" to, gets the meat.

Those are very misleading representations of what Paul teaches us of the inside dynamics of Christian living in this chapter. If those pictures are a discussion of Galatians 5 where a war exits between the "flesh" and the "Holy Spirit," then they can be of help. To apply them to Romans 6 can only result in confusion.

I. Understanding What the "Old Self" or "Old Man" Is

A. The "Old Man" Is a Person's Life Before Becoming a Christian

It is imperative we understand the "old man" or "old self" is the life a person lives before they trust Christ as Savior—it is our "old way of life." It may be a very sinful life or it may be a highly moral life, but it is a life separated from God. That life came to a catastrophic end in crucifixion the moment we received Christ as Savior and Lord.

The word for "self" or "man" is *anthropos*, the generic Greek word for man or humanity, not just the male sex. So we have the study of anthropology, the study of humankind. The same word appears throughout the fifth chapter when speaking of humanity as the family of Adam. All are sinners and under condemnation.

5:12 *"Just as sin entered the world through one man, and death through sin, and in this way death came to all men, because all sinned."*

5:15 *"The many died by the trespass of the one man."*

5:17 *"By the trespass of one man, death reigned through that one man."*

5:19 *"Through the disobedience of the one man the many were made [constituted] sinners."*

The "old man" of 6:6 specifies our condition as sinners as members the family of Adam. Our old way of life ended in crucifixion with Christ when we became Christians.

B. The "Old Self" is Not the Same as the "Flesh" or "Sinful Nature" Discussed in Galatians 5 and Romans 7 & 8

There is a battle in the Christian. The next chapter makes that clear. Romans 6 is *NOT* about that problem. Galatians 5 and Romans 7 do address that inner conflict which I previously described in my personal journey. The "flesh" [*sarx*], or "selfishness" is that dynamic power inside the heart that is opposed to God and is carried over from our pre-conversion life. I suppose Eugene Peterson chose "selfishness" to translate *sarx* is because the primary condition of the human heart from its earliest moments is selfish. Selfishness summarizes how we feel and behave as people separated from God. When a person becomes a Christian their battle with selfishness isn't over. Every believer has within them a drive that is in rebellion against God. It is a carry over from our pre-conversion life. Though it is powerful, the flesh can be defeated at the cross.

God crucified the "old man" with Christ, but *we* are to crucify the "flesh" with its passions and lusts. *We* must confront sinful behaviors and attitudes one by one, day by day, and moment by moment throughout our lives.

II. The "Old Man" Was Crucified When Christ Was Crucified

A. It is Descriptive of a Basic Transaction That Occurs When a Person Trusts Christ

I have made this point several times, but the need for clarification forces me to stress it. Romans 6 is not a discussion about how to live the Christian life, but states what happens when we become Christians.

Why did God crucify the "old man?" Verse 6 has a "so that" phrase, which tells the reader the purpose behind God's action. Through the crucifixion of the "old man" the "body of sin" was rendered powerless. Again, there are differing ideas among interpreters what is the "body of sin." I have concluded that since it obviously has a power of influence and, more likely, of control, it refers to the pervasive power of evil called "the world-system." The world-system is under the control of an unseen tyrant, Satan, whose singular aim is to initiate sin and so destroy people. He knows far more than we that sin brings death, and that is his sadistic delight.

B. It is Not a Crisis of Growth in the Christian Life

This view interprets this chapter as a description of how the Christian lives their life. Some who equate the old man and the flesh, use the term, "old nature." They argue that when a person fully surrenders all he or she has to Christ and asks to be filled with the Holy Spirit, the old nature is crucified. After that experience, a person no longer commits sins. They may make mistakes, but not sins. Such a position is a denial of reality.

The crucifixion of the old man is basic to becoming a Christian. It brings to an end our old unregenerate life and makes us new creations in Christ.

Verse 11 says to "count" this fact as so. "Count" [*logizomai*] means to "(a) reckon, credit, rank with, calculate; (b) consider, deliberate, grasp, draw a logical conclusion, decide" (*DNTT*, III, 822). It is an action of the mind that sets down as true the facts God has stated. To "count" myself "dead to sin" is to accept in the deepest part of my mind that my old life came to an end when I became "fused" with Christ. Therefore, I am not to go on living the same way I did before that event. In *Price Digest* language it reads: "Write in your personal notebook that you are dead to sin." If you are dead, you are not alive. If you are dead to the sins of the old life, you are not going to be going after them as a thirsty person longs for water.

C. When This Distinction is Ignored, much Confusion Can Result

My confusion was, if the old man is my flesh or sinful nature and if that was crucified with Christ, it wasn't working for me. It resulted in guilt, introspection, and self-condemnation that I must really be bad. I have read many commentators and other writers on the Christian life who provide other views on this chapter. But they bring confusion, not clarity. They generally stem from viewing this chapter as instruction in how a Christian can be victorious over sin and equate the "old self" with the "flesh".

John Calvin admitted: "For I do not agree with those who think that he used the word crucified, rather than dead, because he still lives, and is in some respects vigorous" (*Romans*, 224). Those who have felt this chapter is a description of how to live the Christian life end in a quandary about crucifying what is crucified. One writer on the spiritual life said the old man is crucified but comes back to haunt one as a ghost and must be treated as a fantasy, not reality. Or, if the old man is the same as the flesh and is crucified, then a Christian must live in a sinless condition. Yet, I have never met a Christian who did not evidence the behaviors of the flesh at some point.

D. The Problem the Christian Faces is the "Flesh" as a "Law of Sin"

Chapter seven discusses this issue and I will explain it more fully as we study that chapter. There really is something inside the Christian that motivates us to sin. We can refuse to look at wrong motives and sinful behaviors that hurt other people but we must understand that sin in the believer and non-believer alike always brings hurt, pain and suffering.

What the believer has that the unbeliever does not have, is the power of the Holy Spirit who lives in us the resurrected life of Jesus Christ. Because the old man is crucified, we can love even if we don't get loved back. We can be joyful even when we hurt and are going through dreadful challenges. The Christian can have inner peace in the middle of confusion and conflict. We have the power to persevere when we really want to run. We can tolerate other people when they irritate us to the depths of our being. We can gain control over habits. We can do all that and more because we have God Himself, in the person of the Holy Spirit, living in us and through us the supernatural life of Jesus. This separates Christianity from religion.

Conclusion

There is an Ipse. He is the flesh—not the old-way-of-life itself but an expression of that old self. He is set against God and a holy life. He is not crucified. The Christian is commanded to crucify him. The Newman in us is Jesus Himself who has come to live within the believer's heart. He is victorious, having died to sin once, and alive to God forever.

He loves God and what is right. He gives power to change behaviors, even those deeply ingrained.

Galatians 5:24 reads: "Those who belong to Christ Jesus have crucified the sinful nature [flesh] with its passions and desires." We can succeed in doing this because the old self, the old-way-of-life, came to an end the day we trusted Christ. Why did God set it up that way? He wanted a family of men and women, students, boys and girls who were new creations. New creations who had new life—resurrection life. New creations who, because of the residence of God inside them, have power to deliberately sever themselves from sexual lust and chemical addiction. New creations in whom God's love enables them to develop relationships within marriage, family, work, school, the neighborhood that are easily trashed by rage, greed, exploitation and every other form of selfishness.

How is the flesh crucified? Unfortunately, it's not easy. We can't just say a little prayer and never again worry about sexual lust. We can say a little prayer and find the cravings of alcohol, tobacco or heroin don't go away. Crucifying the flesh is not a pretty process. The most hideous death the Romans could invent meant crushing pain, agony and tears, bodies ripped and torn. The cross means brokenness. Most likely our self-centered dreams will be shattered at some point. Crucifying Ipse is a life-long process of facing our inside twists and rank selfishness. We will be forced to tear off the lovely party wrappings of our arrogance and pride to be honest with who we are on the inside.

It all began for me early in the ministry. I had enjoyed popularity in high school and college and was elected student body president at both schools. After graduation I eagerly entered the ministry in Youth for Christ. I was assistant director, had a couple of campus Bible clubs and was soloist for the Saturday night rallies.

Though I enjoyed success in my clubs and work, by the end of the first year I knew I had to do something different. God was directing me into church ministry which I had earnestly tried to avoid. I knew what pastoral work could be like in constantly facing critical, and often downright mean, people. I didn't want to be dissected and pan-fried by those who put on a pious face, quote a few verses, give some money, but in fact are deeply self-centered. In only 18 months I was a broken, confused young pastor of only 24 years. Through the criticism and power plays of church, God forced me to face my own pride and self-reliance. I wanted to be liked, and it cut deeply when I learned my best wasn't good enough. The people-pleaser self had to go to death. Self-reliance required crucifixion.

That was the beginning of a lifetime of God peeling off the layers of the flesh. It has always been hard, never a hilarious, 'Oh boy, I get to be crucified.'

After death, though, comes resurrection. God puts things together again. We come out of the tomb not self-reliant, but Jesus-reliant, not doing our thing but doing His thing, not trusting our abilities but His ability. Our focus is no longer what we can gain and manipulate from people, but how we can serve.

Our old way-of-life was crucified when Jesus died on the cross and we trusted Him as our Savior and Lord. The carry-over flesh now must be nailed to the cross so the resurrection life of Jesus can come through. That life is fruitful. It is satisfying. Mr. Newman will endure through eternity.

For your reflection:

- In the introductory story, I refer to two names: Ipse and Mr. Newman. As best you understood this story, what did Ipse represent in the life of the Christian? What did Mr. Newman represent?

- Some Bibles use the phrase "old man" in Romans 6:6. Others use "old self" and another uses "old way of life." What does your Bible use and which term best communicates with you?

- The "old man" is a phrase used to describe the life a person lives before they become a Christian. It may be a very sinful life or it may be a highly moral life, but it is a life separated from God. When did the "old man" or "old way of life" come to an end for the believer?

- Is the "old man" or "old way of life" the same as wheat the Bible speaks of as the "flesh" or "selfishness?" Why do you think one translator used the term "selfishness" to translate the word other Bibles translate as "flesh?"

- What did God do with the "old man?"

- Verse 11 says to "count" this fact as so. "Count" (*logizomai*) means to a) "reckon, credit, rank with, calculate," b) "consider, deliberate, grasp, draw a logical conclusion, decide" (*Dictionary of New Testament Theology*, III, 822). Will you take that position right now and consider your old way of life over, dead, ended, so that the world system can no longer manipulate and control you?

18

Romans 6:12-14

The Choice is Ours About What Kind of Life We Live

"It is deeply significant here that even to us, new creatures in Christ, and recipients of the Holy Spirit, it is definitely announced to us that we are not under law,—else bondage and helplessness would still be our lot. Note, God does not say we are not under the Law,—the Mosaic Law: (Gentiles never were!). But, God says we are not under law,—under the legal principle. In the opening part of Chapter Seven, Paul will show the Jewish believers, (who had been under law), that only death could release them from their legal obligation; and that they had been made dead to the Law, through being identified with Christ in His death.

"Only when we believe that our history in Adam, with all its responsibilities and demands to produce righteousness, ended at the cross, shall we find ourselves completely free to enjoy these words of heavenly comfort—UNDER GRACE!"[62]

Scripture: Romans 6:12-14

Main Idea: Because our old life ended in crucifixion with Christ, we are to count ourselves dead to sin, not let sin reign in our bodies, and instead to offer ourselves to God.

Introduction

The story was of the farmer who hired a fellow to clean out his barn and pig pens. The farmer anticipated it would

---
62 Newell, 230.

take about a week to accomplish. Within two days the fellow was knocking at the back door saying he needed more work because he had finished the assignment. Being very pleased with the hard-working young man, the farmer put him to work digging post holes. Again, he thought it would take several days, but this amazing man had the work completed in three days.

It was the weekend and the farmer told him to come back on Monday. When the fellow arrived, the farmer took him to the barn and asked him to sort a large bin of potatoes. He told him to put the small potatoes in bin #1, the medium in bin #2, and the large ones in bin #3. At the end of the day, believing he had a winner of a farm hand, the farmer with anticipation checked in to see how much had been accomplished. Not one potato had been placed in any bin.

Exasperated, the farmer exclaimed, "What have you done all day? I gave you two jobs last week that would have taken an ordinary man three weeks to accomplish and you did them in one. Today I gave you a simple job and you haven't done a thing all day." "Well, sir, when you give me work to do, I can get it done. But these decisions kill me."

Decisions about potatoes are one thing, but making right moral choices each day is something else. Any discussion of moral choices involves understanding human nature. Fundamental to human nature is the question of will or volition. To what extent is a person free in their choices? Are our behaviors controlled or caused either by internal psychological factors, or external forces? Are people significant moral beings or merely objects of manipulation?

The Bible presents three important insights about human freedom. First, all humans are subject to the influence of spiritual realities. In some cases, that means control, at other times it is assistance or empowerment. Second, it declares that we are responsible for the choices we make. Whatever the influence of other factors, we choose our behaviors. God will hold us accountable to Him for our decisions. Theologian A. A. Hodge defined volition as "the executive faculty of the soul, the faculty of choice or self-decision"[63]. The third factor is we are spiritual, moral, and rational beings created in the image of God. This factor distinctively sets us apart from all other creation.

Let's recap our studies to this point. A right relationship with God is a gift of God's grace that we experience through faith in Jesus Christ alone. It is not by keeping some moral code or by doing the religious thing. The moment a person trusts Christ, a dramatic severance from the old life under Adam and sin occurs as the believer is crucified with Christ. Because our old life is ended, we have a new base on which to build Christian character and behavior. As a result we are to count ourselves dead to sin, to not let sin reign in our lives, but rather offer ourselves to God.

"In the same way, count yourselves dead to sin but alive to God in Christ Jesus. Therefore, do not let sin reign in your mortal body so that you obey its evil desires. Do not offer the parts of your body to sin, as instruments of wickedness, but rather offer yourselves to God, as those who have been brought from death to life; and offer the parts of your body to him as instruments of righteousness. For sin shall not be your master, because you are not under law, but under grace" (11-14).

---

[63] Archibald Alexander Hodge, *Outlines of Theology* (London: Banner of Truth Trust, 1972), 282.

I. Two Facts We Must Write in Our Hearts (11)

A. We Are Dead to Sin

Up to this point, Paul's argument has emphasized what occurred historically in the crucifixion of Christ and our involvement in that death. Verse 6 declared, "We know that our old self was crucified with Him."

As is true of all Christian experience, we must begin with a knowledge of the facts God has stated. Having understood the facts, we must then act upon them. Understanding what God did in Christ, we are to write it down in the depths of our heart, "We are dead to sin." The verb, "count," is in the present tense meaning a daily, consistent mind-set, a habit of thinking. When temptation throws itself at us in any form, we must learn to say to ourselves and out loud if we need to: "I am crucified with Christ and dead to sin. I don't have to respond."

Sin is presented as a personal power acting upon and within the believer. A personal power influences and seeks to control us. We are dead to that power. We do not have to respond when it demands. We don't have to let sin control us. The one who is dead is freed from sin (7). We are to decisively take on this frame of mind.

B. We Are Alive to God

The mind-set is not totally negative, for that would of itself bring defeat. It is positive. If we are dead to sin, we are also alive to God. There is another power of influence and control, God Himself. Being alive to Him means that we now have the capacity to receive His personal power and make choices of behavior that are right.

Freedom, as one writer defined, is not the right to do what I want, but the power to do what I ought. The 'ought' is obedience to God. It is the power to live a holy life. Being alive to God provides us with the power to do what we ought to do. That will always bring us the greatest happiness.

II. We Control Our Choices About Sin (12)

A. Control is Indicated by the Statement, "Do Not Let"

What does it mean to "*count yourselves dead to sin*"? It means to "not let sin reign [a word referring to a king] in your mortal body so that you obey its evil desires." The tense of the verb for "reign" [present active imperative] translates 'we are not to let sin go on reigning in us as it once did.' The emphasis is on the word "let". We do have a choice. We can say "no" to sin's aggressive demands whether they come from an external source, or from our own natural desires.

Sin is not to reign in our mortal bodies to obey its sinful desires. Choices involve our minds, emotions, and wills. Choices are expressed through our physical body. The body is not evil. The natural drives of the body—appetite, sex, self-preservation—are not evil. However, sin has evil desires. Our natural desires become tools of sin when we seek to find fulfillment in ways opposed to God's plan. Sex is not evil. But sex outside of marriage is sin. Eating is not evil, but eating excessively or eating harmful foods that damage the body is a violation of the God-given drive. Some hold a contrary view to nutritionists. It's called the southern plan. The southern plan says you need lots of fat to slick up the arteries so the blood can flow better. It is not evil to protect ourselves, but when self-protection causes us to withdraw from loving others out of fear of hurt, it becomes sin.

We are not to 'let' sin have control. This requires knowledge of what sin is, and determination to reject the old life and its controlling habits. The world-system of sin has been rendered powerless, so don't let it have power.

B. Control Makes Us Accountable for Our Choices

We are morally accountable regardless of events of the past that have powerfully molded our responses. Prior to becoming a Christian, a person is only accountable for their decision to trust Jesus Christ. Having become a Christian, we are now accountable to not let the sins of the past rule as king over us.

Gary Inrig wrote: "Samson, when brave, strangled a lion; but he could not strangle his own love. He burst the fetters of his foes; but not the cords of his own lusts. He burned the crops of others, and lost the fruit of his own virtue when burning with the flame, kindled by a single woman."[64]

Nothing demands that we live in the failures of Samson whether it applies to sexual drives, seeking significance, or a burning rage inside. God's saving grace enables a person to enter a new life of power in which they can say 'no' to sin. First, a person must hear the gospel and trust Christ. Having come to Christ, we have the power of a new life, the life of the Holy Spirit, to make right choices. God has done His part, the choice of what kind of life we live is ours.

III. We Have Two Options (13-14)

A. We Can Offer Ourselves to Sin

Sin is personified as a personal power which uses our bodily members as weapons of either wickedness or righteousness. The imagery is of a military confrontation of opposing forces using us as weapons. We have a choice of which side we going to be on in any given situation: either sin's or God's.

Again, our physical bodies and members are the means of expression. Our tongues can be used for sin in snide remarks,

---

[64] Gary Inrig, *Hearts of Iron, Feet of Clay* (Chicago: Moody Press, 1979).

thoughtless criticism and put downs. Or they can be used for righteousness in worship, wholesome language, and building up others. Our hands can be used to fight or gesture dirty communications, or they can work and help others.

Our choice is to offer, or present, our bodies to one of the two forces: God or Satan, righteousness or wickedness. "Offer" is a military word and refers to our acknowledgment of superior authority and power in our lives to which we present ourselves.

B. We Can Offer Ourselves to God

The verb tense [first aorist imperative] calls for immediate decisive action. We are people who have been brought from death to life. Because our old life has ended, we are now to offer our complete selves to the new authority in our lives, God Himself. Our bodies, once arsenals in the devil's kingdom are to become weapons in God's kingdom.

Conclusion

There is a reason we are called to offer ourselves to God. Verse 14 states: "For sin shall not be your master, because you are not under law, but under grace." It was God's grace that provided our salvation. The moral code, or law, only facilitated sin's expression. To be religious and to have a moral code cannot save. It sharpens our guilt instead of reducing it, for it pinpoints our failures. In contrast, God's grace gives a power to say "no" that humanity never had before the cross. We were victimized, slaves of sin. Now, because we were crucified with Christ and our old life brought to an end, we have a new power and a new life. We are new creations in Christ. Because of these great truths, sin is no longer to be a master over us.

Verse 14 is both a statement of fact and a promise. The mood of the verb makes it a clear cut statement with no doubt or hesitancy—*"sin shall not be your master."* The future tense makes it a promise as well. Dunn wrote, it is "a promise already being enacted by grace...by enabling from God, the possibility of grace to live now as one will live with Christ in the future."[65] We experience that victory partially now. God promises we will experience it fully when we are in His presence.

The choices we make now are not always easy. They are often very difficult. Sometimes our desires scream at us demanding satisfaction right now. In addition, we carry the baggage of emotional problems from being hurt, abused, or misunderstood that complicates our freedom to choose the right action.

Paul's counter to the reality of these matters is the personal presence of the Holy Spirit as a law of life and power. He gives the strength and power we do not have in ourselves. That's the glory of our gospel and Savior.

Before a person can experience eternal life, they must know they are dead in trespasses and sins. Before a believer can experience the resurrection power of Christ in victory over sin, he or she must count themselves as dead to sin, alive to God, and offer themselves to God as a weapon of righteousness.

Speaking of the future reign of the Messiah, Isaiah wrote: "The fruit of righteousness will be peace; the effect of righteousness will be quietness and confidence forever" (32:17). That promise also applies to our personal lives. As we choose to offer ourselves to God as weapons of righteousness, we will experience His peace, quietness and confidence. To the extent we continue to choose sinful behaviors, we will experience conflict, defeat, and anxiety. Sin always brings

---

65   Dunn, 339.

personal dislocation and disintegration of character. It is the way of death to who you are. Righteousness is the way to harmony, peace and power.

If you want peace and power in your personal life to enable you to turn some things around, then offer your body to Jesus as a weapon of righteousness. How do you do that? Consciously and specifically give God every member of your body: your mind (so you will think God's thoughts); your emotions (so you will love what God loves and hate what God hates); your will (so you will make right choices); your appetites and drives to be under the control of the Holy Spirit.

For your reflection:
- Name the two important facts of verse 11.
- Because of those two facts, what is the believer not to allow to happen?
- Name the two options available to the believer.
- What is meant by "verse 14 is both a statement of fact and a promise?

Do I Have to be GOOD to go to Heaven?

19

Romans 6:15-23

You Can be a Slave to Something that Kills You or to Someone Who Gives Life

"Now the Greeks defined righteousness as *giving to man and to God their due*. The Christian life is a life which gives God His proper place, and which respects the rights of human personality.... That life leads to what the Authorized Version calls *sanctification*. The word in Greek is *hagiasmos*. All Greek nouns which end in *asmos* describe, not a completed state, but a process. Sanctification is not a completed state; it is the road to holiness. When a man gives his life to Christ, he does not stop there and then become a perfect man; the struggle is by no means over. But Christianity has always regarded the direction in which a man is facing as more important than the particular stage to which he has achieved. Once he is Christ's he has started on the process of sanctification."[66]

Scripture: Romans 6:15-23

Main Idea: A person is a slave of either sin which leads to death, or of the gospel which produces life.

Introduction

A primary headline in network news and the daily papers (July 1996) was a government study that demonstrated a dramatic rise in drug use by teens in the previous five years.

---
66   Barclay, 92-93.

The *USA Today* stated one year prior (7/17/95, D1) that teenagers felt the biggest problem they faced was drugs, far outweighing concerns about crime, social pressure, sex or doing well in school. If that was true over two decades ago, how much more so today. Two-thirds of 12th-graders stated illegal drugs are so accessible all kids face the decision whether to try them. The number two factor enabling kids to resist drugs' allure was religion. Our Scripture confronts us with the fact that we can be the slave of something that destroys us or we can become enslaved to Someone who will give us life. What we can't avoid is being a slave.

A *USA Today* (8/9/96, B1) featured the return of heroin to professional life. The title was, "'Chasing the Dragon:' Once designated as a street drug, heroin has become Wall Street's dirty little secret." A couple of years ago, rock hero, Kurt Cobain committed suicide because he was nothing more than a wealthy junkie. Alcohol holds about 35 million Americans in slavery. A *Newsweek* (5/6/96) warned of the danger of herbal abuse. Kids have turned to herbs like Cloud 9 and Herbal Ecstacy (*sic*) to get their kicks and some have died as a result.

It doesn't take a genius to know that drugs bring slavery. So why to people take them? Jesus said the problem is one of the heart. Sinful, self-destructive behavior comes from the heart. Today's psychology says people do these things because of the different experiences and outside influences to which they have been subjected. People are in search of peace, but their lives are filled with anger, bitterness, and turmoil. Where can they find peace? Jesus said peace is an inside matter of the heart, not the result of outside forces working on us. He promised: "Peace I leave with you; my peace I give you. I do not give to you as the world gives" (John 14:27). The old prophet Isaiah wrote: *"You will keep in perfect peace him whose mind is steadfast, because he trusts in you"* (26:3).

A person who has Jesus, has peace. When we have peace, we don't have to turn to a chemical or compulsive behavior to try to get it. We are truly free.

Paul stated in this passage that a person is a slave either of sin which leads to death, or of righteousness [referring to the gospel] which produces life. There are no other options for anyone. Let's look at these options more closely.

The passage begins with a repetition of the question that opened the chapter, "So, since we're out from under the old tyranny, does that mean we can live any old way we want? Since we're free in the freedom of God, can we do anything that comes to mind? Hardly." The Jew as a religious person would have been deeply offended by Paul's argument that the law encouraged sin. The religious view is that rules are a barrier against sin by saying this or that is wrong. If the barrier is removed, then anything goes and moral chaos will result. However, a list of do's and don'ts doesn't stop people from sinning. The rules only point out the fact that we broke them. They don't give us power inside to keep them. The answer to wrong actions isn't a list, but giving our hearts to Jesus to change them.

I. Our Choice Is to Be a Slave of Someone (15-18)

A. We Have Two Options for Masters (15-16)

In verse 13 the believer is told to no longer continue to offer their body as a tool of sin, but to once-for-all and immediately offer their bodies to God as a tool to do what is right.

That command is now explained further. The act of offering ourselves, or presenting ourselves to a higher authority and power, puts us into a slave relationship. This metaphor of slavery was graphically understood by the Roman Christian. Slavery was very common in Paul's day. Paul wrote this letter from Corinth where at least a third of the population were slaves and another third were freed slaves. The Christian community in Rome was most likely composed of slaves and former slaves. A slave was the property of his or her master. They owned nothing. They had no time of theirs own and owned no personal possessions. They were the exclusive possession of their master. They could never do as they liked. Paul uses this word picture to communicate to them, and to us, the heart of his teaching on the dynamics of the Christian life.

You know well enough from your own experience that there are some acts of so-called freedom that destroy freedom. Offer yourselves to sin, for instance, and it's your last free act. But offer yourselves to the ways of God and the freedom never quits.

There are only two options: we are slaves either to sin which leads to death, or slaves of obedience which leads to righteousness. Every person is a slave of one or the other. No other options exist. A person who offers their body to alcohol, drugs, or tobacco will probably end up the slave of that drug. Pornography is addictive and leads to a slavery of sensuality. The tongue is easily enslaved to a critical spirit or to gossiping. We become enslaved to materialism, pleasure, and even work. Sin enslaves.

It is easy enough to understand offering ourselves to sin. What does offering ourselves to obedience mean? In 1:5, Paul wrote of calling people to *"the obedience that comes from faith."* He meant obeying the gospel which requires us to place our trust in Jesus Christ to be saved. The letter concludes in 16:26 stating that the gospel is to believe and obey the revelation of God in Jesus Christ.

Faith in Jesus is more than a flippant, raise the hand, "Yes I believe." To believe in Jesus is to become a disciple, a follower of Him. He is the Master, we are His slaves committed to obey Him. In that relationship, the law's role is to define our obedience. But the law does not give the power to obey its definition of right and wrong. Only grace can do that. Grace provides a change of heart. Grace brings the old life to an end and instills in us a new life which is Jesus himself. He is the power to live in obedience to the law. And obedience leads to a right life.

B. A Testimony of Change of Slavery (17-18)

To assure the Romans they need not be anxious about their standing before God, Paul, who had never met them, rehearses their conversion.

They used to be slaves to sin, but they had *"wholeheartedly obeyed"* what Paul had taught them about God. As a result they were set free from sin to become slaves of doing the right thing.

II. There Are Predetermined Results of Our Choices (19-24)

To convince his readers that grace is not a license to sin, Paul continued to stress the slavery picture. We have one of two choices: to offer ourselves to sin or to righteousness. We do not have a choice of the outcome of our decision. Sin always leads to death and righteousness always leads to life. God has established it as a law of cause and effect. Jesus stated that *"everyone who sins is a slave to sin"* (John 8:34). And the law applies to the Christian.

A. Sin Always Leads to Death (20-21,23a)

"As long as you did what you felt like doing, ignoring God, you didn't have to bother with right thinking or right living, or right anything for that matter. But do you call that a free life? What did you get out of it? Nothing you're proud of now. Where did it get you? A dead end [in some cases, literally dead physically and eternally in hell]. . . . Work hard for sin your whole life and your pension is death."

Two other word pictures are brought into the slavery metaphor. Though it is somewhat awkward, Paul asks what did our slavery to sin 'reap'? What was its fruit? The picture is of a tree of sin bearing its fruit, death. The tree of sin will always produce death. It will never produce anything but death.

The third picture is a soldier receiving his wages, or provisions. As a soldier can expect his government to provide logistic support and feed him, so a person can expect sin to issue its pay which is death. The paycheck of sin is always death, never anything but death.

B. Righteousness Always Leads to Life (22-23b)

"But now that you don't have to listen to sin tell you what to do, and have discovered the delight of listening to God telling you, what a surprise! A whole, healed, put-together life right now, with more and more of life on the way! ... God's gift is real life, eternal life, delivered by Jesus, our Master" (The Message).

Righteousness, obedience, and God are used interchangeably by Paul as the alternate master to whom we offer ourselves in slavery. Verse 23 states the outcome is not a wage but a gift. We do not receive life because we do religious deeds. We receive life when we bring our sinful, broken lives to Him and offer ourselves to Him. The result of that obedient act is the gift eternal life.

Wages and gift are set in contrast. We earn the death of sin by our sinful behaviors. In contrast, eternal life is a gift we receive by faith. It brings us into a right relationship with God.

Conclusion

Verse 19 makes another appeal to us:

> *"You can readily recall, can't you, how at one time the more you did just what you felt like doing—the worse your life became and the less freedom you had? And how much different is it now as you live in God's freedom, your lives healed and expansive in holiness?" (The Message)*

Sin has a downward spiral. Sin is impure behavior. One sin leads to another sin until we become lawless—the word for wickedness. Lord Byron, a poet from the Romantic period, lived a life of sensual pleasure and wrote of the results:

> The thorns I have reaped
> Are of the tree I planted.
> They have torn me and I bleed.
> I should have known
> What fruit would spring
> From such a tree.

In contrast, a right heart generates right behavior. The result is a holy life. Holiness means to be set apart to God as His possession, to be used in His service, and to develop and display His character in our daily lives. In saving us from sin, God's purpose is not only to provide heaven for us, but also for us to demonstrate to the world that living a righteous life is better than living a sinful life.

Getting free of slavery to alcohol or drug addiction is not an easy or simple matter. However, without the inside change of the heart brought about by the Holy Spirit, it is nearly impossible. The statistics of success of drug treatment facilities that do not offer Jesus as the bottom-line, is very low for the dollars invested. Teen Challenge has a success rate of close to 85%.

Nicky Cruz, one of the founders of Teen Challenge, told the story of Gizella, a Hungarian young lady. She was killing herself with heroin. "She could have passed for any of the thousands of young Americans I see enslaved by drugs—thin, distracted, old beyond her years. Her lifetime of potential was hostage to the same merciless captor that had seduced countless others.

"But Gizella wasn't an American. She was a college-educated citizen of Budapest, Hungary. I met Gizella at a Communist drug abuse conference in Budapest. She was in the last, deadly stages of addiction. I was the principal speaker, invited by the Hungarian government. The Lord had put my book *Run Baby Run* into some officials' hands, and they had asked me to help them with their drug problems."

Gizella confronted Cruz in a hallway and said: "'Look, I've read your book and this is my last chance. My friends brought me here from the hospital

"…I'm dying. This is my last mile. What can you tell me?'"

> "I want you to know that the same Jesus who changed me can change you. You must understand this: He died for you. You are precious to Him. He loves you. Everything He touches He changes. He can touch you and change you right now."

In a clear miracle of grace, God did touch Gizella that night to the amazement of communist doctors and political leaders. Later that night, as Cruz told his personal story and God's power to save, Gizella was too weak to finish the service. While she was being carried out to return to the hospital, God touched her. She returned to the stadium to the cheers of the Hungarian crowd and the amazement of the doctors.

> *"Work hard for sin your whole life and your pension is death. But God's gift is real life, eternal life, delivered by Jesus our Master." (The Message)*

For your reflection:
- List some ways people allow themselves to become enslaved to things that control them:
- Verse 15-16 state we only have two choices for masters. What are they?
- If you have asked Jesus to be your Lord and Savior, you are no longer a slave of sin. When did you "wholeheartedly obey" the good news and place your trust in Him?
- We have a choice of which master we will be a slave to; we don't have a choice of the results of our decision. Sin always leads to death and doing what's right always leads to life.

Do I Have to be GOOD to go to Heaven?

20

Romans 7:1-6

Marriage as a Picture of the Christian

"As long as they live, the husband and wife are under the authority of the law of marriage. If the woman leaves the man and marries another man, she commits adultery. But if the husband dies, she is free to remarry because she is no longer a wife. It is death that has broken the marriage relationship and set her free.... In Paul's illustration from marriage, it was the husband who died and the wife who married again. If you and I area represented by the wife, and the Law is represented by the husband, then the application does not follow the illustration. If the wife died in the illustration, the only way she could marry again would be to come back from the dead. But that is exactly what Paul wants to teach! When we trusted Christ, we died to the Law; but in Christ we arose from the dead and now are 'married' (united) to Christ to live a new kind of life! The Law did not die, because God's Law still rules over men. We died to the Law, and it no longer had dominion over us."[67]

Scripture: Romans 7:1-6

Main Idea: The law has authority in a marriage relationship only as long as the husband is alive. Since we died with Christ, sin's authority over the believer has been canceled.

---

67   Wiersbe, 74-75.

Introduction

A number of years ago, the *Presbyterian Life* magazine told of Rusty who had misunderstood a statement from the minister in his uncle's wedding. Later, while playing, he was heard to say, "Rosemary, do you take this man for your awful wedded husband?"

Some of you are crying, not laughing. You landed a husband like that? The parson asked the bride, "Do you take John for better or worse?"

She replied: "He can't be any worse, and there is no hope of his getting any better, so I take him 'as is.'"

Our Scripture states that everyone is born married to sin and the law—an awful husband! When we trust in Christ as our Savior and Lord, that marriage is dissolved through our death, and we are then married to a new groom, Christ Himself—it can't get better than that.

The marriage analogy was also used by Paul in his letter to the Ephesians. There the believer is referred to as the bride and Christ as the groom. The roles are reversed in Romans 7. The believer is comparable to the husband who dies so that the wife can be legally married to another without the relationship being stained by adultery.

Our Scripture makes three assertions about the believer's relationship to the law as illustrated in marriage.

I. The Law Only Has Authority When a Person is Alive (1-3)

A. Statement of Fact

Paul's primary reference to law was to the law of Moses rather than Roman law. For 12 months after a husband's death, Roman law bound the wife to him to mourn his death.

Should she marry in that period of time, she would forfeit her inheritance. [68]

The word for "authority" is the same as found in 6:14: "*Sin shall not be your master.*" Paul is gradually seeking to connect sin with the law. It was a delicate issue with his Jewish audience. He has built his argument to the point where he is confident in making this association. The law functioned to trigger sin in a person. Therefore, if a person was dead, their subjection to sin was broken. That reality also limits the law's authority in a believer.

B. The Marriage Illustration

The marriage union is given very strong language. "A married woman is *bound* to her husband." "Bound" means to be under and carries the idea of subjection. Such submission is not foreign to the New Testament but it is almost repulsive to our society. In our desire to respect a woman's rights in society and the work place, we have consciously or unconsciously discarded this biblical principle. In Ephesians 5 where Paul is using the marriage illustration to shed light on the doctrine of the church and Christ's love for her, wives are commanded to "submit" to their husbands. That, too, is a military word communicating submission to a higher authority. Husbands are commanded to love with the same sacrificial commitment that brought Christ from heaven to the cross in death for sin. That is not an abusive authority, but a saving one. A husband is not told to force his wife into submission, nor is he given any permission to abuse her physically, emotionally, or spiritually.

We must keep all of the pieces of this illustration in place. The wife's voluntary submission to a loving, sacrificial husband is a living picture of God's relationship to us as

---

[68] James D.G. Dunn, *Word Biblical Commentary, Vol. 38, Romans 1-8* (Dallas, Texas: Word Books, Publisher, 1988), 360.

sinners, and ours to Him as our Savior. In that environment, the concept of submission is adamantly mandated.

Our illustration continues, if the wife leaves her husband for another man while he is alive, she is called an adulteress. If he dies and she remarries, she is not an adulteress, for she is "released"—completely absolved or discharged."[69]

II. We Died with Christ (4-5)

A. In Dying with Christ, We Died to the Law

We are still working on the concept of the believer's union with Christ in his death and resurrection, Paul now equates dying to the law with dying to the "old man." He does not say the law has died and therefore is no longer valid nor has a relationship to the believer. Rather, we are the ones who died to the law. The importance of this will be seen latter in this chapter.

The reason God placed us in Christ in crucifixion was to release us to be married to a new master-- *"to him who was raised from the dead."* The purpose of belonging to another is to enable us to bring forth fruit to God. Though the word "fruit" is used, it is not the imagery of a tree, but of a marriage and family. The fruit is defined in 6:22 as a holy life with the end result of eternal life.

Paul moves from "you" to "we" in verse 4. He cannot withhold his own involvement in identification with Christ's death and resurrection.

The old marriage to the law had the fruit of sin resulting in death. Verse 5 should not read as "sinful nature" but as "flesh." "In the flesh" is used here as synonymous with the "old man," our pre-conversion life. This is the first usage of the

---

[69] Fritz Rienecker/Cleon Rogers, *Linguistic Key to the Greek New Testament* (Grand Rapids, Michigan: Regency Reference Library, 1980) 363.

term "flesh" in Romans. It describes the carryover of a sinful element from the old life into the new.

How does the flesh operate? "The sinful passions aroused by the law were at work in our bodies, so that we bore fruit for death." The law is not merely passively defining right and wrong now, it is aggressively enslaving the religious person to sin with the result of death.

The law moves our emotions, our passions, inflaming us to do sinful acts. It pounds upon us as unceasingly as the breakers beat the shore. "Passions" is *pathēmata,* with the English "pathos" a transliteration, and refers to our emotions or feelings. Dunn wrote: "A life ruled by or lived chiefly on the level of the *pathēmata* is almost certain to be a tool manipulated by sin."[70]

I am concerned that a large segment of evangelical Christianity has become primarily emotional. It is understandable that we feel emotionally starved in a sterile scientific age. However, the answer is not to look to church as primarily a source of emotional lift. Some think the primary evidence of an alive church is its emotional content. If the church service doesn't provide an emotional high, these people feel cheated. The point is we must maintain balance between cognitive truth and our appropriate emotional response to the truth. The Psalms are filled with admonitions of praise, joy and exuberance. David was filled with emotional expression to the LORD. We must be the same. The church was emotionless for too long. Let's balance that with emotional exultation of the Lord for His victory over the penalty and power of sin in our lives.

John A. MacMillan, missionary and early editor of the *Alliance Weekly*, forerunner of *Alliance Life*, warned of

---
70   Dunn, 364.

emotionalism in his classical pamphlet on "The Authority of the Believer". Speaking of the spiritual forces of evil in the heavenly realms," MacMillan described them as...

> "an innumerable body of demons, to whose close connection with mankind is due the grosser sins and deceptions, the stirring up of the animal passions, and the incitement to all manner of sensual and sensuous desires.... These beings are at hand in religious gatherings, and are a source of peculiar danger, especially when the emotions are deeply stirred. Many earnest souls, who have been urged to entire surrender, open their beings with the utmost abandon to whatever spiritual force approaches them, unaware of the peril of so doing. Such yielding often provides an opening for the entrance of demons, who under some pretext gain control of the will."

B. Now We Belong to Another

God's way out of our awful marriage to the law is our co-crucifixion with Christ. We die with Christ and we are raised with Him. He is the "other" to whom we are joined in order to bear the fruit of a holy life--a life of victory over sin. The third assertion is...

III. We have been Released to Serve in the New Way of the Spirit (6)

A. The Fact of Our Release

"But now, by dying to what once bound us [the restraint of slavery], we have been released [taken from the sphere of influence of] from the law."

Our emancipation from the slavery of the law that produced sin with the result of death is declared as a fact. It is true. We were once restrained in slavery to the law arousing our passions to sin. But that slavery is ended when we come to Christ. We are released from the law through death. All who have come to Christ have been released from the law's ability to inflame our passions and produce sin in us.

Let's summarize the facts the apostle presents. The law has authority only as long as a person is alive. When they die, it no longer has control. Because we died with Christ, we died to the law and its enslaving power. We are free to live a new life in the Spirit. We are a new creation in Christ. The old has gone; the new has come (2 Corinthians 5:17).

B. We Have a New Life in the Spirit

The next chapter is a great statement of our victory over sin through the power of the Holy Spirit. The subject is introduced to us with this factual statement: "So that we serve in the new way of the Spirit, and not in the old way of the written code."

The written code, the moral code, the lists of do's and don'ts cannot empower us to the new life. That comes only by the gracious ministry of the Holy Spirit in our lives. The "old way" is obsolete, but we keep trying to modernize it. There is nothing wrong with a moral code, especially the one found in the Bible, but it cannot change the heart or empower holiness. Only the Holy Spirit can do that.

We have been released so that we can "serve in the new way of the Spirit, and not in the old way of the written code." Paul said to the Corinthians that the written code kills, but the Spirit gives life (2 Cor. 3:6). Jesus said, "The Spirit gives life; the flesh [meaning the physical or religious good works] counts for nothing. The words I have spoken to you are spirit and they are life" (John 6:63).

Application

In 6:14, Paul made what F.F. Bruce called a "revolutionary" statement: "Sin shall not be your master, because you are not under law, but under grace." To be under the moral or religious code is to be ruled and enslaved to the flesh. To be under grace is to be ruled and enslaved to the Spirit. That is the key to understanding chapters 6, 7, and 8.

The purpose of God saving us in and through Jesus Christ is to bring to an end the old cycle of law/sin/death and to establish a new order of grace/holiness/life. If you have trusted Jesus as your Savior, you are in the new order. If you have not, you are in a quagmire of sinking sand that will eventually swallow you in hell. Break that cycle by coming to Jesus Christ now.

While Paul does not address the divorce issue that is intrinsic to the source passages behind this chapter, he does state the permanence of the marriage relationship. The Christian is to be markedly set apart from this world system in adhering to the concepts of an ancient book, the Bible. It is right when it established the permanence of marriage with a single exception clause of adultery for its dissolution.

Resist the secular humanistic interpretation of marriage that is sold to us on nearly every television program, newspaper, and magazine. The world says, "I don't have to put up with a bad relationship." God says, "You are one of the two people making it bad. I can change you both on the inside by My Spirit, so that a bad relationship can become a good relationship." He did not say that psychology is your answer. Counseling that does not lead to the life of the Spirit, has limited value.

Psalm 1 portrays the effect of walking with God in obedience:

> *"Blessed is the man who does not walk in the counsel of the wicked or stand in the way of sinners or sit in the seat of mockers. But his delight is in the law of the LORD,*

and on his law he meditates day and night. He is like a tree planted by streams of water, which yields its fruit in season and whose leaf does not wither. Whatever he does prospers."

That is the new way of the Spirit that leads to life.

For your reflection:
- When law is discussed, what law is referenced?
- What is Paul's connection of marriage and the law?
- What brings about the end of the authority of the Law to a person?
- State the significance of the believer's death with Christ
- How do we serve in the new way of the Spirit?

Do I Have to be GOOD to go to Heaven?

21

Romans 7:7-25

Winning Over the Internal Conflict

"In this picture, we see the law sternly condemning the sin from which it could not save. Our old husband could tell us of the right and punish us for the wrong, but he had no power forever to cleanse the evil from our nature, or give us the power to keep his own commandment, and when we disobeyed, he could do nothing but strike us down and at last slay us with the sword of his righteous judgment....

"The picture is a beautiful one; we are represented as a woman, lying in her blood at the feet of her former husband, who has bruised and beaten her for her falsity and crimes, and at last has taken her very life. There she lies, a poor hopeless, lifeless thing, but as she lies in her blood, lo! a glorious Being passes by. It is the Son of God, the Prince of Life. He beholds her in her lifelessness and shame. He looks upon her with intense compassion.... His heart goes out to her with intense and Almighty mercy; He touches her with His wand. He lifts her into new life. He raises her from the dead. He washes her from her blood and stains. He clothes her in His own white raiment. He adorns her with His own loveliness. He makes her beautiful...and gives her His love. He makes her His wife. He marries her to Himself, and He imparts to her all that He is and all that He has, and makes her the joint heir of His glory and His kingdom."[71]

---

71   Simpson, 151, 153-154.

Scripture: Romans 7:7-25

Main Idea: The flesh functions as a law of sin affecting every area of the Christians life. There is victory only in Jesus Christ.

Introduction

Let me guess. Five of the couples or families here this morning had some kind of disagreement or fight before coming to church this morning. Sometime this past week a few of you were drunk or close to it and others took an illegal drug. In the last six months, some have either committed adultery or fornication outright or did so in their fantasies. This week too many viewed some form of pornography. A significant number spoke profane or vulgar words or told some dirty stories. We all faced jealousy, pride, greed, gossip, deceit and cheating, or lusting for something you don't have. If you didn't get nailed by this list you are definitely among the Hall of Famers. But aren't we all a neat bunch of people sitting here in church?

What is wrong on the inside of us? We agree that the Bible is true, that obeying God's Word is the best way to live, yet we keep doing the wrong thing. Is our problem not trying hard enough? Yet is seems the harder we try, the more frustrated we become with our failures. Some give up trying to change in some areas because it seems hopeless. So we put on our Crest smiles, a splash of cologne and come to church where we fake our way through the day. We are like the Pharisees which Jesus described as white-washed graves--clean and nice on the outside but rotten on the inside.

Have you decided that's the way you are, and its no use attempting to fuss about? Ignore your sinfulness and get on with life, you think. Inward change is not easy because we do not like to face our sinful selves.

I was a high school student attending a Christian school. I had those inside forces at work as a maturing young man and so found this chapter of Romans fascinating. When the pastor of my church invited me to preach on a Sunday evening, I chose this passage. Can you imagine? I relied heavily on William Newell's *Romans Verse by Verse*, and did the best I could trying to understand it. I think of that now, and chuckle. I think the pastor and congregation did as well.

It is only natural that we look at the great apostle as made up differently than us. After all, he had some direct experiences with God most of us don't have, and he wrote most of the New Testament. In this passage, Paul lets us see inside his life. He had an on-going battle with sin. We can all be encouraged from his experience and the solution he provides to the conflict on the inside.

I. Our Problem is Not the Law ((7-13)

A. The Question: Is the Law Sin? (7)

The "law" is the Torah, the first five books of the Bible which includes the Ten Commandments. If the law is connected in some way to our sinful behavior, is it sin? "Certainly not."

How is the law connected to sin? It identifies sin. For example, says Paul, I would not have known that covetousness was sin except the law said, "Do not covet." By simply saying that some desires are wrong the law triggered that wrong desire in me. All but one of the Ten Commandments is cast as a negative statement. Why? We were born as sinners and sin comes naturally. It is a power in us that compels us to do what is wrong. Therefore we must be told to not do what we naturally do. The song in the Broadway musical, "Annie Get Your Gun," celebrates sex as doing what comes naturally.

Unless God had told us certain things are wrong, we would never know. Paul did not choose the first nine commandments to illustrate his point. He chose the tenth one. He knew what it was to have wrong desires. But he isn't just autobiographical, he is speaking for every person.

Two different words are used for "know" in verse 7. It could read this way: "Indeed I would not have experienced what sin was except through the law. For I would not have understood what coveting really was [and my on-going problem with it] if the law had not said, 'Do not covet.'"

In choosing covetousness, Paul put his finger on something that is universal. The old rabbi's felt that wrong desires, lust, covetousness, was the root from which all other sins sprouted. James 1:15 states that lust conceives and gives birth to sin.

B. The Law Triggers Sin into Action (8-13)

When the law said, *"Do not covet,"* inside Paul sin triggered a desire for the very thing being forbidden. After all, forbidden fruit is always the sweetest. While there is often a direct connection of coveting and sexual immorality, it broadly includes all that is selfish and grasping.

What do we covet? We want more recognition or attention from others. We want someone else's position or possessions. Married people lust after a different spouse and create fantasies of that relationship. Employees covet the boss's job. We desire a certain car, or dress, or house like.... Where are you discontent?

Throughout the years, churches have attempted to define Christian behavior. It has usually ended with a legalistic list of restrictions. Another approach attempted to get at the issue without the list. The bylaw read, "Behavioral Standards of the Christian." In the middle of the statement it read: "The basic issue is to love God with our whole heart, soul, mind and strength and our neighbors as ourselves. Unthankfulness and covetousness are inconsistent with loving God and our brother." An unthankful heart is wanting things to be different than they are now, and so we gripe. Where are you unthankful? In what areas are you coveting? If those behaviors are identified and rejected a Christian is reflecting a Spirit-controlled life.

The very commandment that was intended to bring life brings death. The culprit is sin on the inside, working its deceit by telling me that I am being cheated. If I had a different spouse, house, car, more money, or a hit of cocaine, I would be happy. The same way that Satan deceived Eve—the same word is used—into eating the forbidden fruit, he deceives us into thinking that someone or something else can make us happy.

The problem is not that there is something wrong with the law, because it is holy, righteous, and good. The function of the law is to point out how bad we are on the inside, that we cannot solve our problems by having a high moral code. We need a Savior who will not only bring forgiveness of sins, but who will also change us on the inside.

Our problem is not the law or the moral code…

II. Our Problem is the Law of Sin Inside (14-23)

A. We Face a Constant Internal Conflict (14-20)

The law, or moral code, is spiritual, but we are unspiritual, or of the flesh. We are sold as slaves to sin. The conflict is summarized in verse 15ff:

> "I do not understand what I do. For what I want to do I do not do, but what I hate I do. And if I do what I do not want to do, I agree that the law is good…. Now if I do what I do

not want to do, it is no longer I who do it, but it is sin living in me that does it."

There is nothing of the flesh, or sinful nature, that is any good. Before any of us can learn a victorious life in Christ, we must come to accept how sinful we are on the inside. Jeremiah reminds us that *"The heart is more deceitful than all else and is desperately sick; Who can understand it? I, the LORD, search the heart"* (17:9-10a NASB) Everyone who is a true Christian had to come to the place of accepting their own sinfulness and the impossibility of self-salvation. As Christians, we must also come to the place of full admission of our inner sinfulness and our inability to change ourselves on the inside.

We become Christians by accepting the free gift of forgiveness and eternal life in Christ. We will only be victorious over sin as we understand the depth of our sinful hearts that can only be changed by the Holy Spirit. We do not change our hearts by keeping a moral code. We keep the moral code because God has changed us and by His Spirit gives us power to obey his Word.

B. The Culprit is the Law of Sin (20-23)

What is it on the inside? Paul seems to talk like a schizophrenic with two "I's". But he isn't divided. There is an "I" sold under sin and its fleshliness, and an "I" delighting inwardly in the Word of God. They are the same "I".[72] "In my inner being I delight in God's law." But there is a law of sin that wages war against me and takes me prisoner.

The agony is intense. *"What a wretched man I am! Who will rescue me from this body of death?"* The one who was crying out in desperation was a man who was a religious fanatic. Paul was a Pharisee who kept the religious rituals

---

[72] Dunn, 390.

without error. Yet his religion, his high moral code could not change him on the inside.

He did not ask, "What must I do now?" He knows he is whipped. Do you feel whipped in trying to win the battle against sin on the inside? That's the most helpful point you could possibly come to. God can't help the self-sufficient, the person who feels they can handle it. God is here to help the sinner. If you know you are whipped, there is a Savior.

Conclusion

No one can escape Paul's struggle with lust, with coveting. How do we handle the problem?

Jesus is the answer to what's wrong on the inside. "Thanks be to God—through Jesus Christ our Lord!" There are four aspects to the spiritual dimension of inside change. One is to recognize the activity of the flesh, to take it to the cross and ask God to crucify it. Two, is the ministry of the Holy Spirit that will be discussed in Romans 8. Three is discipline. Four is personal therapy with a seasoned, godly believer or professional.

Christian psychologist and author, Larry Crabb, compared our lives to an iceberg. Our visible and observable lives are above the waterline. That includes the things we do, our conscious thoughts and feelings we sense inside us. The great mass lies beneath the waterline. That is the art that sinks the ship and includes our motives and attitudes of our heart, those strange impulses and urges that overwhelm our ability to resist, and painful memories and raging emotions we prefer to keep hidden. He wrote that the Christian community presents three options for dealing with this inside issue.

The first is to shape up and do the right thing. Just obey God's commands because they are good and right. Let's do this! There need in this frenetic culture to spend time in reading the Bible and being quiet for a period of time every day. Satan never rests. We are to be alert, firm in our faith, strong and courageous (1 Corinthians 16:13).

Crabb wrote: "So many have come to me for professional counseling after years of doing their Christian duties without experiencing the expected benefit. They wonder what went wrong. Rising earlier for devotions simply has not helped; they're tired, discouraged, disillusioned."[73]

The second option is the special work of the Holy Spirit. The stubborn effects of sin that are a part of the Fall are only effectively countered by the Holy Spirit's inner work in our hearts. How that is experienced differs according to denominational positions. In this model, a definite work of the Spirit brings substantial healing to the soul, the inside. Crabb pointed out the weakness of limiting ourselves to these two options. "Problems such as a fear of romantic involvement that began with sexual abuse in childhood or low self-esteem planted by inattentive parents or strong urges to do weird things" are not addressed in these two options (48).

The third option is to work through the obstacles to growth that are preventing winning the inside battle. That is where Christian therapy will continue to be needed. However, therapy is limited. Crabb wrote: "More often than not… psychological efforts do not resolve the deepest issues, which are spiritual. Change through counseling often involves working through deep problems rather than repenting of deep sin" (49).

The three options are not a matter of either/or; rather both/and. They need to work together to provide the most

---

[73] Larry Crabb, *Inside Out: Real Change is Possible If You're Willing to Start from the Inside Out* (Colorado Springs: Navpress, 1988), 45ff.

complete resolution to the inside battles we all face. To follow through more, Crabb wrote: "It is my view that an inside look is necessary as we continue to live responsively before God, but that its direct purpose is not to promote self-acceptance….. An inside look can help me to face my dependency on God in a manner that requires me to grapple with what it means to deeply trust. It can also expose my determination, in all its subtle ugliness, to manage life on my own. Such exposure pushes me toward deeper repentance and more thorough obedience" (64).

Some things to look for include deep anger or resentment, sexual lust, the drive for accumulation of things and money, an obsession for beauty or achievement. Resolution includes the full surrender of our hearts and asking the Holy Spirit to take full control. Then, we need to seek to understand the beneath-the-surface iceberg that will destroy us if we don't deal with it either in therapy with a counselor or a mature trusted friend.

Prayer, confession, repentance, surrender. Lord make me honest.

Jesus is the answer to what's wrong on the inside. *"Thanks be to God—through Jesus Christ our Lord!"* He can change us on the inside by his Spirit. How that happens is the subject of Romans 8.

For your reflection:

- It is hard to be honest with inside distortions. We easily find excuses as to why we do wrong things. Read through David's prayer in Psalm 39 after the prophet Nathan confronted him about his adultery with Bathsheba and the murder of her husband, sins this great lover of God found ways of excusing. Maybe you aren't guilty of those sins, but what are the sins you are white-washing?

- Why do you think there is a knee-jerk reaction in us to respond positively to what we know is wrong?

- What does Paul mean by the "law of sin"?

- The chapter concludes with an exultant expression. What is it and what does it say to you/

- St. Augustine (354-430)

"My inner self was a house divided against itself. Why does this strange phenomenon occur? The mind gives an order to the body and is at once obeyed, but when it gives an order to itself, it is resisted. What causes it? The mind commands the hand to move and is so readily obeyed that the order can scarcely be distinguished from its execution. Yet the mind is mine and the hand is part of the body. But when the mind commands the mind to make an act of the will, these two are one and the same and yet the order is not obeyed.

"Why does this happen? The mind orders itself to make an act of will, and it would not give this order unless it willed to do so; yet it does not carry out its own command. But it does not fully will to do this thing and therefore its orders are not fully given. It gives the order only in so far as it wills, and in so far as it does not will, the order is not carried out....

"When I was trying to reach a decision about serving the Lord my God, as I had long intended to do, it was I who willed to take this course and again it was I who willed not to take it. It was I and I alone. But I neither willed to do it nor refused to do it with my full will. So I was at odds with myself. I was throwing myself into confusion. All this happened to me although I did not want it, but it did prove that there was some second mind in me besides my own. It only meant that my mind was being punished. My action did not come from me but from the sinful principle that dwells in me (Rom. 7:17)."[74]

---

[74] Augustine, "Confessions," *Devotional Classics*, Foster & Smith (HarperSanFrancisco, 1993), 52-53.

Do I Have to be GOOD to go to Heaven?

22

Romans 8:1-8

How We Have Resurrection Power

"The righteousness of the law is not discarded but brought to fruition. All that God did in His Son for our redemption was 'in order that the just requirement of the law might be fulfilled in us, who walk not according to the flesh but according to the Spirit' (v. 4). The demands of the law are met when the righteousness of Christ is imparted to the believer by the Spirit, as well as imputed by the Father. The latter is the essence of justification. The former is the essence of sanctification.... Righteousness *of* the law, that is the righteousness which the law demands but can never provide, is gloriously possible when the Spirit applies to our hearts the full benefits of Christ's atoning death. Our Lord is Himself possessed of that perfect righteousness and it is unique to Him. He alone has attained to God's moral standard and no one else ever will apart from Him. But He gained the goal not merely as a decoration: He won the prize so that He might share it with us. His righteousness is offered to believers through the Spirit. It becomes a rich reality in experience. That is the whole aim and intention of what Paul is here expounding. The just requirement of the law is to be fulfilled in us."[75]

> **Scripture: Romans 8:1-8**
> **Main Idea: the indwelling power of the Holy Spirit becomes effective in the believer by developing a mind set on the Spirit.**

---

75   Wood, 29.

Introduction

Several years ago, I was privileged to serve on the national board for my denomination. When this particular meeting was over, I was driven to the airport by a gentleman who had previously owned an asphalt paving company. During the Korean War, he flew over 100 sorties as a top and side gunner on B-29's.

He was serving at that time as an elder in his church. Part of his ministry was conducting a Bible study in the state prison near his city. He told me two fascinating and dramatic stories of inmates who had come to Christ. Both men were in for life with no chance of parole. They were multiple murderers.

One said he had no memories of any affection or love from his mother or father. He could not recall ever being told he was loved, or receiving a hug. "Now I could tell you about discipline—don't do this or else. But I could not understand love." He had received Christ as His Savior, but this deficiency had never been resolved.

Recently, an organization came to the prison for a seminar and to bring the inmates some dinner. Prison food is not the greatest. He and some other inmates stole a couple of cases of the dinners. He never thought anything about. But that night, he had a knot in his stomach. The next morning, it was still there, and there that night. Not understanding what was the cause, he prayed: "Lord, if what I did was wrong, I ask you to forgive me." Immediately, the stomach problem went away.

He said, "For the first time, I felt what love is. I knew God loved me, but I had never felt love. I have experienced grace in my life, but for the first time I understood grace. Now

I have love in my mind, and love in my heart. I have grace in my mind, and grace in my heart."

The second inmate was a sex-murderer. After attending several Bible studies, he talked to the Lord one night in his cell. "Why is it that those men are so happy, and I'm so miserable, he asked God. The answer came so clearly, he thought God had spoken audibly. "Because you are a sinner." "What?" "You are a sinner." "How do I get rid of my sin?" "You must receive Christ into your heart." He prayed there in his cell, "Lord, I ask you to come into my heart, take away my sin and give me the joy these other men have." Immediately he was changed and knew it.

These two case stories emphasize that Jesus alone can change the heart. These men were not changed by knowing murder is wrong, violent rape is wrong, stealing is wrong. They were wrong on the inside and Jesus is the only one who can change us on the inside.

Most of you would not identify yourself as a criminal, but you know that sin is a power on the inside that causes you to do the wrong thing. The wrong might be in sexual behavior, temper, lying, a dirty mind, or bad language. Or it might be pride, self-righteousness, independence from God, gossip, or resentment. In any case, to change requires more than education or self-determination because sin as a power is greater than our human will-power.

I. We Receive Resurrection Power Through Jesus Christ (1-4)

A. Jesus Was Made a Sin-Offering (1-3a)

The transition into chapter 8 begins with two particles and is translated, "therefore." It indicates a conclusion to the foregoing argument. Sin, as an inner power, uses the moral code as a means of stimulating sinful behavior. The law, or moral code is not evil, but holy, righteous, and good, yet its function is not to produce right behavior but to highlight the reality of sin as an inner power. Everyone knows the conflict: we want to do right, but inside a power works against us and we fail. The only one who can deliver us from this wretched body of death is Jesus Christ our Lord. These verses tell us how.

The celebration of communion reminds us that through His death, Jesus satisfied God's demands against our sin. He was made a sin offering.

That He was sent by God (v 3), indicates He was with the Father as the eternal Son and came to earth to become our Savior. As a human being, He was subject to all the pressures of sin that we face, but He did not sin. Being without sin, God made Him an offering for sin, in the same way a lamb without defect was used as a sacrifice in Old Testament ritual.

The result? All who are "in Christ Jesus" are without condemnation. When we are forgiven through Christ, God removes all condemnation. Why? "Because through Christ Jesus the law of the Spirit of life set [aorist tense means decisively in the past] me free from the law of sin and death." As one of those two prisoners expressed it: "For the first time in my life I am free." Yet he will spend the rest of his life behind bars.

A person is placed "in Christ" when they put their trust in Him. In addition, God works to change the inside. Through the Spirit of life, a power is given that over comes the power of sin working in these wretched bodies of death. Sin is always working through the flesh to cause wrong attitudes and actions. But there is a greater power than sin. It is the Holy Spirit. He overcomes sin on the inside. In the same sense, the Christian has both the law of sin and death at work in them and at the same time, the law of the Spirit of life that is victorious over sin.

The answer to sin is not the moral code. No one really has a problem not knowing right and wrong unless there has been a distortion that has damaged their conscience. We know what we ought to do, but we are weak on the inside. The flesh is strong to do wrong, but weak to do right. It was so in the Old Testament and New Testament eras, and it is so in the 21st century. The law, or moral code, is powerless because it cannot change the sinful heart.

B. Jesus Condemned Sin's Power (3b-4)

We are without condemnation, but sin is under condemnation. Jesus judged sin and won victory over it.

What was God's reason for this dramatic action of His Son? "In order that the righteous requirements of the law [the Torah] might be fully met in us, who do not live according to the flesh [sinful nature] but according to the Spirit." "Fully" is a key word. It means much more than simply doing what is right. A person can do the right thing for the wrong reason. To fully meet the requirements of God's law the heart must be right. The motivations behind the actions are as important to God as the actions. True righteousness is more than mechanically doing what some moral code tells us. It is being right in our attitudes and motives. That comes when the Holy Spirit gives us the desire to do what is right and then the power to actually do it.

Jesus conquered sin on the inside. In doing so, He conquered sin in the flesh and lives within the believer to give us the same victorious lifestyle. The "law of the mind" (7:23) might give assent to the moral code but is too weak and fails to produce the right behavior. There are enormous implications for education and political theory in this fact. It is the Spirit that enables a person to do what is right. Religion that does not change the heart through regeneration by the Holy Spirit is bankrupt. No other religion offers this provision for changed behavior.

II. Resurrection Power Flows Through a Mind Set on the Spirit (5-8)

A. Our Mental Focus Determines the Direction of Our Lives (5)

The original word translated "minds set" refers to a settled way of understanding, to hold an opinion, or to maintain an attitude. There are two mental attitudes available. We can have our minds set on the flesh and do what sin desires, or we can set our minds on the Spirit—referring to the Holy Spirit. Which one we choose will determine the direction of our lives. We can choose the mind-set, but we cannot choose the outcome. We want to have the flesh and life, not the flesh and death, but that is not the way it works. This is written to Christians, not to the secularist.

B. The Spirit Mind-Set Produces Life (6)

"The mind-set on the Spirit is life and peace." There isn't anyone who doesn't want life and peace. God put in us the desire for eternal life. It is part of the human make-up. He also made us to enjoy peace. The goals are common to all humans regardless of race, education, or social status. But our strategies to reach the goals are naturally contrary to God's way because we are sinners.

C. The Flesh Mind-Set Produces Death (7-8)

Any person, Christian or not, who is convinced that life is power, or money, or sex, will experience the tragic death that mind-set generates. Sin, the flesh, always brings death. If we buy into the philosophy behind the slick advertisements in the media, we will bring death on ourselves.

Let's put church clothes on the flesh mind-set. It says the way to heaven is by going to church, being a good citizen, politically correct, non-racial, helpful to the poor, a non-substance abuser, and semi-generous to benevolences including the church. The end result is the same: it will lead to eternal death in the same way as sexual immorality will take its toll emotionally, mentally, and in many cases, physically.

Applied to marriage and family relationships, it means when we attempt to make our spouse or sibling meet our needs for security and significance, we will destroy what we so desperately long for. Our deepest needs can only be met in Christ. The flesh always tries to avoid going to Christ with our needs and longings. The Spirit always runs to Christ. The flesh will bring death every time, and the Spirit will satisfy every time.

Application

There are three action steps basic to this passage:

Before a person can know God's full empowering presence, they must first come into a personal relationship with God. To become a Christian requires that we face our sinful status before a holy God. There is only one Savior and that is the Lord Jesus Christ. When a person places their trust in Him as their Savior, God takes away their sins, all of them, and makes the person a daughter or son.

The second action point is to begin to develop a mind-set on the Spirit. In verse 6, Paul refers to this as a mind controlled [*phronēma*] either by the flesh or the Spirit. The idea is the mental inclination or purpose. It is used only in this chapter. It is possible to place our faith in Christ as Savior and have a mental purpose that focuses on the flesh. I know Christians who are more concerned about money, status, sex, or partying, than they are about living a godly life. That only brings death.

Basic to a Spirit-controlled mind is a Spirit-controlled life. God's counteraction to the power of sin in our lives is the Holy Spirit. He alone can conquer sin in us. Asking the Holy Spirit to fill and control us is a deliberate choice. That is why Paul commanded us in Ephesians 5:18 to be filled with the Spirit. The word for 'fill' means to literally cram a net or level up a hollow. Paul prayed in Ephesians 3:19 that we might "*know [God's] love that surpasses knowledge—that you may be filled to the measure of all the fullness of God. Now to him who is able to do immeasurably more than all we ask or imagine, according to his power that is at work within us.*" Both phrases get at the same point. We Christians can't live a holy life on our own. We need God in His fullness to give us inside power.

To be filled with the Spirit requires that we make a clean break with sin, the flesh, and our self-centered determination to run our lives our own way. We must be willing to submit fully to God. When we are willing to do that, then we need to surrender our entire life to Him. Submit to God your mind, emotions, will, job, money, pleasure and recreation, family, sexual desires and drives, your wretched body that serves sin. Give it all to God.

Then, by faith ask God to take control your mind and to fill you with the Holy Spirit. Invite Him to be your teacher, companion, friend, to make Christ real to you, to live in you the very life of Christ. Ask Him to win the battle with sin.

A third action point is to develop a spiritual mind-set each day. This is where the disciplines of the Christian life come in. We cannot have a mind-set on the Spirit and fill our minds with the cheap and sleazy stuff in films, music and television.

Instead, we must consistently read the Bible, pray, memorize key Bible verses, fellowship with Christians in a supportive relationship and serve God. This is NOT to say Christians can't go to movies, enjoy music, novels and books that have good content, and so forth. It may sound stifling and dull to some, but the point is, it works in producing wholeness in our lives. If that is what you want, this is how you get it.

By the power of the Holy Spirit, God uses the law or moral code to bring spiritual renewal and life. David wrote: "The law of the LORD is perfect, reviving the soul." Revived soul comes as we obey God. An obedient life will bring the peace, fulfillment, and joy we long to experience.

Gerhart Tersteegen was a layman in Germany over 250 years ago. He became a lay minister whose advice was sought by people from around the globe. A little book, *The Quiet Way*, is a compilation of some of his letters and thoughts. On the inner life, he wrote on February 29, 1736: "Whatever your state may be, never let anyone rob you of these two fundamental truths: (1) that God *is present* everywhere, and particularly in your heart; (2) that God loves you dearly and would have you entirely for Himself" (54).

He continued: "It is as if there were a little secret room in your heart where your best friend lives and waits for you. And so your love must urge you now and again to purchase some time, and if possible, some outward loneliness, so that you can go to your friend in the little room and talk to Him privately, and tell Him how you are and that you want to love Him truly. And when you go back again to your business, let it be as if you took your friend by the hand and begged Him to come with you and keep you company while you work, and take care of you. And that He will do most willingly" (56).

For your reflection:
   List three points in this sermon that are important to you, either in thinking or action.

23

Romans 8:9-11

Resurrection Life Is Ours Now

"In every spiritual transaction, there is an interplay of the divine and the human. Inasmuch as, on the divine side, sanctification is a work which God alone can effect, it *must* be appropriated 'by faith'. On the human side, there must be self-separation from all controllable wrong in the life; complete self-yielding to Christ; obedience to the written Word of God; and a prayerful determination to live only to His glory. Sanctification is not real unless it expresses itself in obedience to the divine law—and obedience means 'works'....

"Let us summarize and clinch this. That which *prepares* on the human side is a resolute renunciation of all known wrong in thought and behavior over which our will has control, and an utterly honest yielding of our whole being to Christ. That which *occurs* from the divine side is the Holy Spirit's infilling of the yielded believer. That which is thereupon *effected* is an inwrought moral and spiritual renewal into holiness, issuing in perceivable transfiguration of character."[76]

Scripture: Romans 8:9-11

Main Idea: Because Jesus rose from the dead, the believer has the person of the Holy Spirit living in them to overcome the power of sin.

---

[76] J. Sidlow Baxter, *A New Call to Holiness: A Restudy and Restatement of New Testament Teaching concerning Christian Sanctification* (Grand Rapids, Michigan: Zondervan Publishing House, 1973), 142, 143.

Introduction

Paul cried in despair: "What a wretched man I am! Who will rescue me from this body of death?" He wrote that, not of his life before becoming a Christian, but as a Christian.

Augustine described his pre-conversion life in similar terms. His *Confessions* is one of the most dramatic diaries ever written. He wrote of his life in Carthage:

> "To Carthage I came, where they sang all around me in my ears a cauldron of unholy loves. I loved not yet, yet I loved to love, and out of a deep-seated want, I hated myself for wanting not. I sought what I might love, in love with loving, and safety I hated, and a way without snares.... To love then, and to be beloved, was sweet to me; but more, when I obtained to enjoy the person I loved. I defiled, therefore, the spring of friendship with the filth of concupiscence, and I beclouded its brightness with the hell of lustfulness.... I fell headlong then into the love wherein I longed to be ensnared" (13).

Perhaps you have found yourself snared by the power of your inner lusts. You struggle to get free, but you can't. You have made resolutions, became religious, turned over the new leaf, only to find yourself back at square one. That whirlpool can quickly lead to a jaded despair. In a Broadway play of the sixties a young man who had dropped out of school and was estranged from his parents was hooked on drugs. In hopeless despair, he said: "How I wish life was like a notebook, so you could tear out the part where you've made all the mistakes and start over with a page that is fresh and clean." While we cannot delete the past from our personal history, Jesus does give to us a new start. He offers total forgiveness of sin. More, He will personally come to live in us by His Holy Spirit and begin changing us on the inside.

Is there any hope for the human heart to really change? Can we be different? Can we change on the inside? The gospel of Jesus Christ says, "Absolutely. If anyone is in Christ, he is a new creation." We become new creations the moment we trust in Christ. But there is another fact, too. The full experience of that new creation is yet to come. That is why hope is a dominant theme in the New Testament.

I would love to tell you that if you receive Christ as your Savior and Lord, your problems are over. But I can't. I can tell you there is coming a day when the problems will be gone, and you will enjoy a pain free eternity. That is guaranteed to us by the resurrection of Christ. This side of heaven, we experience a mix of victory and defeat. Jesus assures us of the future, but also a taste now of what that future will be like.

"Who will rescue me from this body of death? Thanks be to God—Jesus Christ our Lord." Let's gain a glimpse of how. In this passage, two statements are emphasized. First, victory belongs only to people in whom the Holy Spirit lives. Second, the Holy Spirit gives resurrection life now, not just in the future.

I. The Spirit Lives in Every Christian (9-10)

A. A Christian is a Person in Whom the Spirit Lives

The word, "Christian," is used in a descriptive sense to refer to an advanced culture. It can be used in a general sense to refer to anyone who belongs to either a Protestant or Roman Catholic church. Further, we use Christian to mean behavior that is good, or acceptable, such as being kind, generous, self-controlled. "Its the Christian thing to do," we say.

In the New Testament, it was first used of the believers in the city of Antioch, and was more a slur than a compliment. The unbelievers saw believers as "little Christs." What makes a person a Christian? A person must have the Holy Spirit living in them. Jesus said, "You must be born of the Spirit." Paul wrote a person is not under the control of the flesh if the Spirit of God lives in them.

The only way the Bible says we can have the Holy Spirit living in us is through faith in Jesus Christ. You can be a decent person morally, a religious person, but unless you have the Spirit of God, you are not a Christian in the biblical use of the word. "If anyone does not have the Spirit of Christ, he does not belong to Christ." The Holy Spirit is the Spirit of Jesus Christ. He comes to live in us the life of Jesus.

B. The Christian Is Controlled by the Spirit, Not the Flesh

The text reads, "You, however, are not in the flesh [meaning under the dominion/control of the flesh], but in the Spirit [under the dominion/control of the Spirit], if the Spirit of God lives in you." When a person genuinely repents of their sin and receives Christ, God establishes a basic change. The power of the flesh, the sinful nature inside us, is broken. How? First, the old man was crucified with Christ. Then, the Holy Spirit literally comes to live in our bodies to bring new attitudes, new desires, and a love for obeying God.

At conversion, a person comes under the rule of the Spirit who begins to make them a new creation.

C. The Christian Experiences the Conflict of Death and Life (10)

"But if Christ is in you, your body is dead because of sin, yet your spirit is alive because of righteousness."

The body is not sinful, but the body is the target of the sin that is in us which Paul termed the flesh, or sinful nature. In the last chapter, the apostle spoke of the flesh as the law of sin and death. The flesh is against God, doesn't like the rules, wants to do its own thing, loves to get thrills, thinks really good sex is with lots of partners. The Bible's standards just don't fit today's world. The flesh worships money, power, possessions, sensuality. It wants to get high on drugs. It is the source of pride, self-centeredness, anger, drunkenness. The flesh is anti-God, or more mildly, hangs the "Please don't disturb" sign on the door of the heart.

That is the power of sin on the body. We are addictive creatures. The majority of Americans are addicted to something: alcohol, drugs (prescription or non-prescription), nicotine, TV soaps, pornography, sex, or gossip. I wish we were addicted being truthful, kind, loving, or joyful. Sin enslaves us with destructive behaviors. It works through our bodies to do its evil.

As the body is the tool of sin, so the human spirit is the tool of the Holy Spirit. When we trust Christ, God unites our spirit with the Holy Spirit. He is the power in us to break the chains of the flesh.

Some ideas of how we gain victory in the Christian life portray sin as a cancer tumor that needs to be surgically removed. British scholar and author, J. Sidlow Baxter, used the metaphor of a blood disease that affects every part of a person's life. There is an antidote for the disease of sin, it is an infusion of the Holy Spirit. The disease will not be totally eradicated until we are in heaven, but we can experience the power of the Spirit of life now. The flesh, assures Baxter, is not a tumor of sin that can be removed by spiritual surgery. It permeates our whole being and only the counter work of life filled and controlled by the Holy Spirit can effectively live victoriously.[77]

---

[77] The reader can consult Baxter's volumes on sanctification: *His Deeper Work in Us; Our High Calling; A New Call to Holiness.*

II. The Spirit Gives us Resurrection Life and Power Now (11)

A. The Spirit Raised Jesus from the Dead

In his opening remarks to the Romans (1:4), Paul said Jesus was raised from the dead by the Spirit who is holy, and thereby powerfully declared to be the Son of God. He returns to that theme here. How did the corpse of Jesus come to life? The same Spirit that participated in the creation of the universe, came to that corpse and gave it life. When Jesus came out of the tomb alive, He defeated hell and sin and dramatically demonstrated that He was God who alone is man's Savior.

B. The Same Spirit Gives Life in Our Death

The clincher is, the same Spirit that brought a corpse to life will give life to our mortal bodies enslaved to sin. There is a two-pronged concept in this verse. One, in the future resurrection the believing dead will be raised out of their graves--even those whose dust has been scattered in the winds and seas. We, too, shall live. The grave and funeral service are not the end. They are a door to eternity. The Christian will be raised to life eternal with Jesus. In contrast, the unbeliever will be raised to eternal damnation in hell. There won't be any party there, either.

Two, we can experience that resurrection power of the Spirit in these mortal bodies now. We do not have to wait until we die. Bodies gripped with the enslaving power of sin can be set free to be the slaves of righteousness. The sins that control and manipulate us can be defeated. Minds that are polluted with lust, bodies that are chained with habits, can be set free to become like Jesus Christ in purity and goodness. We'll see more of the "how" in the next chapter.

Application

Maybe you're in a quagmire, in despair over the disappointments of life. Life has lost its spark. You wonder if it's worth going on. You feel like the fellow on the bridge who was going to jump off. A policeman came along and tried to talk him out of his action. "Let's take ten minutes to talk about this. You take 5 minutes to tell me why life is so bad you have to end it this way. Then I'll take 5 to tell you why you should live." The fellow thought that was okay. At the end of his five minutes, the policeman climbed up beside him and they both jumped.

There is hope, not only ultimately for eternity, but right now. Our lives can be different.

Jesus said, "You will know the truth and the truth will set you free.... I am the truth.... If the Son sets you free, you will be free indeed." Freedom is not the right to do what I want, it is the power to obey God and do what I ought to do. It is victory over the law of sin inside me. It is the resurrection power of the living Christ in me, setting me free from the law of sin and death.

Paul experienced that reality, and so did Augustine. You can too. The first step is to become a Christian by repenting of your sin and placing your complete trust in Jesus Christ as your Savior and Lord.

For your reflection:
- Do you in any way identify with Augustine's testimony? If so, how would you describe your struggle?
- How do you understand the difference between the old man/sinful nature and the flesh?
- How is the resurrection life of Jesus experienced by the believer?

24

Romans 8:12-17

Wow! What an Inheritance

"The old cross is a symbol of death. It stands for the abrupt, violent end of a human being. The man in Roman times who took up his cross and started down the road had already said good-by to his friends. He was not coming back. He was going out to have it ended. The cross made no compromise, modified nothing, spared nothing; it slew all of the man, completely and for good. It did not try to keep on good terms with its victim.

"God offers life, but not an improved old life. The life He offers is life out of death. It stands always on the far side of the cross. Whoever would possess it must pass under the rod. He must repudiate himself and concur in God's just sentence against him. What does this mean to the individual, the condemned man who would find life in Christ Jesus? How can this theology be translated into life? Simply, he must repent and believe. He must forsake his sins and then go on to forsake himself. Let him cover nothing, defend nothing, excuse nothing. Let him not seek to make terms with God, but let him bow his head before the stroke of God's stern displeasure and acknowledge himself worthy to die.

"Having done this let him gaze with simple trust upon the risen Saviour, and from Him will come life and rebirth and cleansing and power. The cross that ended the earthly life of Jesus now puts an end to the sinner; and the power that raised

Christ from the dead now raises him to a new life along with Christ."[78]

Scripture: Romans 8:12-17

Main Idea: Those who have the Holy Spirit are children of God, heirs of God and Co-Heirs with Christ.

Introduction

Newsweek Magazine reported June 13, 1994 (Vol 123:24, p. 50) that Jacqueline Kennedy Onassis, left the bulk of her estate to her two children. The value of the estate was estimated at the time to be in the $200 million range. Caroline and John Jr. inherited her 15-room Fifth Avenue apartment, its contents, other properties including the Martha's Vineyard compound and $250,000 a piece in cash. Various other individuals were named to receive significant sums of money and personal items.

You may have some wealthy relative somewhere through whom you are hoping to receive a nice sum. Far more important than worldly wealth which will only last for a few short years is the spiritual wealth God offers to those who belong to Him.

Our Scripture begins with 'therefore,' indicating a summary or conclusion. At this point it will help us to summarize the last few paragraphs.

In computer terminology, 'default' refers to the setup of the software as written by the programmers. The program will automatically follow those settings unless the operator deliberately chooses a different setting and so alters the

---

[78] A. W. Tozer, *Man: the Dwelling Place* of *God: What it really means to have Jesus Christ living in You*, compiled by Anita M. Bailey (Christian Publications, Camp Hill, PA 17011, 1966), Chapter 10, "The Old Cross and the New".

program. When those temporary replacements are removed, the program returns to its default settings.

Chapter seven illustrates that the human default setting is sin. That is not how God made us, but that is the consequence of Adam's sin. Romans 5:12 reads that "sin entered the world through one man, and death through sin, and in this way death came to all men, because all sinned." In chapter 7:15 Paul confessed of his personal experience: "I do not understand what I do. For what I want to do I do not do, but what I hate I do." Then he stated it was sin in him driving his behavior.

The opening of this chapter emphasizes the importance of a mind-set on either the flesh or the Spirit. A mind that focuses on the flesh will produce death. A mind focused on the Spirit will result in life and peace.

If the Holy Spirit is in a person, they belong to Christ. The Spirit who raised Jesus from the dead will give life to our mortal bodies enabling us to live in the Spirit rather than the flesh. Those in the Spirit have life and power.

The conclusion of this is "we have an obligation—not to the flesh" but to the Spirit.

I. A Christian is Under Obligation (12-13)

A. We Are NOT Obligated to Live to the Flesh

"Obligation" simply refers to one who owes someone something. This exhortation makes no sense if it isn't possible for a Christian to live according to the flesh. However, Paul has stressed with strong language that we must understand that the flesh can only result in death, never in life. He uses the personal pronoun, "we," to include himself—"We have an obligation."

Our obligation is NOT to the flesh to live according to it. If you are tempted to ask the "why" question, Paul says:

"For if you live according to the flesh (sinful nature), you will die." There is a two-fold application to the question of what kind of death we die. Galatians 6:8 states, "A man reaps what he sows. The one who sows to please the flesh, will from the flesh reap destruction; the one who sows to please the Spirit, from the Spirit will reap eternal life." The flesh brings death to self-esteem, our inter-personal relationships, our emotional well-being, and even to our physical life. A second aspect is spiritual death. Paul gives no comfort to the person who makes verbal claims to being a Christian and then continues on to live in the same behaviors of the flesh with no indication of a desire to change. Living after the flesh proves one does not have the Holy Spirit. If you do not have the Holy Spirit, you do not belong to Christ.

B. We Are Obligated to Put the Flesh to Death

A parallel expression to this verse is found in Galatians 5:24: *"Those who belong to Christ Jesus have crucified the flesh with its passions and desires."* In Ephesians 4:22-24 we are commanded to *"put off your old man, which is being corrupted by its deceitful desires; and be made new in the attitude of your minds."* And in Colossians 3:5: *"Put to death whatever belongs to your earthly nature."*

The specific reference is to the misdeeds of the body. It is the present tense stating something that is on-going in our daily life. We can't get a spiritual shot that inoculates us from sin. Dunn wrote: "The deeds of the body are the actions which express undue dependence on satisfying merely human appetites and ambitions."[79]

Esau is an Old Testament example of the principle. He was willing to sell his future, his inheritance as the oldest son with its spiritual rights, in order to satisfy his temporary

---
79   Dunn, 449.

appetite. As a result, his younger brother, Jacob, inherited the family blessing.

Today's emphasis for the flesh includes the vanity of beauty—body-building, slim, lithe, bodies. We spend billions on diets, health clubs, and beauty aids. Success as measured by income and position is another appeal to the flesh. It will find every means to bend the rules in order to make a buck. Our culture undulates with steamy sex appealing to our flesh to find fulfillment in promiscuous sex. Everything in our culture seems driven by sexual themes, which parallels Paul's day.

"Put to death" is present tense meaning a sustained effort. It is a daily, moment by moment, conscious effort by the Christian in his journey to the Celestial City. Living a holy life is not easy. It demands our highest efforts.

II. The Obligation Is Based Upon Sonship (14-17)

A. The Spirit of Life is the Spirit Who Makes Us God's Children

The argument continues that the person who by the Spirit puts to death the deeds of the body is one led by the Spirit. All who are led by the Spirit are sons of God. We are back to verse 9 in which we are told that the one who has the Spirit is not controlled by the flesh, but by the Spirit. And if the Spirit is in a person they belong to Christ—they are sons of God.

It is clear. Anyone who has been born of the Spirit is changed on the inside and begins to respond to the Spirit. Their behaviors begin to change. They can't use the same language. They cannot continue in a sexual relationship outside of husband/wife marriage, if the Holy Spirit is in them.

The child of God knows the reality of the Holy Spirit crying out to God inside their heart, calling Him, 'Abba,

Father.' To be adopted is to gain a new family relationship with all of its rights, privileges, and responsibilities[80]

"Abba" is an Aramaic expression used in prayer. It was used by Jesus and so found its way into Gentile worship because of its identity with Him. "Jesus' use of 'Abba' most probably implies a sense of intimate sonship on the part of Jesus."[81] We are able to enjoy the same endearing and sacred relationship He knew as the God-man. Paul emphasizes a strong emotional content in saying the Spirit cries, "Abba, Father." Use of both terms with different words communicates a spontaneous delight in God.

How do we know the Spirit is in us? How do we know we are led by the Spirit and are sons and therefore heirs? The Spirit "testifies", confirms, that we belong to God. It was a word "used in the papyri where the signature of each attesting witness is accompanied by the words 'I bear witness with and seal with.'"[82] Our sonship is not determined genetically by racial association as descendants of Abraham, but spiritually, as people born of the Spirit.

B. God's Children Are Co-Heirs with Christ

I suppose most people fantasize about some rich relative who would someday die and leave to us a fortune. Most of us wouldn't handle it with Christian stewardship because we don't manage what we now have with God's principles. Far better than earthly fortune, the child of God is a co-heir with Jesus to all of the riches of God.

To what extent are we accepted by God? To the fullest extent of His acceptance of Jesus. We are in Christ, and in Christ we share His position of sonship. Ladies, you want a

---

80   Rienecker, 365.
81   Dunn, 453-454.
82   Rienecker, 366.

beautiful home, the role of a princess? Do you want to get rid of the wrinkles, stop the aging process? Men are you wanting to be important, to feel you are something? Do you want power? All that we long for we will enjoy, not for a few short years, but forever. However, its only ours in Christ.

Paul's argument throughout this letter is our salvation is not the result of human good works, but a gift of God's grace. There is a stigma attached to belonging to Jesus. He was rejected. The world hated Him. He told His disciples to not be surprised when the world hated them when it hated their Master first.

We are co-heirs, we are God's children, we will enjoy His blessed inheritance forever, IF we share His suffering. In the last letter of Paul, 2 Timothy, he quoted an early church hymn (2:11-13):

"If we die with him, we will also live with him; if we endure, we will also reign with him. If we disown him, he will also disown us; if we are faithless, he will remain faithful, for he cannot disown himself."

Paul's own experience was one of suffering:

"We always carry around in our body the death of Jesus, so that the life of Jesus may also be revealed in our body.... Our light and momentary troubles are achieving for us an eternal glory that far outweighs them all."

Conclusion

We have a fantastic inheritance as Christians. It is Jesus Himself and through Him, we have all the heavenly Father has given to His Son. C. S. Lewis wrote: "God designed the human machine to run on Himself. He Himself is the fuel our spirits were designed to burn, or the food our spirits were designed to feed on. There is no other. That is why it is just no good asking God to make us happy in our own way. God cannot give us a happiness and peace apart from Himself, because it is not there. There is no such thing."[83]

You and I are under obligation to the Spirit who has made us sons and co-heirs with Christ. We are to be led by the Spirit in putting to death the deeds of the body with a default to sin. We can by the Spirit counter-program our bodies to not respond to sin and the flesh. We can say 'no' to what is wrong. We are under obligation to the God who has so greatly enriched us to do so.

So, let's quit playing around about living the Christian life. Call sin what it is. Take the Holy Spirit to give power to your weak and wretched body, and to live in you the victorious life of Jesus.

For your reflection:
- What is the 'default' setting of humanity?
- To what is the Christian NOT obligated?
- Why are we not obligated?
- What is the Christian obligation?
- Who is an Old Testament illustration of putting the flesh to death?
- Name the basis of our obligation.
- What is the believer's inheritance?

---

[83] *Mere Christianity*, quoted in Servant, Jul 1994.

25

Romans 8:18-25

What a Fantastic Future

"The reason we groan is because we have experienced 'the firstfruits of the Spirit,' a foretaste of the glory to come. Just as the nation of Israel tasted the firstfruits of Canaan when the spies returned (Num. 13:23-27), so we Christians have tasted of the blessings of heaven through the ministry of the Spirit. This makes us want to see the Lord, receive a new body, and live with Him and serve Him forever. We are waiting for 'the adoption,' which is the redemption of the body when Christ returns (Phil. 3:20-21). This is the thrilling climax to 'the adoption' that took place at conversion when 'the Spirit of adoption' gave us an adult standing in God's family. When Christ returns, we shall enter into our full inheritance. Meanwhile, we wait and hope. 'For we are saved by that hope' (Rom. 8:24, literal translation). What hope? 'That blessed hope and the glorious appearing of the great God and our Saviour Jesus Christ' (Titus 2:13). The best is yet to come! The believer does not get frustrated as he sees and experiences suffering and pain in this world. He knows that the temporary suffering will one day give way to eternal glory."[84]

Scripture: Romans 8:18-25

Main idea: Though we experience suffering now, we have a glorious future as God's children.

---

84   Wiersbe, 93.

Introduction

Vance Havner wrote in *Moody Monthly* (6/74): "There are a lot of questions the Bible doesn't answer about the Hereafter. But I think one reason is illustrated by the story of a boy sitting down to a bowl of spinach when there's a chocolate cake at the end of the table. He's going to have a rough time eating that spinach when his eyes are on the cake. And if the Lord had explained everything to us, what's ours to come, I think we'd have a rough time with our spinach down here."

If you don't like spinach, then the illustration works. If you happen to like the tart green leaves and don't like chocolate, turn the story around. A lot of life is eating spinach. Occasionally we have chocolate cake.

Children of God go through suffering. It is not optional. In our culture, we do all we can to eliminate pain. A sinful world under the control of Satan, the god of this age, will be predominantly painful.

Why be a Christian? Because God has promised a future when the injustices, hurt, and suffering of this life will be banished forever. That is the glorious inheritance of God's children.

I. Suffering is the Reality of the Present (18-21)

A. Our Glorious Future Outweighs Our Present Suffering

The Holy Spirit testifies we are the children of God through authoring the strong cry in our hearts, "Abba, Father." As children, we are heirs of God, co-heirs with Christ to the vast riches of God. But there is a conditional clause tacked on to the promise: *"if indeed we share in his sufferings in order that we may also share in his glory."*

That seems to be a very dark view of life. We want fun and excitement, peace and prosperity, and we're willing to pay almost anything to get it. Christianity is supposed to offer the abundant life, and suffering isn't what most of us have in mind when we hear Jesus say: "I have come to give you abundant life." We can only make sense out of the picture by understanding what is now is not what will be.

Paul is so certain of the future glory he begins the paragraph (v. 18) by saying, "I consider" *(logizomai)*. It means to come to a studied conclusion like a mathematical calculation. The conclusion is life is a mix of suffering and glory. God gives us enough taste of the glory to come to enable us to endure the suffering of the present.

The sufferings include the physical sufferings of sickness, injury, and deformity. Also, the pain of emotional, physical, and sexual abuse, the sorrow of death, and the hurt of broken friendships and promises is part of suffering. Spiritual suffering involves the agony of wrestling with the flesh, our failures to fully obey God, and combat with the devil as our enemy.

What is the glory that is to come? We will have new bodies of immortality. This mortal will put on immortality. Those who have died will be raised with a new body. Those who are alive will be instantly changed. Our emotional twists and warps will be resolved. No longer will we carry around the sense of failure and worthlessness. We will not try to use other people to meet our inner needs. Jesus will make us complete emotionally. And the devil will be banned from heaven. All the areas of suffering we know now will not be ours in the future.

B. Creation Itself Waits for the Coming Glory

A great revelation is going to take place when Jesus returns. Part of the revelation will be a glory in us, and a glory through us to the universe. Salvation, which we experience in part now, will be completed *in* us. Our sonship will be blazoned across the universe in a drama that will make the Oscar program look like child's play.

Creation is in "eager expectation" of that event. It refers to one who scans the skies searching the distant horizon for the break of dawn. Presently, creation is subjected to a frustration and sense of futility, not by its choice, but because it was imposed by God when man fell in sin. Because of man's sin, creation has been abused and devastated. As a result, inanimate creation joins with the children of God to hope for a future when all creation will be liberated from the bondage of decay.

Not only do people suffer decay, so does creation. The whole universe is running out of energy. Our magnificent and aged redwoods do not live forever. Everything is subject to death. In the Revelation, John wrote of trees that bear all manner of fruit twelve months a year. There will never be a dormant stage nor a time to cut the trees down because they are too old to produce anymore.

However, the decay of humanity is a tragic thing. Our life-span is very brief, though we are living longer than our ancestors ever dreamed. Worse is our moral decay. Using the same word, Peter wrote of the corruption (decay) that is in the world through lust. Our culture is totally adrift in a putrid sea of relativism. We have no standards of right or wrong and we have thrown out the Bible as a narrow, bigoted book of restrictions. Having done so, moral decadence is plainly evident.

Back in the nineties, NBC news ran a piece on the drunkenness of our university students. The problem is not a glass of wine with a dinner, its "Animal House" John Belucci binge drinking. A tragic story was of a beautiful young co-ed who got so drunk with her boyfriend they both fell from an overpass to railroad tracks below. She was killed. Alcohol is responsible for 50% of the traffic fatalities in our country. It is the culprit behind most of the violent crimes committed every year. Yet, the advertisements continue to sell alcohol as the passport to the good life.

Here is the Jeff Dahl Story (*Wall St Journal* 3/18/91):

"One tense day in August 1982 my brother vanished. Strung out on drugs, Jeff kicked in our parents' car door that afternoon—because they wouldn't give him $35.... Afraid and frustrated, my father told his 27-year-old son never to come home."

Shortly before the father, a wealthy IBM executive, died in May, 1988, he made a final wish: "Find Jeff." So, Jonathan began the hunt for his brother, a skilled guitarist, and champion swimmer with a 130 plus IQ. A long and frustrating search for one among millions of homeless people led him to New York, Connecticut, Florida, and Colorado.

Last December, after two years of searching, Jonathan found Jeff in Denver. He was now 35. "Jeff still wore his blond hair in the same Elvis Presley hairdo from high school; his eyes were the Windex-blue I remembered. But his face looked haggard and bloated, and his swimmer's build had become potbellied. The kid in my wallet had become a middle-aged man."

He had now gone from the more expensive drugs to marijuana and Vodka because they were cheaper. "Because of his addiction my brother had spent almost half his adult life at drug rehabs, drunk tanks and mental wards." He had tried more than once to kill himself. "I just didn't think anyone cared about me," he confessed.

There was no happy ending to the story written by Jonathan, a writer for the *New York Times*. Jesus came to save the lost. He died and rose again to make the Jeff Dahls of the world sons of God who will one day be restored to authority over creation.

II. Hope is Something in the Future (22-25)

A. We Groan as We Wait

The whole creation is groaning burdened with imperfection. We forget telephone numbers, names, and what we did last week. Klutzes that we are, we drop and break things and have to repetitiously redo work because of errors. We are plagued by self-doubt, jealous of other people's success or expertise, wish that we could be better, or do things better. We botch up our personal relationships with friends, our marriages, and our family. On one hand, we are envious of others, and on the other hand, we think everyone ought to be like us.

Every time a tornado rips through a town uprooting trees, collapsing buildings, picking up vehicles and dropping them a block later, killing people, creation groans. It groans because of the devastating drought in Africa. Hurricanes gathering winds of terrifying power and piling waves upon waves evidence a creation groaning for a new day. Floods, earthquakes, tidal waves all speak of creation out of control.

That was not God's original plan. When man was created, God gave to him authority to subdue the earth and rule over it. Sin broke that authority and ever since, man has struggled to regain control of what he lost. Maurice Irvin wrote in the *Alliance Life*: "We see God allowing man to use a bit of his potential power and authority through science.... But man is so corrupt God dares not let him have back too much of the dominion he lost. Because man who was to rule creation is a fallen being, creation is subject to aimlessness and frustration. It is under the bondage of corruption" (5/25/83).

Jesus, the God-man demonstrated that control. He spoke to the winds and the waves to be still and they obeyed Him. Creation groans, waiting for the day when the sons of God will be revealed and restoration of proper order in creation will be accomplished.

B. We Hope for What We Do Not Have

"In this hope we are saved." The groaning of our heart is for a release from this wretched body of death. We long to be freed from the power of sin in us. We yearn for the day of no sickness or accident, when we will experience an uninterrupted joy and peace that flows like a river.

Hope is something yet future. We don't hope for what we now have, we hope for what we do not have. We hope for our resurrection bodies. We hope for a full salvation that delivers us from all the twisted thought patterns and subtleties of sin. We hope for a day when our deepest longings are completely met. That is the promise of Christianity.

Christian psychologist, Larry Crabb, has written extensively on this. Suffering is designed by God to create in us a passion for Him. He wrote: "My body writhed in pain as I cried out: 'God, I don't know how to come to you. Please let me find you.'"

True passion for God is a work of the Holy Spirit, but we must cooperate with that work by facing certain facts about ourselves and life, facts that make us run either toward the Lord or from Him. The Spirit reveals just enough about God to move us to the next level of personal honesty. If we face the realities He enables us to face, He gives a fuller vision of God. If we refuse to believe that God can keep us regardless of our pain, we quench the Spirit and He reveals no more of God.

"The Spirit deepens our passion for God when we develop an awareness of ourselves that immobilizes us in a state of spiritual alertness, one in which we are eager to hear the voice of God."

Crabb reveals there are five truths about ourselves that we must face:

4. Our deepest longings go unmet in this life because we are not made to live in this world. We were designed for heaven, and only there will we be satisfied.
5. Other people's lives demonstrate the importance of knowing God better, and we should cultivate relationships with them.
6. We are incurable selfish, wanting relief from our pain more than forgiveness for our sin.
7. The Holy Spirit is a person working in our lives.
8. Suffering is the inevitable but must not become the focus of life. Future hope is more important than present relief. We go through the cycle of suffering that brings us to immobilization where all we can do is trust the Lord. Each time through the cycle, "our focus is drawn more easily to Christ, and slowly we change."[85]

Conclusion

A few years ago Andre' Kole, the talented Christian illusionist, told this personal story. His wife, Aljeana, was smitten with a brain tumor. For two years, she endured

---

85   Larry Crabb, "Finding God", *Today's Better Life*, Winter 1993 (Vol. 3, No 2).

incredible suffering. Gradually, she lost the use of her arms and legs and couldn't move her head or body. She became totally blind. Day after day she could do nothing but lie helplessly in bed. Kole wrote: "While Aljeana was still able to do some speaking, she always shared a poem that ended with these lines: 'We should not long for heaven, if earth held only joy.'"

You long for heaven, even if you are not a Christian. All religions focus on the basic yearning in the heart for immortality. Jesus said, "I am the way, the truth, and the life. No one comes to the Father except through me." He invites you today to put your trust in Him as your personal Lord and Savior.

For your reflection:

What are some specific steps you can take when hit by adversity?

1. Accept that suffering is part of God's growth plan.
2. Look through the suffering to see God and patiently ask Him to enable you to grow through the experience, even though you don't understand it.
3. Find things that bring an internal lift to your heart: listen to music that communicates God to you; go to a special place like the ocean, where you can soak up the environment of God's creative love and power.
4. Pray with honesty and thanksgiving.

Do I Have to be GOOD to go to Heaven?

26

Romans 8:26-27

Help in Prayer

"In any study of the principles, and procedure of prayer, of its activities and enterprises, first place, must, of necessity, be given to faith. It is the initial quality in the heart of any man who essays to talk to the Unseen. He must, out of sheer helplessness, stretch forth hands of faith. He *must* believe, where he cannot prove. In the ultimate issue, prayer is simply faith, claiming its natural yet marvelous prerogatives—faith taking possession of its illimitable inheritance. True godliness is just as true, steady, and persevering in the realm of faith as it is in the province of prayer. Moreover: when faith ceases to pray, it ceases to live."[86]

Scripture: Romans 8:26-27

Main Idea: in the weakness of our life-struggles and humanity, the Holy Spirit intercedes for us.

Introduction

On July 20, 1976, the Viking I spacecraft touched down on the surface of Mars. Programmed to work until 1994, it pleased scientists by performing beautifully and sending back information whenever it was asked—that is, until November 19, 1982. On that day the Viking flight team at the Jet Propulsion Laboratory radioed some instructions up to the spacecraft's computer, expecting an appropriate response.

---

[86] *E. M. Bounds: His Works on Prayer* Electronic Edition STEP Files Copyright © 2007, QuickVerse. All rights reserved.

But no answer came. The "uplinked" message from earth was not acknowledged, and no "downlink" reply was ever given. Despite concentrated efforts by a team of experts, the spacecraft remained silent.

The Holy Spirit is our "uplink" who brings our prayers to God. The link is always there. The computer will never crash. When the message is garbled, He decodes it in language that agrees with the heart of the Father.

Many, many times in preparing sermons I exhaust my resources to find an illustration or story that works well, or I try to make an outline come together. Too often I come up with nothing, drop my head in my hands and cry to God, "Lord, I'm blank. I just don't have it and I have to stand in front of your people on Sunday and give them a word from you." In those times an involuntary groan has come. Paul wrote what the Holy Spirit does inside us in prayer.

I have been frustrated by my inability to express any prayer that brings relief to the burden on my heart. I have felt totally weak and inadequate. Often, I don't know how to pray about an item. In a true sense, I groan on the inside about these things. I have experienced a level of depression because of feeling helpless in dealing with people problems, family and personal issues, and areas of ministry.

Because we are in this world and are imperfect creatures of weakness, we need God to help us in our prayer life. These verses assure us of that unlimited resource. Three simple statements summarize our text: we are weak; prayer is our resource, but we do not know how to pray; the Holy Spirit helps us pray.

I. We Are Weak

"The Spirit helps our weakness"

"Weakness" is singular so it is not the Spirit helps our weakness*es*. "This is our total inability to do anything for ourselves or for the creation in which we live."[87] Not that we don't have many weaknesses, but there is one fundamental weakness that encompasses all others in the matter of prayer. And that is…

II. Prayer is Our Resource, But We Do Not Know How to Pray

The previous verse ended with our waiting patiently for what we do not have. While we wait for the fullness of our salvation, we groan and creation joins us longing for the great revelation that will set us free.

As we wait for relief, we are constantly confronted with the question of how to pray about specific things. We do not know what the will or purpose of God is in many, many matters. We do not clearly perceive what is right, or what God is wanting to accomplish. When the issue relates to us personally, our prayers are corrupted by our desire for relief from our suffering, or by other deviant wants of our sinful nature. In those cases, it's very easy to pray for the wrong thing.

The problem is much deeper than not knowing what words to use. It is the inability to grasp God's intention.

William Barclay suggested two reasons we can't pray correctly. One, we simply do not know the future. We cannot accurately predict one hour from now, so how can we pray properly about things we think ought to happen in the future? Two, in any given situation we don't know what is best for us, for God, or for others for whom we are praying. We may think

---

87   Donald Grey Barnhouse, *Romans: Expositions of Bible Doctrines Taking the Epistle to the Romans as a Point of Departure*, Vol. 3 (Fincastle, Virginia: Scripture Truth Book Company,1959), "God's Heirs,"141.

we know what should or should not happen, but we are grossly ignorant at best.[88]

As one author expressed it: "Notwithstanding our faith and calling, we are still troubled with many infirmities and are very far from being rid of them. None are specified here, for all are included—our ignorance, our conscious failures, our earthiness, our worldliness, our selfishness, our deadness, our inconsistencies, our faintings, our weakness, our emptiness. But against all our infirmities and every department of our sin, the Comforter teaches us to balance the strength of Christ—His fullness against our weakness and emptiness, and all the grace that is in Christ against all the need that is in us."[89].

That brings us to the one who helps us:

III. The Holy Spirit Helps Us in Prayer

A. He Prays with Deep Compassion

Jesus told His disciples when he was preparing them for His death and departure to heaven, that He would send to them a *paraklētos*, a Counselor, to be with them. That counselor is the Holy Spirit.

"Counselor" (*paraklētos*) means one who comes alongside to help. "Helps" refers to someone who shoulders a burden. It is used only twice in the New Testament. The other occasion was when Martha asked Mary to help her with the meal (Luke 10:40). In Psalm 89:21 God said of David, "My hand will sustain him; surely my arm will strengthen him." The same Greek word is used to translate the Hebrew.

The Holy Spirit helps us pray. "The Holy Spirit indwelling the saint [believer], comes to the aid of that saint in his spiritual problems and difficulties, not by taking over the responsibility

---

88 William Barclay, *The Letter to the Romans* (Philadelphia: The Westminster Press, 1957), 116-117.
89 Ibid., 194.

for them and giving the saint an automatic deliverance without any effort on his part, but by lending a helping hand, allowing him to work out his problems and overcome his difficulties, with His help."[90] The idea is very familiar to every parent. When a child is an infant, the parent does everything for the child. As the infant grows to a toddler, the parent begins to allow the little person develop their abilities and gradually decreases assistance. As the child grows and matures, the goal of the parent is to prepare their child for life on their own by guiding them with wisdom and freedom of choice. When the direction of choices take a side trip, the parent, still there to direct, provides the necessary restrictions and maybe some tough love.

In this instance, the help of the Spirit is in not knowing how to pray or even praying for a result that isn't in alignment with God's will. So, the Holy Spirit interprets our prayers, correcting our expression before the Father. The goal is for us to learn more of the Father's mind and heart and therefore pray more frequently in concert with the will of God.

The application goes beyond how we pray. Our burden is not just spiritual, it is the totality of our being: a body of decay, a wretched body bound to sin, a heart that is deceitful and desperately wicked are the things the Spirit shoulders for us. That is why Peter could tell us to cast our anxieties on the Lord for we are His personal concern (1 Peter 5:7 JB Philipps). God has given us in the Spirit a personal caddie to shoulder our weaknesses.

The Spirit is deeply moved with our need. Hebrews states we do not have a high priest [speaking of Jesus] who is indifferent to or unaffected by our weaknesses. Rather He

---

[90] Kenneth S. Wuest, *Wuest's Word Studies: From the Greek New Testament, Vol. One, Romans* (Grand Rapids, Michigan: Wm. B. Eerdmans Publishing Company, 1955), 140.

sympathizes with us for He was tempted in every way yet was without sin (Hebrews 2:18). Because of this fact, He prays for us with deep compassion.

There is a specific reference back to verse 23. We groan, creation groans, and the Spirit groans. The Holy Spirit is our ID card proving our membership in God's family. The Spirit groans in prayer what language is incapable of expressing; *i.e.*, God's compassionate love for us. Our Shepherd is not distant from us, He is right with us in our struggles and is praying for us. F. F. Bruce wrote: "It covers those longings and aspirations which well up from the depths of the [human] spirit and cannot be imprisoned within the confines of every day words."[91]

B. He Prays for Us According to God's Will

We do not know the mind or will of God, but the Father knows His own mind, and He also knows the mind of the Spirit. "The Holy Spirit interprets our prayers to God."[92] The same word used back in verse 5 meaning "mind-set" is used here of the Spirit. The Father knows the Spirit's mind-set. As the Spirit prays for us with groaning that cannot be translated into language, God understands. He knows what the Spirit is praying, He understands what we are saying when we groan unable to put our feelings into words.

The Spirit's groanings are His prayers of intercession for us. Intercede is a "picturesque word of one who 'happens on' *(entugchanei)* one who is in trouble and 'in his behalf' *(huper)* pleads 'with unuttered groanings [instrumental case] or with 'sighs that baffle words.'"[93] An early church father, Chrysostom, gave the analogy of a little boy in Constantinople

---

91   FF. Bruce, *The Letter of Paul to the Romans*: Tyndale New Testament Commentaries (Grand Rapids, Michigan: Inter-Varsity Press,1989), 165.
92   Archibald Thomas Robertson: *Word Pictures of the New Testament, Vol. IV* (Nashville, Tennessee: Broadman Press, 1931), 377.
93   Denney quoted by A. T. Robertson, Ibid., 377.

who loved his father very much. Wanting to give him a present when he returned from a trip, the little boy gathered a bouquet of flowers and assorted weeds. The mother took the arrangement and separated out the weeds so when the father returned, he received a beautiful arrangement of flowers. When we present our prayers to God loaded with weeds, the Holy Spirit, searching our hearts to know what we are really desiring, removes the weeds and arranges the prayer to harmonize with God's will for us.

There could be no greater assurance than to know when we are in a world of hurt, God Himself is there groaning, coming alongside to shoulder our weakness, and to intercede for us before the throne of God. It is precisely this dependent mind-set on the Spirit with which we are to live all of the time, not just when we are hurting. The spiritual unraveling of our lives is always caused by our natural desire for independence. God wants us to live with our eyes on Jesus, depending on *Him* to lead, empower, and comfort us. He said in John 15:5: "Without Me you can do nothing." Paul wrote:

> *To keep me from becoming conceited because of these surpassingly great revelations, there was given me a thorn in my flesh, a messenger of Satan, to torment me. Three times I pleaded with the Lord to take it away from me. But he said to me, 'My grace is sufficient for you, for my power is made perfect in weakness.' Therefore, I will boast all the more gladly about my weaknesses, so that Christ's power may rest on me. That is why for Christ's sake, I delight in weaknesses, in insults, in hardships, in persecutions, in difficulties. For when I am weak, then I am strong (2 Corinthians 12:7-10).*

Conclusion

A. J. Gordon wrote that "the ministry of the Comforter consists in His effectuating in us that which Christ is accomplishing for us on the throne.... The keynote of all true intercession is the will of God.... It is the Spirit's deepest work in the believer to attune his mind to this exalted key."[94] It is the ministry of the Holy Spirit to cause us to understand the will of God so that we pray God's will. He is doing His work today.

"Whenever God is ready to do something with His people, He always sets them to praying," wrote Dr. J. Edwin Orr, the late writer on revival.

Puritan theologian Jonathan Edwards predicted an increase in prayer movements with each generation of believers, culminating with a great one near the year 2000. That movement, said Edwards, would be characterized by a conviction that what was happening was of God, not of man; it would be a corporate expression and have revival as its agenda.[95] There was a significant movement of prayer at that time.

How are we to pray? The Psalms, Jesus' prayer in John 17, Paul's prayers in Ephesians 1 & 3, Philippians 1, and Colossians 1 give us excellent guidelines. Those are really the Spirit's prayers put into our language for our benefit and use.

For your reflection:

Write your prayer for the deepest longing of your heart.

---

94   A. J. Gordon, *The Ministry of the Spirit* (Philadelphia: AmericanBaptist Publication Society, 1894), 148-149.
95   "Today's growing prayer movement signals hope for the world" by David Bryant. *National & International Religion Report*, Mar 6, 1995 (Vol 9, No 6), Pages 1-4.

27

Romans 8:28-30

God Is Determined That We Will Win

"Since God is love, and the center of His love is Christ, He must have His plan center in the person and the work of His Son. As we read the entire Bible we can come to no other conclusion than that God the Father never had a thought apart from the Lord Jesus Christ and His glory. And then, here is the most amazing fact of all: the plan of God includes the glory of the elect, the glory of those who are the called according to His purpose.

"Our lives are not the haphazard result of the moving of blind chance. All that comes to pass in our lives is according to the eternal plan of the all-wise, all-powerful and all-loving Father. When we understand this, we will never be moved by the accusation of some that we believe in fatalism. Fatalism comes from blind chance; but the divine plan comes from the mind and heart of the all-loving Father. It is for this reason that we are well assured that everything helps to secure the good of those who love God, those whom He has called in fulfillment of His design."[96]

Scripture: Romans 8:28-30

Main Idea: God has purposed to achieve His original goal in creating humanity that we are like His Son, Jesus Christ.

---

96   Barnhouse, Vol. III, "God's Heirs", 151.

Introduction

In looking at the back side of stitchery one could conclude that the artist was not very good. When we turn it around it is plain to see that it is beautiful. People are like stitchery. We have jangled and loose ends on one side, but in the end, we will be a beautiful illustration of God's masterful handicraft. The same illustration can be drawn from a craftsman who takes a plain block of wood and goes to work to create a beautiful bowl, statute or some other work of art.

Many times, we feel life is a meaningless patchwork of random events and suffering. If we can allow ourselves to believe what God says about us and His magnificent future, we will see a cohesive and beautiful picture of our life.

Every one of us has been through adversity, some type of suffering. We have all dreamed about things being different. Inside we have even groaned at times in wanting to have life different than what we are experiencing. We think it ought to offer something better and so we chase after different experiences seeking to find that elusive thing called happiness, a state in which we think our disappointments will be banished.

Up to these verses, Paul has talked about suffering. He said our present suffering is insignificant when compared to the glory of our future. In fact, he said all of creation is in the pit of suffering, not just human beings. The animals also long for a new world of harmony and peace. If you are searching for some answers to the paradoxes of life, there are plenty of ideas to pursue. I want to present to you what the Bible teaches about God's plan for you and me. I think you will find it makes sense. I hold that the Bible is God's infallible Word to us defining who He is, who we are as human beings created in His image, and why we have the problems that mess us up. We see the jangled loose ends of the stitchery and we need to see the front side of the finished product. These verses will help us do that.

> *"And we know that God causes everything to work together[f] for the good of those who love God and are called according to his purpose for them. For God knew his people in advance, and he chose them to become like his Son, so that his Son would be the firstborn among many brothers and sisters. And having chosen them, he called them to come to him. And having called them, he gave them right standing with himself. And having given them right standing, he gave them his glory" (New Living Translation).*

Two basics give us understanding about how life works: God is active in all of life; God's goal is to shape all humanity to be like the original, His Son, Jesus.

I. God is Active in All of Life

The God of the Bible is not the god of the Deist, a removed, unconcerned creator who wound up the universe to let it run down. Neither is He the god of the pantheist where everything is god. He certainly isn't the god of the humanist that says you are a god. Just look inside yourself and you will find everything you need for happiness and success. He isn't some god of New Age channelers who worship the devil and don't know it because he has camouflaged himself as an angel of light. God is transcendent, over all of creation yet inside creation as the power behind life, the One who makes life tick, actively involved in every aspect of our lives. God is the subject of this sentence, the One who does the acting. He is making His stitchery work of art.

A. God Works for Our Good

Our Scripture breaks into an on-going statement: "And we know that God causes everything to work together for the good." We begin with the powerful statement, "and we know." It is knowing both intellectually and in experience. The statement stands out because we live in a culture that stridently tells us through the academia and media that there is no absolute truth. You can't "know". After all, it is politically incorrect and naive in a pluralistic society to say one religion is true and others are false. We are repeatedly told that everything is relative. They jabber none-stop like a pack of monkeys—their evolutionary ancestors—trying to drown our ears in the cacophony of their impassioned arguments against the existence of truth. By their asserting the absolute of non-truth, they contradict their own position that there is no absolute truth. What we know is that the God who created the universe loves His people and works on their behalf to transform suffering and evil events into something good for them.

Paul assured us that the Holy Spirit Himself prays for us when we don't know how to pray because we don't understand what is best for us or those we are really concerned about. The reason we can be sure that God is working for our good is because God Himself is praying for us. God knows how limited we are in our narrow perspective of life that causes us to be confused and baffled by events.

God's involvement in our lives is down to the detail. Both suffering and blessing are included. We more easily accept events or experiences we call *'good'* but God is also involved in suffering as well. He works in it all for something good. Good conveys that we will benefit from all of the suffering and non-suffering events. God commands us to rejoice in and during our suffering, not just when it's all over and we see good comes out of it.

Suffering is a very complex issue. Sometimes we suffer because of our own choices, choices made in ignorance or rebellion. At other times people suffer as victims of another's evil. In our day, some are trying to make every form of suffering the result of victimization. No one is responsible for their behavior, it seems. People are only victims. That is not only unbiblical, it just doesn't fit reality.

B. God's Involvement Is Directed on Two Conditions

1. "Of those who love God." This is the first occurrence in Romans to the special word for *'love'* that describes love as primarily a matter of the will, not just an emotion. God is the initiator of love. Ours is responsive. We love because He loved us first. As people who were separated from God by our sin, we don't seek God, God seeks us. You may be reading this because life isn't working right and you think maybe the spiritual side of things might hold a clue. The reason you are asking the questions is not because *you* are seeking God, but *God* is seeking you and putting into your mind the questions about Him. You are here because God loves you and wants you to know Him and to share eternity with you.

If our heart is to love God, we can have the assurance that He is working all of life for our good.

2. And are called according to His purpose for them. Not only is this promise given to people who love God, but also to those who want to fit into His plan for their lives. God's purpose for every person is to know Him, to experience His forgiveness of sin, to restore us to the dignity of the first humans He created. God wants to have a huge family of sons and daughters upon whom He can lavish is generosity. He is the true Daddy Warbucks. Why doesn't all humanity enjoy

His goodness now? Because of sin. The Bible makes it plain that the essential problem humanity is facing is a sinful heart that has broken the most fundamental of all relationships: our relationship to the God who created us and who loves us.

The Bible uses the word *'redemption'* to describe God's aggressive action to buy back a lost people to make them His own once again. How did He do that? The price was His Son dying on the cross in payment of our sin. We can experience God's forgiveness by placing our trust in Jesus Christ as our personal Lord and Savior. God will instantly remove the barrier of sin and make us His children. He wants to rescue you from the sin that will certainly destroy you not only in this life but eternally.

God is active in all of life to bring good to His people. The conditions of experiencing His goodness are that we love Him and fit into His plan for us.

II. God's Goal is For Us to Be Like Jesus Christ

A. God's Involvement is Based on His Sovereign Power

God knows everything. The technical word for this is omniscience. *'Omni'* means all, *'science'* means knowledge. Not only does He have complete knowledge, but He "knew His people in advance." God knows you. He knows your thoughts, your desires, every action, and He knows whether or not you are going to respond to His love. Christianity is not merely a factual or intellectual interaction with some propositions. It is relational. God loves us and wants a relationship with us. He will be true to that relationship and He wants us to be true as well.

He determined that the people He knew in advance would be shaped like His Son, the Lord Jesus Christ. Jesus, then, became the number one Son in a long list of sons and daughters. God will have a huge family. Every person in that family will be a winner. All His family will enjoy the fabulous glory of heaven for eternity. That is big time winning.

God's plan is for each of us to be like His Son. Does that mean we will all look like Jesus—males in our thirties? Hardly. We will be like Jesus in character. Here's the caveat, He is in us through His Holy Spirit. Our bodies are literally His home. Because of that reality, He will live in us His life of moral goodness. We will love with His love. We will be filled with His joy and peace. We may still be plagued by the thoughts and addictions get the best of us occasionally, but they will not drag us down in misery and self-destruction. He is our victory in life.

To achieve this wonderful objective required enormous suffering. God Himself had to become one of us, take our sins upon Himself, and die in our place under God's judgment. As Jesus had to suffer, so we as sons and daughters who are in the process of being changed to become like Him, have to go through suffering. The way to glory is through suffering. God will bring to completion the good work He started. In the same way as stitchery requires a long process of detailed stitching to become a finished product, so God is taking us through a long process to make us winners.

One person used the illustration. To make a carving of a horse from a block of wood, the sculptor knocks off everything that doesn't look like a horse. To make us like Jesus, God knocks off everything that doesn't look like Him.

B. God is Following a Four Step Plan
- He intimately knows those who will be in His family.

➤ Then He calls those people to belong to Him. This is not simply an invitation. God's call carries with it the desired response. He gives us the desire to say yes to Him.

➤ He brings His people into a right relationship with Himself.

➤ He will finally make them all winners by sharing with them His eternal glory. God created us to belong to Him. Sin fouled up the whole picture and separated humanity from God. Because we are separated from God we do all kinds of destructive things. Jesus came to reclaim us and bring us into His glory.

Application

Centuries ago an Italian violin maker, Antonio Stradivari, was turning out his magnificent instruments. He made it a rule that no violin should ever leave the shop until it was as near perfection as human care and skill could make it. He said, "God needs violins to send His music into the world, and if my violins are defective, God's music will be spoiled."

Bending over his workbench in Cremona, Antonio Stradivari, who died December 18, 1737, issued a vow that has remained for more than two and a half centuries: "Other men will make other violins, but no man shall make a better one." There is no more valued violin in all of the world, than a Stradivarius.

God is making His Stradivarius violins. He is shaping His people by knocking off everything that doesn't look like His Son. When He is done, every one of His people will be a demonstration throughout all eternity of His craftsmanship. You can be one of His people if you will come to Jesus, face your sin in repentance, and place your trust in Him as your Lord and Savior.

Inherent within the promise is a warning. If a person refuses to love God and fit into His purposes for their life, the events of life—both the good and bad, the successes and failures—will not bring good, but evil. Life will not make sense, God will not make them into winners. They will be losers regardless of how much education, money, power or prestige they gain. In the end, they will face the judgment of a righteous God.

We can accept the bumps in life's road when we know what kind of future God has planned for us. That future can be yours as a free gift of God's outrageous grace. He loves you and wants you to enjoy all he is getting together for the future. What do you do now? If you have never read the book of John in the New Testament, take the time to read a chapter a day in the next 30 days and get acquainted with Jesus.

For your reflection:
- Do you see your life as the back side of stitchery or the front, or something in between?
- Where do you see God working in your life now to make you more like Jesus?
- In what areas of Christian living are you experiencing frustration?
- How do these verses give you strength?

Do I Have to be GOOD to go to Heaven?

28

Romans 8:31-39

We Are Conquerors Plus!

"Can we ever wonder enough at the miracle of our conversion?—at the mystery of our regeneration"—at the solemn, glorious, thrilling truth that each of us 'in Christ' is a very 'temple of the Holy Spirit'? Oh, the gracious mystery of it! We are not only regenerated; we are *indwelt*! Familiarity with this, instead of dulling our wonder, should ever deepen it. Even our mortal bodies are now His temples (1 Cor. 6:19). Think what it means. Not only does it give unspeakable sacredness to the physical frame, it hallows individual *personality*. Every Christian is meant to be a living temple; a cleansed, renewed, transformed, Spirit-filled temple of God, expressing in a unique way the life and love of the indwelling Christ! *That* is Christian holiness. To such holiness the New Testament calls us."[97]

Scripture: Romans 8:31-39

Main Idea: Our greatest assurance is that there is no hardship or power that can separate us from the love of God.

Introduction

One of the greatest challenges the Christian faces is to maintain the poise of assurance of God's love in times of trial and hardship. Our natural response when hit by a tidal wave

---

[97] J. Sidlow Baxter, *His Deeper Work in Us: A further enquiry into New Testament teaching on the subject of Christian Holiness* (Grand Rapids, Michigan: Zondervan Publishing House, 1967), 23-24.

of hurt or disaster is to ask, "Where is God, does He love me, does He care?" There is no stronger passage in the Bible affirming God's love for us than these last verses of Romans 8. C. S. Lewis wrote: "On the whole, God's love for us is a much safer subject to think about than our love for him." I am thankful my relationship with God and eternal future are not contingent on the perfection of my love for God.

Paul presents a series of questions to set the stage for his dramatic lines of assurance. I am reading from the *New Living Translation*:

> "What can we say about such wonderful things as these? If God is for us, who can ever be against us? Since God did not spare even his own Son but gave him up for us all, won't God, who gave us Christ, also give us everything else?
>
> "Who dares accuse us whom God has chosen for his own? Will God? No! He is the one who has given us right standing with himself. Who then will condemn us? Will Christ Jesus? No, for he is the one who died for us and was raised to life for us and is sitting at the place of highest honor next to God, pleading for us.
>
> "Can anything ever separate us from Christ's love? Does it mean he no longer loves us if we have trouble or calamity, or are persecuted, or are hungry or cold or in danger or threatened with death? (Even the Scriptures say, "For your sake we are killed every day; we are being slaughtered like sheep.") No, despite all these things, overwhelming victory is ours through Christ, who loved us.
>
> "And I am convinced that nothing can ever separate us from his love. Death can't, and life can't. The angels can't, and the demons can't. Our fears for today, our worries about tomorrow, and even the powers of hell can't keep God's love away. Whether we are high above the sky or in the deepest ocean, nothing in all creation will ever be

able to separate us from the love of God that is revealed in Christ Jesus our Lord."

Let's look at the five basic questions Paul poses and answers about God's love for you and me:

I. The Rhetorical Question: "What can we say about such wonderful things as these?"

It is a sweeping "all" that encompasses everything Paul has said about salvation as the act of a faithful, gracious God. The immediate preceding context of the eighth chapter places the action on God, rather than on us. This is truly a "celebration of God's faithfulness."[98] Words cannot convey the wonders of God's grace to us in Christ. God's love is wonderful.

II. The Question of Ultimate Power: "If God is for us, who can be against us?"

The "if" is not a question, Is He for us? It is an affirmation of fact, "since God is for us." Regardless of what form suffering or hardship takes, God is for us. We can inscribe that in stone and walk in its comforting light all day. God is *for* you!

Of course, there are many opponents who are against us, but none can be victorious. Why? God is for us, and no one can defeat Him. He is greater than all other powers. Who is this God? He is the Almighty. He is the God who contains the entire universe in Himself. He is the Creator who is infinite in His knowledge, power, justice, and love. He is holy, the only One who perfectly loves what is right and hates evil in every form. He is thoroughly good and never does anything from evil motive.

---

[98] Dunn, 509.

III. The Question of Ultimate Generosity: "Since God did not spare even his own Son...won't God, who gave us Christ, also give us everything else?"

A. The Depth of God's Love Cannot Be Questioned

He gave His *Son* to die on the cross. That is ultimate in terms of physical suffering, but far more in spiritual and emotional agony. The custodian in Ingmar Bergman's film, "Winter Light" was horribly crippled and lived in constant pain. As he reflected on Jesus' crucifixion he said, "The pain in my life goes on and on, in my back and in my bones…. It's not the physical pain that burdens me about the Crucifixion, but that He had given so much, He had loved so much, He had healed so much—and nobody cared. Nobody understood. When He died, He seems to have died absolutely uselessly; utterly alone; utterly, utterly abandoned."

People have pain. In spite of all our advanced technology in the medical sciences, the development of the discipline of psychology, the pain goes on—physical pain, emotional trauma, spiritual suffering. Whatever life has dealt you God loves you. Nothing can separate you from His love. He knows pain as no other being in the universe has experienced pain. He knows what it is to be misunderstood or rejected. He was nailed to a cross with crude, jagged spikes cruelly driven through His wrists and feet. He was innocent, sinless, yet He was made sin and took on Himself the wrath of a holy God that belonged to us.

The assurance of our position in God's love was His surrender of Jesus to death on the cross. On the basis of God's ultimate expression of love, Paul draws a conclusion.

B. If God Gave His Son, He Won't Stop There with His Generosity

"All things" most likely refers to a restoration of humanity to authority over creation. David declared: *"You made him [humankind] ruler over the works of your hands, you put everything under his feet"* (Psalm 8:6).

God's plans for us do not terminate with death. A glorious future that defies our understanding awaits us. The ultimate triumph was the reducing the roar of death to a whimper and literally swallowing the grave in life. The "all things" also includes His promise to supply all our needs according to His riches in Christ Jesus.

IV. The Questions of Ultimate Authority—both are loaded

A. "Who Dares Accuse Us Whom God has Chosen for His Own?"

The setting is the final judgment scene. God is the judge. Satan and all the detractors against Christianity—all the opposing religious and philosophical points of view who see things differently—are ready to point out the hypocrisies, failures, blunders, and stupidity of Christians throughout the ages. There are millions of complaints and charges. God says to them, "Bring them on, let's hear the charges." Not one dares to step forward to bring an accusation. Why? It is not possible to bring a charge against someone when the highest judge in the universe has chosen that person, and justified him or her of all charges against them.

The word, "justifies," or "given us right standing with Himself," is in the present tense meaning God's action is on-going. He not only justified us when we trusted in Christ, He continues to do so in the present, and will in the future.

Because of that, no one can bring a charge when God has acquitted a person.

B. "Who Then Will Condemn Us?"

The answer God gives to all who would accuse this motley batch of sinners He calls His saints is that Jesus His Son died completely satisfying God's justice for a payment for sin. More than dying, He rose again from the dead conquering sin, death and hell. No prosecutor has an argument that can counter those facts. The highest law of justice in the universe has been satisfied.

But that is not all Jesus has done to exonerate the sinner in the presence of God. He is now interceding for us. The portrait of Jesus as our high priest is presented more fully in Hebrews and 1 John. To be at the right hand of God is a picture taken from Psalm 110:1. The right hand denotes power, being at the right hand of God denotes a position of special power and honor. This right-hand reference can be found in Mark, Acts, five times in Hebrews, Ephesians, Colossians, and 1 Peter.

With Jesus at the right hand of God interceding for us there is no one in all the universe who can win a court case against us. And by the way, the lawyer's fees are all paid. The poorest people anywhere can afford to have Jesus defend them before the court of heaven.

V. The Question of Ultimate Assurance: Can Anything Ever Separate Us from Christ's Love?"

To clinch his argument that salvation is God's work from start to finish, not the result of a person keeping a religious code or doing religious things, Paul assures us nothing in the universe can alter our relationship with God.

Dunn insightfully wrote the "sufferings as are about to be listed should be seen as evidence of union with the crucified one, not a cause for doubting his love."[99] Yet, that is just what our flesh does the moment adversity crashes in on us.

The English word for "trouble" or "tribulation" comes from the Latin for a "flail." A flail was a long broomstick-like devise with a shorter stick attached by a leather thong. With that instrument, a worker would beat wheat to separate the kernel from the chaff. Sometimes we feel like life is flailing us with adversity. Christians have no immunity from such adversity. What we can know for certain is that none of it can separate us from the love of God.

"Calamity" or "hardship" comes from two words, narrow and space, and carries the idea of being hemmed in, boxed in on a dead-end street. We may find ourselves there, but it cannot separate us from the love of God. It certainly is no fun time, but God has not abandoned us in that situation.

"Persecution" is a primary theme in the New Testament. Jesus said we are blessed "when people insult you, persecute you and falsely say all kinds of evil against you because of me." Peter echoed the same thing: *"if you suffer as a Christian, do not be ashamed, but praise God that you bear that name"* (1 Peter 4:16). Paul's letter to the Christians in Philippi states: *"For you have been given not only the privilege of trusting in Christ but also the privilege of suffering for him"* (1:29 NLT).

Pain and love were joined together on the cross. Paul prayed that we might grasp *"how wide and long and high and deep is the love of Christ, and to know this love that surpasses knowledge."*

---

99 Dunn, 504.

In the Old Testament, a recurring key word identifying God's love for us is a word meaning loyal love and often translated as "unfailing love". It was a favorite of David in his psalms. God is committed to keep His promises. Because He does, nothing can come between Him and us.

A theologian/scholar reflected at his retirement: "The longer I live the more value I put on God's sheer Grace, which I take simply to be what by our human standards we would call His 'extravagant goodness.' The utter persistence of His love: it is our sole hope."

Conclusion

There is no question in Paul's mind about his future. The tense (perfect passive) underlines Paul's complete certainty when he says "I am convinced." I hope you are likewise so convinced about God's commitment to you—not yours to Him, but His to you. We falter, we are fickle, we vacillate. He never fails. From what was likely an early hymn, Paul wrote to his young associate: "

> *"If we died with him, we will also live with him; if we endure, we will also reign with him. If we disown him, he will also disown us; if we are faithless he will remain faithful, for he cannot disown himself" (2 Timothy 2:11-13)*

Sandra and I relaxed after we had enjoyed a lovely dinner at a local restaurant. I picked up the current edition of *Reader's Digest* (Dec 96, 121-126) and read a very touching story of Kim and Krickitt Carpenter.

Kim was a university baseball coach, Krickitt Pappas worked at a sportswear firm in Anaheim. They met over the phone when Kim called the firm about an order. He was so impressed with her buoyant spirit, he kept calling, each time asking to speak with Krickitt as his sales representative.

She was a gymnast and knew the sports scene very well. The inevitable happened. They discovered they were both committed Christians and at every turn found something more to love in each other.

Kim invited Krickitt to New Mexico to watch his team play. They had first talked in September 1992 and by June 1993 Kim asked Gus Pappas for his daughter's hand in marriage. They were married September 18, 1993, in Scottsdale, Arizona. It was a fairy tale romance.

However, tragedy struck ten weeks later. Barely beginning their life together, they were involved in a terrible automobile accident. Krickitt received very severe head injuries. It was questionable whether she would live. Three weeks later, as they asked her several questions to assess her condition. Kim was in the room. "Where does the sun rise?" the therapist asked. She looked puzzled and said, "North." "Who is the President?" "Nixon." "Where do you live?" "Phoenix." That was where they had lived before she was married. Kim began to get excited. Then the question: "Who are you married to?" "Her voice was flat and emotionless, and her words stabbed at Kim's heart: 'I'm not married.' Stunned, Kim backed out of the room. In the hallway, he wept openly, slamming his fist against a wall. God, help me! Help Krickitt and me."

It became a long rehabilitation. Krickitt's memory of the year before her marriage was completely gone. Her attention span was extremely short. She referred to Kim as "that guy" and even asked him why he didn't go home.

"'Because I love you' was his unwavering response." In the fall of last year (1995), Kim went into counseling. The therapist asked him, "What made Krickitt fall in love with you?" "He thought of all the love and affection he'd shown her during their courtship. He was her sweetheart. Then he considered how he had acted since her injury. He was more like a parent or coach. Finally, it struck him: Start over! *Win her back*!" He began to court her again. It felt awkward but he kept at it.

Krickitt began to see how compassionate and generous Kim was. Her counselor suggested they renew their vows and she enthusiastically agreed. On Valentine's Day of this year, Kim "went down on one knee as he had done the first time, and with a bouquet of flowers in one hand, asked Krickitt to be his bride." Krickitt commented, "People think we're getting married a second time to make my memory come back, but I have accepted that that part of my life is erased." On May 25, she held out her hand to Kim and said, "I thank you for being true to your original vows, and I pray that I might be the wife you fell in love with." In addition to their original wedding rings, they gave each other new rings to commemorate their second vow of love. An accident that in essence made his wife a different person did not take away Kim's love of her. In the same vein, no trouble or calamity, no persecution, or hunger, or cold, not death, life, angels, or demons, our fears for today, our worries about tomorrow, or hell itself can separate us from the love of God.

We are conquerors plus. We are big-time winners. Nothing, nothing or no one in the entire universe, can separate us from the love of God in Christ Jesus. May He be praised!

For your reflection:

Of the five rhetorical questions looked at in the sermon, which one or ones held the greatest meaning for you?

29

Romans 9

Is God Unjust?

"To many modern readers chapters 9-11 form a parenthesis in the course of Paul's argument. Had he proceeded straight from 8:39 to 12:1, we should have been conscious of no hiatus in his reasoning. He has just pointed forward to the culmination of God's purpose of grace, the glory that is to be revealed in the children of God. What more can he say than press home on his readers their responsibility to live in this world as befits heirs of the glory to come? If 'I appeal to you therefore' (12:1) came in at this point, we should be quite ready for it.

"Not so Paul. The problem with which he proceeds to grapple was one of intense personal concern to him. He gloried in his ministry as apostle to the Gentiles, and rejoiced in their salvation. But his own kith and kin, the Jewish nation, had for the most part failed to accept the salvation proclaimed in the gospel, even though it was presented to them first. What then? Should they simply be written off as 'unworthy of eternal life' (Acts 13:46)? No indeed: they were his own people, and he neither would nor could dissociate himself from them. He too, like so many of them, had once opposed the gospel, but he had been arrested by the risen Jesus and set on the Christian way. How he longed that they too might have the scales removed from their eyes! Indeed, if their salvation could be purchased by his own damnation, right readily would he consent, if such a thing were possible, to be 'anathema from Christ' for their sakes. The ingathering of the Gentiles, no matter on how extensive a scale, could never compensate for the defection of his nation, which caused him such unceasing mental anguish."[100]

Scripture: Romans 9

Main Idea: as a sovereign, holy God, whatever He chooses to do is just.

Introduction

This chapter focuses on one of the issues about God I have encountered repeatedly over the years. How can God be just when there is so much... [you fill in the blank]. The controversy might be the horrible images of malnourishment, or the slaughter of war. It is usually some inhumanity that man commits against man, not something God does. It is argued that if God were almighty, He could stop all of this. He could cause rain to fall in northern Africa to bring crops, for instance. I begin with a red-hot topic in today's society to set-up our analysis of Romans chapter nine: abortion.

The central debate of the pro-abortion movement is the woman's right to choose. Early in the debate, *Newsweek* (1/14/85) featured a special report, and the issues in the debate haven't changed since. In a primary picture of pro-choice demonstrators in San Francisco, one woman held a sign: "Keep your laws and your morality off my body." I have a cartoon of six panels of a woman in monologue: "He kissed me and I melted," reads the first panel. "My heart pounded at his touch. His embrace sent the blood coursing through my veins. I was overcome with passion! I couldn't refuse. Now I'm pregnant and I want an abortion. After all, a woman should have control over her body."

---

[100] Bruce, 171-172.

The argument assumes that because a baby is inside a woman's body it is her body. We accept that no one has unlimited rights to destroy a person outside the womb—though partial birth abortion comes close. We are protective of a person's right to life once they are born to the extent that if an intruder comes into my home, I better kill him. If I only maim him, I will probably go to prison.

Our society has ostensibly embraced that a fundamental human right is the right to exist. For the pro-abortion side to win their argument with justice, they must prove that the fertilized egg in a woman is not human—and that they cannot do. Another sign in that same *Newsweek* article read: "A woman's life is a human life." An inconsistent argument when considering destroying human life. No one has ever declared the baby's life as non-human because it cannot be done. In fact, all scientific evidence is that the fetus is fully human from the earliest stages of the sperm's penetration of the egg. We have said it is not viable human life until it can exist outside the womb. The Supreme Court arbitrarily established that at the second trimester.

If justice refers to playing by the rules, then the crucial issue is who and how are the rules made? In our country, we say congress writes the rules and the courts interpret them. During the nation's early years, law had another external rule it used to measure the justice of its laws and that was the Bible. The three most often quoted sources included the Bible, and the other two cited more biblical references than any other documentation. Today, the Bible is ignored and the latest Gallup, Quinnipiac, Harris, or some other opinion poll becomes the basis of law.

In the Bible, God is His own rule. There is no external authority to which He turns about a matter, and there is no other authority that can be applied to Him. He is always just and is so because He is perfectly holy. God loves the right and hates the wrong with perfection. As a result, "there is a consistency in God, a 'straightness' about Him.... In all eternity God has never done a crooked thing."[101]

Paul was charged that his gospel made God unjust. If salvation was God's work in choosing, calling, and justifying the sinner, then those who are not called are being treated unfairly. To the point, if salvation was God's work alone, then it looks like, in the case of Israel, His plan did not work. Most of the Jews of Paul's day were not believers. Paul was not harsh and condemning toward his own people. Instead, he was deeply emotionally involved with their plight.

I. Paul's Compassion was That His People Would Enjoy Eternal Life (1-5)

Facing the charge that he did not care about his own race of people, Paul countered in strong terms that he not only agonized over their estrangement from God, he was willing to be cursed if it would result in their salvation. That would not work because Paul was not qualified as a savior. His level of compassion is simply amazing. I might be willing to die to save my wife or children from the ravages of some disease, but to be eternally damned is something else.

II. God Makes Choices Because He is God (6-21)

Israel had a great religious system through which Christ eventually came into the world. But religious practice and heritage fall short of making a person right with God.

---

[101] R.C. Sproul, *The Holiness of God*, (Wheaton, Ill.: Tyndale House Publishers, 1985),143.

A. Illustration One: the True Children of Abraham (6-9)

Even in Jewish terms, Paul effectively destroyed any perception that a right relationship with God based on natural, human decent. He stated that being in the blood-line of Abraham would not guarantee one's place in God's family.

Abraham fathered Ishmael and Isaac. Ishmael was Abraham's son through his wife's servant. Though he was Abraham's son he did not participate in the blessings of God's promise to Abraham. Isaac, the son his wife Sarah bore to him, was the one God accepted because Isaac was born as a result of God's promise, not man's desire or action. It is an involved story. In brief, Abraham was 100 years old and Sarah was 90 when Isaac was born. They had been without children until God promised them Sarah would have a son.

Many people I have talked with think that because their parents were Christians, or at least religious, they were okay. We can't get to heaven based on our parents' religion or even because we do religious things.

B. Illustration Two: Rebekah's Twins (10-13)

Isaac fathered two sons, twins. It was not the older that inherited the promises of the covenant, it was the younger, Jacob. God made His choice *before* they were born and had done either good or bad things. The reason was to clarify that salvation is *not* a result of our keeping the moral code or doing the religious thing. More than that, Paul quoted a passage in Malachi where God said He loved Jacob and hated Esau (Malachi 1:2,3).

The question is raised, is God unjust because this is so? Not at all. Why? Because God said to Moses in Exodus 33:19: *"I will have mercy on whom I have mercy, and I will have compassion on whom I have compassion."* God can do what He wishes because He is sovereign. What He does is just, because He is holy.

Without any irreverence to God, you remember a few years back the joke going around, Where does a 1,000 pound gorilla sit when he goes to a football game? Anywhere he wishes. Respectfully, God does whatever He wishes because He is God. If He saves someone, it is *not* because that person is good and another bad. Salvation is *not* a result of keeping the moral code or of doing religious things. Eternal life is *not* a reward given to the good guys and kept from the bad ones. "It does not, therefore, depend on man's desire or effort, but on God's mercy."

C. Illustration Three: Pharaoh (14-18)

Pharaoh was the monarch ruling in Egypt when Israel was detained as slaves after Joseph's death. When God chose to free Israel from slavery—which is an illustration of our salvation—He made Pharaoh a stubborn man who would not listen to Moses' pleas.

God told Pharaoh, "*I raised you up for this very purpose, that I might display my power in you and that my name might be proclaimed in all the earth*" (Exodus 9:16). To this day, the Exodus is celebrated by Jews world-wide. It tells God's power to save His people. In hardening Pharaoh's heart, He was having mercy on Israel.

D. Illustration Four: the Potter (19-21)

To answer the challenge that such a person as Pharaoh who was chosen to demonstrate the power of God cannot be blamed in the day of judgment, Paul replied with an illustration of the potter. Jeremiah used the same picture to make a similar point.

A potter has the right from the same batch of clay to make a drinking cup for the king or a chamber pot for a ditch-digger. It is his choice and the clay can't fight it.

III. All of God's Actions Focus on Salvation (22-33)

A. In Fact, God has been Extremely Patient with Humankind (22-24)

In the process of making His power known in the case of Pharaoh, God endured enormous hostility and rebellion from Pharaoh. God's reason for all of His actions is to extend the mercy of His salvation to sinners who deserve the full wrath of God in hell. The purpose in bringing Israel out of Egypt was to fulfill His plan to provide the world with a Savior. It was to "make the riches of his glory known to the objects of his mercy—even us."

B. Illustration One: Hosea (25)

Hosea married a prostitute named Gomer. The first child she bore, Hosea accepted as his. The next two, he refused to accept. The one was called, "not loved" (*Lo-Ruhamah*), and the other, "not my people" (*Lo-Ammi*).

Hosea was referring to God's consistent plan to have a family of sons and daughters out of every race and people on the earth. All those nations other than Israel were to become a part of the family of God. That is still His plan and that is the reason for a church's commitment to taking the Gospel to all people groups.

C. Illustration Two: Isaiah (27-29)

God had promised Abraham that his seed would be as the sands of the sea, yet only a small number of Israel, a remnant, has been saved. Apart from God's mercy in providing a remnant of people, there wouldn't be any Jews left. And that has stayed true down through the holocaust.

D. People Have the Option to Believe or Disbelieve (30-33)

Anyone can be made right with God. It is not by keeping the moral code or doing the religious thing. It is by faith alone—the faithfulness of God to His promises. The evidence of that promise is the cornerstone God laid in Zion, none other than Jesus, who died as the sinless human and became sin as the Son of God to provide salvation. "The one who trusts in him will never be put to shame."

Conclusion

A. W. Tozer wrote on God's justice: "God's justice stands forever against the sinner in utter severity. The vague and tenuous hope that God is too kind to punish the ungodly has become a deadly opiate for the consciences of millions. It hushes their fears and allows them to practice all pleasant forms of iniquity while death draws every day nearer and the command to repent goes unregarded. As responsible moral beings, we dare not so trifle with our eternal future."[102]

Justice is personal in the Bible. Every person has broken God's law and stands guilty before Him. There is only one way anyone is made right with God. God requires each person to turn from our sin of self-righteousness and rebellion to trust Jesus as Savior and Lord. It is not complicated, but it is a very difficult for proud humanity to do so. It is humbling to accept our guilt before a holy God. We want to believe that we can correct the problem by doing good things. We want to believe that we are basically good, that we have made some mistakes, but we can overcome them in some way by our own efforts.

God's solution is stated a number of ways in the Bible. The religious person, such as the Jew in Paul's day, will miss

---

102   A. W. Tozer, *Knowledge of the Holy*, (New York: Harper & Row, 1961), 95.

out on God's salvation unless they place their faith in God's Savior as the core of their religious belief. What is the faith that God requires? In the next chapter, Romans 10:9-10 it assures us: *"If you confess with your mouth that Jesus is Lord and believe in your heart that God raised him from the dead, you will be saved. For it is by believing in your heart that you are made right with God, and it is by confessing with your mouth that you are saved."* That was the way to God 2,000 years ago for Jew or any other race, and it is still the way into His acceptance.

Simply state your faith in prayers: "Jesus, I believe You are the Lord and Savior. I believe You died and rose from the dead to take away my sin and guilt. I ask You to come into my life and change me on the inside. I receive your gift of eternal life. Thank You for hearing and answering this prayer."

Anyone who turns away from Christ as their only salvation will be damned to an eternity separated from God and all that is loving and good. And there isn't anyone in the universe who will be able to challenge God's justice in doing so. There is One who loved you and me enough to literally experience hell to rescue us from God's just judgment. That person is Jesus.

We have a rule in our society that respects human life, except in the case of a baby in its mother's body. That is unjust. If we applied the same criteria of mercy and salvation to the abortion issue, then the only cases of mercy would be the endangerment of the mother's life and the birth of a deformed child doomed to a meaningless existence. Yet those are less than 2% of the cases. Morality in those instances is questionable, but some use it as a defense of select abortion. Ninety-eight percent of all abortions are for reasons of personal convenience.

Norman Geisler wrote of our culture that "when all the arguments are reduced to the bottom line, they amount to this: man is an animal and undesired animals can be weeded out of the human herd".[103] Most people would say, that is not just. I'm very thankful God did not view us that way. Instead, He saw people who were rebellious sinners who needed a Savior, and He became that Savior.

He loves you and died for your sins. If you will put your trust in Him, you will not be disappointed. God, in justice, will banish your sins into non-existence and welcome you into His family as His gift of love to you.

For your reflection:
- The debate on the right to life and the woman's right to her body continues with intensity today. What direction do you see this taking in the future?
- What is your reaction to Paul's statement he was willing to be damned if that would bring salvation to his Jewish people?
- Paul lists four illustrations of the sovereignty of God. Which one[s] do you feel are the strongest to support his argument?
- How does Paul describe God's patience?

---

103   Norman Geisler, *Kindred Spirit*, Autumn 88.

30

Romans 10

Obstinate or Responsive

"Paul is very clear in Romans 9 concerning the sovereignty of God and the election of those who are saved. Now, however, Romans 10 deals with the responsibility of those who are lost, for Paul makes it equally clear that one is lost because he rejects the truth as it is in Jesus Christ, because he rejects the Word of faith. So, if we have God's sovereignty in Romans 9, we have the other side of the coin, man's responsibility in Romans 10; man is responsible for his own lostness.

"Much more space could be devoted to this theme of the sovereignty of God and the responsibility of man, but we would not come to the place where we found a neat compromise between these two paradoxical truths; the Word of God teaches both to be true: God is sovereign, man is free and responsible. We cannot finally resolve these two truths which to us seem to contradict each other...."[104]

Scripture: Romans 10

Main Idea: the primary issue for any person is to first hear the gospel of God's grace in salvation, then, having heard, to respond in faith.

Introduction

Communication is a very complex science and practice. The difficulty is easily illustrated in our everyday experience.

---
104   Halverson, 193-194.

How many married people feel their spouse doesn't understand them, or they don't understand their spouse? How many parents feel their kids don't understand them? How many kids feel their parents don't understand them?

I read there are 600,000 words available to us in the English language. Of these, an educated adult uses 2,000. And the most used 500 have, according to standard dictionaries, 14,000 different definitions. Each common word must be used to cover a wide range of 'meanings.' Some words have 100 or more different meanings.

Sports Illustrated quoted Astronaut Michael Collins speaking at a banquet that the average man speaks about 25,000 words a day and the average woman 35,000. "Unfortunately, when I come home each day I've spoken my 25,000 and my wife hasn't started her 35,000."

In a seminar I attended many years ago, it was explained that in the communication process there is a sender and a receiver. In between the sending and reception of messages are filters the message passes through on both sides of the process. Those filters place meaning on words, tones of voice, body language, sentence structure, etc. The common practice is a sender might be convinced they have said a "square," but it is received by the hearer as a "triangle." If the sender is fully convinced they have accurately described a square and that any problem of understanding is in the listener or receiver, there cannot be communication. The same is true if the receiver is fully convinced they have heard and interpreted the message correctly. The result is both go away fully believing communication has taken place when in fact neither has understood the other. That happens all the time in every day conversations.

The *Reader's Digest* printed this incident sent in by a reader: A department store clerk was demonstrating the efficiency of a window cleaning device by smearing margarine on the glass and cleaning it off again. Quite impressed, a woman asked her, "How much margarine do I have to use?"

There is a saying: "I know you think you understand what I said. But I am not so sure you realize that what you heard is not what I meant."

Communication becomes even more complicated in religious matters, because the subject matter is in abstract concepts. For example, when Jesus came to Berkeley Divinity School, he asked the professors, "And who do you think I am?"

They answered, "You are the eschatological manifestation of the *kerygma* in which we recognize the ultimate significance of our interpersonal relations."

Jesus said, "What?"

In this passage, the issue is hearing the gospel and understanding what God has said. I'm afraid that our filters constructed by sin and human limitations have caused most people to hear a triangle instead of a square.

I. It Takes More Than Religious Enthusiasm to be Saved (1-4)

A. Paul's Desire was Israel's Salvation (1)

There is no indication of anger or retribution in Paul toward his people. In the previous chapter, he said he was willing to be damned if it would result in his people receiving eternal life. A Jew himself, he was deeply concerned over his people's lack of understanding and their stubborn resistance to Jesus as Messiah and Savior. His prayer was that Israel would be saved.

B. Israel had Zeal but did not Understand Salvation (2-4)

Many people hold the Charlie Brown view of faith: As long as you are sincere it doesn't matter what you believe. That is not the Bible's point of view, and certainly not Paul's.

The Jews were very religious. Paul, trained in Judaism was also a devoutly religious man. Both were zealous, *i.e.,* enthusiastic, in their faith, but it takes more than enthusiasm to be right with God. As one has said, "Zeal without knowledge is like the bottom half of a double-boiler—full of steam but doesn't know what's cooking." That was Paul before he met Jesus, and he indicted his people with the same problem.

There are only two options on how to go to heaven presented by religion. Judaism and all other religions including New Age religion, present some concept of personal works. In unpolluted Christianity—and it has been polluted by various groups throughout history—heaven is an absolutely free gift we receive by faith totally apart from keeping a moral code or performing religious ritual.

Paul said his people had attempted to establish their own righteousness rather than receiving the righteousness that comes from God.

(Verse 4) *"Christ is the end of the law so that there may be righteousness for everyone who believes."* The word for "end", *télos*, can mean goal or termination. Christ is the goal because He perfectly obeyed the law. By fulfilling the law, He terminated the law as a way to righteousness and made it possible for anyone to come to Him and be saved.

II. God's Message Must First Be Heard (5-15)

A. The Contrast of Moses and Faith (5-8)

Paul utilized quotations from two books of Moses: one from Leviticus 18, and two from Deuteronomy 30. In Leviticus 18:5, Moses wrote: *"The man who does these things will live by them."* In that chapter, Moses listed a long series of moral and sexual restrictions. Paul only refers to the principle of doing what the law says. Interpreters differ on what the word "live" means. Does it mean to live eternally, that by keeping the law a person will gain eternal life? Or does it mean that by keeping the law a person will enjoy the wholesome benefits of living within the boundaries of how God set up life to work?

The first view is the error of all religion: by doing religious things or keeping a moral code, we will make it to heaven. Paul's answer is simply no one has ever perfectly kept the law; therefore, no one can be saved by keeping a moral code or doing religious ritual. That is why the world needs a Savior—One who perfectly kept the moral code, and then paid the penalty for humanity's failure to keep the same code, and so their sin. Salvation must be available to us not by law-keeping, but through faith in the Savior.

The second is the appropriate response a Christian should have to the moral law of God. I need to be obedient because in doing so I will be rewarded with a wholesome life.

Deuteronomy presents a different emphasis. It called Israel to trust God from the heart, that is the *"righteousness by faith."* Moses' promise was that God would change their hearts if they would choose to give themselves fully to Him in a faith-commitment. To trust God would bring life; to trust in themselves by turning to other gods would bring death and destruction. That is the word of faith Paul found in Moses.

They did not have to do something such as ascend into heaven to bring Christ down, or to raise Him from the dead. All that was needed was a word of faith in Jesus of Nazareth who had already done these things. He came, lived, died, and rose again.

B. The Word of Faith Defined (9-13)

God requires two things of any person, young or old, poor or wealthy, educated or not, to be saved from their sins:

First is confess with your mouth, "Jesus is Lord." I want you to say it with me: "Jesus is Lord." That Jesus is Lord means He is God Almighty, the sovereign God Who is enthroned above all other powers. There is no God higher than Jesus. He is the King of kings and Lord of lords. There is no other name through which we can be saved from our sins than the name of the Lord Jesus Christ.

The second is believe in your heart God raised Jesus from the dead. Jesus died, actually, really died—all-the-way-dead. God raised the dead body to life and He is alive today. It was not just an out-of-the-body experience. It was a true physical resurrection. The resurrection is the one ultimate authentication that everything Jesus claimed to be and do is true.

Why confess with the mouth? The gospel is word. Paul calls it the "word of faith." It is something communicated through words involving a herald or preacher—one conveying a message from someone who has commissioned him. God "calls" people to trust in Him—the call involves words. Therefore, we are to use words to declare our faith. That confession states Jesus is Lord. We should have no problem understanding the process Paul is referring to here. We are bombarded with words from cultural preachers; they are called commercials. It is estimated that the average American is exposed to 1,500 commercial messages every day.[105]

It is not enough to go through the mechanics of saying words. The heart is involved as well. A person must believe with their core inner self that Jesus proved His lordship by rising from the dead.

What happens when we do those two acts of faith? We are saved. What does 'saved' mean? An equivalent phrase is to have eternal life. In salvation God forgives all of our sins and comes into our lives to be Himself the gift of eternal life. That's all there is to it. Nothing complicated. But it works!

To prove it, Paul quotes from Isaiah that "Anyone who trusts in him will never be put to shame." If you trust in Jesus, not your works, you'll not be disappointed at the judgment. In another reference Paul quoted the Old Testament prophet, Joel: "Everyone who calls on the name of the Lord will be saved."

C. Getting the Word of Faith to People (14-15)

Our primary task as Christians is to be God's means of getting this good news of the word of faith to people who are desperately trying by their religious good works to get to heaven. It is also why we must be Great Commission people in our neighborhoods and our daily contacts.

III. Having Heard the Message, People Must Respond in Faith to Be Saved (16-21)

A. Israel Heard and Was Obstinate (16-19)

The charge cannot be made they did not hear. Nor can anyone reading this book say they haven't heard. Israel was obstinate and did not accept the word they heard. I hope you don't make the mistake of joining them.

---

105   "To verify." *Leadership*, Fall 1990, p 129

B. Others Now Hear Who Respond in Faith (20-21)

These verses describe the contrast of the response to the Gospel among non-Jewish people known as Gentiles, and the rejection of the Gospel by the people to whom God has constantly held out His hands of invitation.

Conclusion

A fundamental spiritual flaw basic to all fallen, sinful people is the idea that we can work our way to heaven, that we can establish our own righteousness. God has communicated to us a square, and we insist on making it a triangle. We do so to our own damnation.

There are several side-spurs within Christianity that add something to trusting Jesus alone for salvation. These groups declare Jesus is the Son of God, that He died on the cross and rose again, but they slip in a plus factor that we also have to do something. We must keep some moral code, or a certain day, or be baptized a certain way, or do some special act of penance, or a thousand other things. Someone has rightly said that religion is spelled "d o"; Christianity is spelled "d o n e".

The Bible declares that to be saved we must "confess with our mouth that Jesus is Lord." And we must believe in our heart—the complete inner self that directs behavior—that Jesus rose again from the dead. If we do those things, we will be saved. Anyone who trust in Him will never be put to shame. Everyone who calls on the name of the Lord will be saved."

Sir Winston Churchill is reported to have written: "Broadly speaking, the short words are the best, and the old words best of all." The words of the Gospel are short, simple, straight forward and old. They are the best of all. We are to be the commercials of giving those words to people who are lost and separated from God. There is an old gospel song that stated, "I love to tell the old, old story of Jesus and His love." Let's not be ashamed of the Gospel, it is the power of God.

For your reflection:
- As you think about your journey to faith, was there a time where you had the wrong understanding of how to gain a right relationship with God?
- What is religion's error about salvation?
- What is the emphasis of Deuteronomy as stated in this message?
- Name the two aspects of the word of faith in 10:9-10.

Do I Have to be GOOD to go to Heaven?

31

Romans 11

Where Do We Fit in God's Plan?

God does not "fly by the seat-of-the-pants", simply taking what comes next and making spontaneous on-the-spot decisions. Before creation, God knew all that would occur in individual personal decisions, cultural developments, and national events. He knew there would be a man name Abraham through whom He would establish a people, and through that people bring to the world a Savior. He knew His specially chosen people would turn their backs on Him and that He would then take His salvation to the nations of the world. If God had such detail all mapped out, then He also has a plan for each of us.

Scripture: Romans 11

Main Idea: Through Israel's hardened heart, the door was opened to give the gospel to the Gentiles.

Introduction

Charlie Brown is at bat. STRIKE THREE! He has struck out again and slumps over to the bench. "Rats!" he says, "I'll never be a big-league player. I just don't have it! All my life I've dreamed of playing in the big leagues, but I know I'll never make it."

Lucy turns to console him. "Charlie Brown, you're thinking too far ahead. What you need to do is set yourself more immediate goals." He looks up. "Immediate goals?" Lucy says, "Yes. Start with this next inning when you go out to pitch. See if you can walk off of the mound without falling down!"[106]

At the opening of a new year it is axiomatic to think of where we are going. Goals are set, plans to reach the goals are developed and, as a result, renewed energy and motivation set the juices flowing through our system. Planning, both long-term—which is now about 3-5 years—and short-term, is a vital part of business and personal life.

God is the master planner. Before any of creation existed, God knew all that would happen once He created angels, the universe, and humankind. God doesn't get any surprises. His knowledge and plans are not only macro in nature to cover the universe, but also micro in coming down to you and me.

Our passage emphasizes God's plan to have a people through whom He would bring the Savior, not just for one small ethnic group, but for all ethnic groups on the earth. Paul's first point is that…

I. God Has Always Had People Who Have Believed in Him (1-10)

A. Paul Illustrates This Fact (1)

Paul's definition of God's saving work in which all the people of the world have become recipients of His grace, seemed to exclude the chosen nation of Israel. He denies this is so, and proves God has included His people by using the commonly understood concept of a remnant of believers. Ladies understand the word, 'remnant', as left over pieces of fabric. The Bible uses the term to refer to the minority group who were true followers of the LORD in Israel.

Paul used his own case to prove his point that God has always had people who have believed on Him in every period

---

[106] Dexter Yager and Ron Ball, *The Marks of a Millionaire*, (Wheaton, IL, Tyndale House Publishers), 21.

including the present. He was himself not only a descendant of Abraham, he was also of the tribe of Benjamin. His name was Saul, after the family's hero, King Saul. Paul, a Jew, was a believer in Jesus and a recipient of God's salvation.

Not only was Paul an illustration of a Jew being saved, but Elijah was, too.

B. Elijah Illustrates This Fact (2-6)

You recall the story. Elijah felt he was the only believer in the LORD left in Israel. God said, "Not so, I have reserved for Myself 7,000 who have not bowed the knee to Baal." It is important to notice who does the action in that statement. He did not say 7,000 had kept their faith strong. God said **HE** had reserved 7,000. Faith is the *result* of God's saving work in the heart of a person, not the *cause* of it. God is always the initiator, not humankind. No one seeks God; God seeks people. There is a critically important factor in faith that Paul emphasizes later. These could appropriately be called *believers*, but Paul's emphasis was on God's choosing as the source of faith.

There were believers in the day of Elijah. There were believers in Paul's day, and there are believers today. Unfortunately, the saved are not the majority, they are a remnant—meaning a small part that is left over.

Why weren't there more believers in Israel and Judah?

C. Israel's Failure Was Due to a Hard Heart (7-10)

I live with a wonderful lady who occasionally drifts into la-la land in an afternoon rest. In that state, she isn't asleep, but she is hardly aware of anything going on around her. The word for it is a 'torpor', described as a suspension of movement. If I suddenly shouted or clapped my hands, it would bring some folks out of the torpor they are in now. But since I am basically a kind man, I'll not disturb them. You tell them they missed some good stuff, but also ask them if they enjoyed their little journey. Those who were not the chosen remnant were put into a spiritual torpor. "God gave them a spirit of stupor." Is that the condition of some people you know? Would someone else describe you as a person who was in a spiritual daze or la-la land?

That spiritual daze led to a hardness of heart. The word refers to being callused with a loss of feeling—no response to God and to spiritual things. There are a lot of people who have become hard in their hearts because they think the church is full of hypocrites and Elmer Gantry preachers. Unfortunately, there are some of those types around. However, the church is made up mostly sinful people, forgiven, changed, and being changed who are trying to get it together step by step through God's power. None of us will ever get it together completely, but we can learn to allow Jesus to live His perfect life in and through our imperfect humanity. That is true Christlikeness.

It is a terrible thing to develop a hard heart. God takes our choices seriously. If we line Him out, then the consequences of that choice take over.

Paul methodically built his case that God's plan was much larger than the people of his day thought. God included all humanity, even the despised Gentiles.

II. God's Plan Included All Humanity (11-24)

Israel's failure had benefits:

A. Israel's Failure Proved God's Grace to Them (11)

Paul was an illustration that Israel was not completely thrown out of God's plan. The promises of God assured a future redemption of the nation. Neither the world nor the

Jews have seen the last of God's dealing with the nation of Israel.

B. Israel's Failure Facilitated the Spread of the Gospel to the Gentile World (11-12)

"Again I ask, did they stumble so as to fall beyond recovery? Not at all! Rather, because of their transgression, salvation has come to the Gentiles to make Israel envious. But if their transgression means riches for the world, and their loss means riches for the Gentiles, how much greater riches will their fullness bring!"

The book of Acts is a record that Paul and others went first to the synagogues with their message of salvation in Jesus Christ. When rejected they turned to the Gentiles who heard and responded.

Paul states, that if the loss of Israel has resulted in making the Gentile world spiritually rich, which it has, how much richer will we be when Israel is made spiritually whole?

C. Inclusion of the Gentiles was to Motivate Israel Through Jealousy (13-16)

Through God giving His salvation to all people it was also hoped the Jewish world would want to be included. Thank God millions have become believers, but only a remnant. In the same way, only a small percentage of the Gentile world can be classified as true believers.

D. Gentiles Have No Room for Arrogance (17-24)

To help his readers understand his warning, Paul used the metaphor of an olive tree, a frequent reference in the Bible. However, he reversed the usual order. Usually, the good olive branch was grafted into the wild olive trunk, much like the walnut growers. Instead, Paul has the wild olive branch grafted into the good olive tree and thereby becoming a productive branch. Israel is the good olive tree. All the Gentile nations are wild branches grafted into the good trunk of Israel.

Because we are grafted branches, there is no room for arrogance on our part. Though Israel, God's chosen nation is under His judgment, Gentiles have no room to brag. If God didn't spare the natural branches, He is not going to spare the grafted ones if they are careless with His grace as was Israel.

Verse 22: *"Consider therefore the kindness and sternness of God: sternness to those who fell* [meaning Israel], *but kindness to you, provided that you continue in his kindness"*. I mentioned the key factor of faith. Here it is: faith is continuous. It is not a once-for-all decision, it is a continuous attitude of trust and commitment to Jesus as Savior and Lord. We are to *"continue in His kindness."* Don't be careless and sloppy about your relationship to the Lord. The genuineness of our faith is evidenced by our walk of obedience with Him.

III. God Will Bring the Nation of Israel Back to Himself (25-36)

A. Israel's Hardening Is Only Partial (25-32)

For the last 2,000 years God's focus in salvation has been upon the Gentile nations of the world. When the completed number is fulfilled, God will turn the hearts of Israel from hardness and rejection to faith. It is assured by the promises of God to the patriarchs. His promises and call are irrevocable.

> *Zechariah 12:10 states: "And I will pour out on the house of David and the inhabitants of Jerusalem a spirit of grace and supplication. They will look on me, the one they have pierced, and they will mourn for him as one mourns for an only child, and grieve bitterly for him as one grieves for a firstborn son."*

A similar statement is made in Matthew 24:14:

"This gospel of the kingdom will be preached in the whole world as a testimony to all nations, and then the end will come."

This verse was a theme verse in the life of A. B. Simpson, founder of the Christian and Missionary Alliance. He wanted to share in the preaching of the gospel to the last nation and people on earth and so bring back Jesus. When that day comes, the hardened hearts of Israel will become soft and receptive to Jesus as their Messiah, Savior, and Lord.

Because of His magnificent inclusive plan...

B. God is to be Praised for His Unsearchable Wisdom (33-36)

In a majestic expression of praise, Paul's heart bursts in a powerful statement of God's greatness and glory. The God who planned it all before creation, is also the God who has a plan for you and me and is carrying out that plan! Let's read together this great statement of praise:

"Oh, the depth of the riches of the wisdom and knowledge of God! How unsearchable his judgments, and his paths beyond tracing out! 'Who has known the mind of the Lord? Or who has been his counselor' (Isaiah 40:13)? 'Who has ever given to God, that God should repay him' (Job 41:11)? For from him and through him and to him are all things. To him be the glory forever! Amen."

Application

There is a warning of presuming upon God's goodness, as did Israel. We must hold in balance the kindness—coming first in order—and the sternness of God. The word for 'kindness', refers to the goodness of God. "It is the grace which pervades the whole nature, mellowing all which would be harsh and austere."[107] God is love, but He is also just, He is 'severe'. This is the antonym of kindness. It literally means to cut off, as the farmer prunes dead branches. Our relationship with God is based upon His saving acts on the cross and the resurrection. God requires a response of faith that is much more than a one-time decision. Faith by its nature is continuous. Nurture your faith. Don't let the weeds of the cares of life, or the pursuit of the madness of pleasure and money choke out your trust in God. Don't let the spirit of pluralism or the disappointments of life make your heart like a piece of concrete. Keep it soft through thankfulness and praise.

In a real sense, the United States has been a favored nation because of the strong spiritual roots based upon biblical truth. But now those roots have become diseased and the whole tree of the nation is sick. We are spiritually drowsy and have become callused toward God. The Bible and the church are being cited as the cause of the nation's problems. Some feel the answer is to throw God out and get rid of the repressive restrictions of a moral code. We are ripe for God to cut off the branch.

You are not going to go to heaven because you are an American. A person can be forgiven of their sins only through trusting in Jesus as Lord and Savior. I invite you to come to Him today.

There is a strong word of comfort in this chapter. God works through disobedience to bring mercy to the sinner. Parents who grieve over children who have thrown their faith to the rubbish heap can gain strength in knowing He is still a saving God. If you have lived a rebellious and careless life,

---

107   Spiros Zodhiates, *The Complete Word Study Dictionary New Testament* (Chattanooga, TN: AMG Publishers, 1992), #5544, 1482.

God will forgive you and receive you. Will you come to Him now?

For your reflection:
- God has always had people who follow Him. List two "proofs" of this:
- What was the cause of Israel's failure as God's people?
- To whom does the word, "Gentiles", refer?
- What did Israel's failure mean to the Gentiles?
- Paul used the metaphor (word picture) of an olive tree to portray the place of Gentiles in God's plan. Identify the trunk of the tree.
- Who is the olive shoot?
- Because Gentiles are "grafted branches", what should our attitude be?
- What is the future of Israel?
- What warning can we take from this chapter?
- What assurance can we receive?

Do I Have to be GOOD to go to Heaven?

32

Romans 12:1 2

Our Most Important Personal Commitment

"There are then two things to be considered here—the first, that we are the Lord's—and secondly, that we ought on this account to be holy, for it is an indignity to God's holiness, that anything, not first consecrated, should be offered to him. These two things being admitted, it then follows that holiness is to be practiced through life, and that we are guilty of a kind of sacrilege when we relapse into uncleanness, as it is nothing else than to profane what is consecrated."[108]

"Then there is the *irrevocable attachment*. What do I mean by that? I mean that the Lord doesn't want any experimenters about. Some movie actor wrote a book one time called *Try Jesus*. I never read the book. I wouldn't be caught dead reading it. 'Try Jesus.' All this experimentation—I don't believe in it. I believe we ought to be suicide bombers. We ought to tie ourselves in the cockpit and dive on the deck and if we go out, we go out. Sink or swim, live or die, irrevocably attached in love and faith and devotion to Jesus Christ the Lord.

"Christians ought to be those who are so totally committed that it is final. This weak looking back over your shoulder to see if there isn't something better—I can't stand it. One time a young man came to an old saint who taught the deeper life, the crucified life, and said to him, 'Father, what does it mean

---
[108] Barnhouse, 451.

to be crucified?' The old man thought for a moment and said, 'Well, to be crucified means three things. First, the man who is crucified is facing only one direction.' I like that—facing only one direction. If he hears anything behind him he can't turn around to see what's going on. He has stopped looking back. The crucified man on the cross is looking in only one direction and that is the direction of God and Christ and the Holy Ghost and the direction of the edifying of the church, the direction of sanctification and the direction of the Spirit-filled life.

"And the old man scratched his scraggly gray hair and said, 'One thing more, son, about a man on a cross—he's not going back.' The fellow going out to die on the cross doesn't say to his wife, 'Good-bye, honey. I'll be back shortly after five.' When you go out to die on the cross you bid goodbye—you're not going back! If we would preach more of this and stop trying to make the Christian life so easy it's contemptible, we would have more converts that would last. Get a man converted who knows that if he joins Jesus Christ he's finished, and that while he's going to come up and live anew, as far as this world's concerned he's not going back—then you have a real Christian indeed. The old man went on, 'Another thing about the man on the cross, son; he has no further plans of his own.' I like that, too. Somebody else made his plans for him, and when they nailed him up there all his plans disappeared. On the way up to the hill he didn't see a friend and say, 'Well, Henry, next Saturday about three I'll come by and we'll go fishing up on the lake.' He was going out to die and he had no plans at all.'"[109]

Scripture: Romans 12:1 2

Main Idea: having been saved by God's grace, the believer is to commit him or herself fully to God.

---

109   A. W. Tozer, *Total Commitment to Christ* (Camp Hill, Pennsylvania: Christian Publications, 1995), Quick Verse

Introduction

William Booth, the great founder of the Salvation Army stated: "When I got the poor of London on my heart and caught a vision of what Jesus Christ, the reigning Lord, could do with those people, though I knew there were many with greater training, greater wisdom, greater intelligence, greater power than William Booth, I was determined that the living Christ would have all of William Booth that there was."

Church history has more of the not-so-great who have made a significant impact than it does of the intellectuals, the powerful, the talented, or the wealthy. It may well be that the more gifted and blessed that we are, the more we tend to rely upon ourselves, and the less upon God. Therefore, God is not able to display His power because we haven't given to Him all there is of us. Does God have all of you?

A chicken and a pig took a trip together. After many miles and hours on the road, they got hungry. Finally, the sharp-eyed chicken spotted a restaurant. Approaching the door, they read a sign: "Ham and eggs: Our Specialty!" "Hold it!" shouted the pig. "What's the matter?" asked the chicken. "Plenty. All they want from you is a little donation. They are asking me for total commitment!"

After clearly and emphatically stating and restating that our salvation is a free gift of God's grace received by faith, and not a result of our keeping a moral code or doing the religious thing, Paul now begins a discussion of the ramifications of that wonderful truth. His first statement is that God's gracious love should evoke a total commitment of ourselves to Him. God doesn't want the comfortable donation from us, He wants us, all of us.

> "Therefore, I urge you, brothers, in view of God's mercy, to offer your bodies as living sacrifices, holy and pleasing to God—this is your spiritual act of worship. Do not conform any longer to the pattern of this world, but be transformed by the renewing of your mind. Then you will be able to test and approve what God's will is—his good, pleasing and perfect will (Romans 12:1-2 [NIV]).
>
> "So, here's what I want you to do, God helping you: Take your everyday, ordinary life—your sleeping, eating, going-to-work, and walking-around life—and place it before God as an offering. Embracing what God does for you is the best thing you can do for him. Don't become so well-adjusted to your culture that you fit into it without even thinking. Instead, fix your attention on God. You will be changed from the inside out. Readily recognize what he wants from you, and quickly respond to it. Unlike the culture around you, always dragging you down to its level of immaturity, God brings the best out of you, develops well-formed maturity in you (Eugene Peterson: The Message)."

I. Why We Should Commit Ourselves to God

A. Because Salvation is a Gift of Grace

The "therefore" forces us into more than the immediately preceding verses. It is the whole of the argument to this point that Paul has in mind. "In view of God's mercy" centers on the argument of the first eleven chapters. The word for 'urge' or 'beseech' [KJV] refers to someone coming alongside to encourage. Paul invites us to join him in his commitment to the Lord. The motivation for us to respond is God's mercy—the forgiveness of sins and eternal life that God has freely given. His mercy is unearned and undeserved.

B. Because Salvation is Available for Everyone

The preceding verses emphasize God's goodness to graft the wild olive branches of the Gentile nations into the good olive tree of Israel. God's plan is expressed in John 3:16 that God so loved the entire world that He gave His only Son. A plan so generous and complete deserves a response of love and commitment in return.

The commitment Paul calls for is stated to people who have placed their personal trust in Jesus Christ as Savior. There is, of course, a commitment in coming to Christ. This takes the next step towards becoming a fully devoted follower. Having told us why, Paul now tell us how to commit ourselves to God.

II. How We Are to Commit Ourselves to God

A. We Are to Present our Bodies as Living Sacrifices

To get a better understanding of this language we need to review Old Testament worship. Leviticus is the worship manual of Old Testament worship. The "burnt offering" is described in chapter 1. Verse 9 states the priest is to burn all of the animal being offered on the altar: the inner parts, the meat, the skin. "It is a burnt offering, an offering made by fire, an aroma pleasing to the LORD."

In New Testament terms, our most important personal commitment is to offer our bodies to God as living sacrifices. We are not dead animals to be burned by fire. We are alive and to be just as totally committed to God as the animal. We are to present our bodies as Mary and Joseph *presented* Jesus to the Lord. Ephesians 5 states that Jesus will *present* us to Himself as a glorious church, in the same way a bride *presents* herself to her groom.

Our bodies may be tall or short, well developed or limited in function, good looking or homely, thin or large, blue or brown eyes, black or red or no hair. It doesn't matter, God wants our bodies. It doesn't matter what we have as personal talents and gifts. God made them all and will use them all for His glory.

Who in the Godhead wants our bodies? The Father needs no body for He is spirit. The Son, Jesus, has a body, but the Holy Spirit needs our bodies to work through to accomplish the will of God in our lives. He needs our minds to think His thoughts, our lips to speak His word, our hearts to love others, our feet to take us where He wants us to go, our hands to do His work.

B. Such Commitment is Reasonable Worship

A Greek scholar wrote: "'Reasonable service' or worship is to be understood as that service to God which implies intelligent meditation or reflection...."[110] We sing hymns of praise and speak words of adoration to God in worship. However, it is empty religious ritual if we have not given our bodies to God. Our reasonable response to God's mercy is to give Him our bodies. The word 'holy', carries a basic meaning of 'set apart to God'. It also means to be morally pure. Our bodies can either be instruments of pure living or immoral living. We can tell the truth with our tongues or we can deceive with words. We can live sexually pure lives or we can live immoral lives. God deserves and desires holy bodies. How can we give to Him holy bodies when we have all sinned? By receiving the forgiveness and cleansing given to us in Christ. He makes the impure, pure. Jesus comes to live in our bodies by His Spirit to change us from the inside out.

---

110 Spiros Zodhiates, *The Complete Word Study Dictionary, New Testament* (Chattanooga, TN: AMG Publisher, 1992), #2050, p 923.

1 Corinthians 6:19 reads: "Do you not know that your body is a temple of the Holy Spirit, who is in you, whom you have received from God? You are not your own; you were bought at a price. Therefore, honor God with your body."

Giving ourselves fully to God is the highest act of worship of which we are capable, and every believer can do it. You don't have to know a lot of the Bible or perfect Sunday school attendance to qualify. Just do it. Give Him your mind, tongue, hands, feet, eye and ears. Give them to God.

III. Three Results of Our Commitment to God

A. We Are to No Longer Conform to the World's Pattern

Phillips' translation is good, *"Don't let the world around you squeeze you into its mold."* Or, Peterson's rendition: *"Don't become so well-adjusted to your culture that you fit into it without even thinking. Instead, fix your attention on God. You will be changed from the inside out."* Unfortunately, Christians are not distinctive from the world in values or behavior. We gripe as much or more than the other guy. We want to participate in the same entertainment. Our sexual behavior is too often no different than the non-Christian. We are as driven to accumulate money and things as the next person. We shave our tax reports, pull shady deals, tell the dirty stories the same as the person who makes no spiritual claims.

If you have given your body to God, then it is His body you are involving in adultery or fornication. It is His tongue you use to utter profanity and vulgarities, His eyes you cause to look at porn, His ears you constrain to hear gossip and slander. We compromise Jesus' integrity when we cheat in business or in school.

The great Bible teacher, F. B. Meyer wrote: "Thousands of Christians are like water-logged vessels, they cannot sink; yet, they are saturated with so many inconsistencies, worldliness and little permitted evils that they can only be towed with difficulty into the celestial port."

Nationally renowned Christian businessman, Fred Smith, visited Russia shortly after *perestroika* began to open the country up to Christianity. Membership at the Moscow Baptist Church was 5,600 with an attendance of 6,000. The pastor told Smith, "In Russia, we have no four-wheel Christians." He coined the phrase to describe people who ride to church only for their baptism, Easter morning service, the Christmas program, and their own funeral.

God accused Israel of wanting to "be like the nations, the peoples of the world, who have served wood and stone" (Ezekiel 20:32). "Do not follow the crowd in doing wrong," God said in Exodus 23:2. Instead of obeying God in separating themselves from the nations of Canaan, the psalmist accused Israel of "mingling with the nations and adopting their customs" (Psalm 106:35).

Paul commands us to *"not conform any longer to the pattern of this world."* What is that pattern? John tells us all that is in the world is *"the cravings of the flesh, the lust of the eyes, and the boasting of what he has and does"* (1 John 2:16).

Rather than conforming to the world...

B. We Are to be Transformed Persons—a 2nd result of our commitment to God.

How can we become transformed? By allowing our minds to be renewed. The word for *transformed* is the English "metamorphosis", the change a worm goes through to become a butterfly. That's a fitting comparison. God wants the wormy sinner to become a beautiful, holy person. For that to happen, our thought patterns have to change because behavior is generated in the mind. God's change agent for the mind is His Word, the Bible. We are to read it, meditate on it, and memorize it. The psalmist said he hid God's Word in his heart as a preventative to sin. By doing so, our minds are made new. God changes us from the inside out through this process. The Bible is not a decoration on the coffee table. Did you spend time in Gods' Word this week? What kind of behavior characterized your life? The only way to change our thinking and through that our behavior is to know and apply God's Word asking God to bring about His change by His Spirit. Then we choose to live it out.

A third result of our commitment to God is. . .

C. We Will Prove God's Way is Best

We cannot test and approve of what God's will is, that it is good, pleasing, and perfect, until first we make our most important personal commitment. The word, 'perfect', carries the idea of completion or maturity. That is why Peterson translated this: *"God brings the best out of you, develops well-formed maturity in you."* The people who are willing to give themselves without reserve to the Lord will find He is easy to live with. He is not a harsh dictator who delights in ruining our lives. Quite the opposite. He delights in giving the best to His devoted children. Some Christians have dropped along the side of the road muttering to themselves that the Christian life isn't what it's cracked up to be. The fact is, they aren't in a position to make that judgment, for they never gave their bodies—their lives—totally to God. Therefore, they cannot test and approve the will of God. Are they Christians? Yes, they are going to heaven, but they will never know the fullness of joy and peace, or the power of God working in and through them that God intends for them to experience.

Conclusion

At the beginning of this century, William Borden was heir to the Borden Dairy Estate, graduating from a Chicago high school a millionaire. A century ago, that was worth a lot more than today's eroded dollar. His parents gave him a trip around the world. Traveling through Asia, the Middle East, and Europe, gave Borden a burden for the world's hurting people. Writing home, he said, "I'm going to give my life to prepare for the mission field."

When he made this decision, he wrote in the back of his Bible two words: "No Reserves". Turning down high-paying job offers after graduating from Yale University, Borden entered two more words: "No Retreats".

Completing his studies at Princeton Seminary, Borden sailed for China to work with Muslims, stopping first at Egypt for some preparation. While there he was stricken with cerebral meningitis and died within a month. In his Bible underneath the words, "No Reserves," and "No Retreats," he had written two final words, "No Regrets".

Offer your body to God. The verb form of 'offer' indicates we do the acting, we make a decisive act. God may take your body overseas to serve others, he may leave you where you are to be light and salt in a dark and deranged world. You will have your struggles and disappointments, but he will never abandon you, and in the end, you will not have any regrets.

Chuck Swindoll tells the story of a house church in the former Soviet Union several years ago. They had to meet in secret to avoid reprisals from the communist government.

"One Sunday these believers arrived inconspicuously in small groups throughout the day so as not to arouse the suspicion of KGB informers. By dusk they were all safely inside, windows closed, and doors locked. They began by singing a hymn quietly but with deep emotion. Suddenly, the door was pushed open and in walked two soldiers with loaded automatic weapons at the ready. One shouted, 'All right--everybody line up against the wall. If you wish to renounce your commitment to Jesus Christ, leave now!'

"Two or three quickly left, then another. After a few more seconds, two more. `This is your last chance. Either turn against your faith in Christ,' he ordered, `or stay and suffer the consequences.'

"Another left. Finally, two more in embarrassed silence with their faces covered slipped out into the night. No one else moved. Parents with small children trembling beside them looked down reassuringly. They fully expected to be gunned down or, at best, be imprisoned.

"After a few moments of complete silence, the other soldier closed the door, looked back at those who stood against the wall and said, 'Keep your hands up—but this time in praise to our Lord Jesus Christ, brothers and sisters. We, too, are Christians. We were sent to another house church several weeks ago to arrest a group of believers....'

"The other soldier interrupted, 'But, instead, we were converted! We have learned by experience, however, that unless people are willing to die for their faith, they cannot be fully trusted.'"[111]

---

[111] Charles Swindoll, *Living Above the Level of Mediocrity* (Edison, NJ: Inspirational Press, 1995).

For your reflection:
- How much of your life (mind, emotions, will, sex, family, possessions, work, entertainment, etc.) have you given to God? 10%, 40%, 70% 100%
- What specifically do these verses command us to give to God, and why?
- What does the word "holy" imply?
- Name three outflows of a life fully committed to God

33

Romans 12:3-8

We Need to Think Sensibly About Ourselves

"Healthy self-esteem is important because some of us think too little of ourselves; on the other hand, some of us overestimate ourselves. The key to an honest and accurate evaluation is knowing the basis of our self-worth—our identity in Christ. Apart from him, we aren't capable of very much by eternal standards; in him, we are valuable and capable of worthy service. Evaluating ourselves by worldly standards of success and achievement can cause us to think too much about our worth in the eyes of others and thus miss our true value in God's eyes."[112]

Scripture: Romans 12:3-8

Main Idea: if every believer went through a sensible analysis of themselves, and functioned in the church according to God's gifting of them, the church would not have been so divided down throughout its history.

Introduction

One of the developments within evangelical Christianity in the last thirty-five years has been emphasis upon spiritual gifts and tools of assessment that help us identify where we fit in the body of Christ. Bruce Bugbee has pioneered in this field and developed a program called, "Networking".

---

[112] *Life Application Bible Commentary: Romans* Copyright © 1992 by The Livingstone Corporation. Electronic Edition STEP Files Copyright © 2002, Parsons Church Group, a division of FindEx.com, Inc. All rights reserved.

In *Discipleship Journal*, Bugbee emphasized that when a church identifies spiritual gifts, passions, and relational styles, numerous benefits result. There's new enthusiasm when a person's God-given profile is matched with needs in the church. More people are enabled to get involved when they're helped to find the right niche for service. When people understand that serving is not optional, and that they're designed for ministry, they take greater responsibility for areas of need in the church's life. This results in less turnover in ministry positions.

He also pointed out that when people are making contributions to God's work, they have less time to complain and criticize, so there are fewer interpersonal conflicts. They have a better understanding of the challenges and difficulties of ministry. In addition, people personally involved in ministry tend to give more generously, and they have greater love for others.[113]

Christianity requires a personal, individual commitment to Christ. Each person must individually place their trust is Jesus. To commit one's body to God is a personal commitment. Those are personal commitments, yet they place us into the social context of group relationships. Believers are a family, a building of stones, a body of many parts functioning in unity.

The word picture Paul uses here and in 1 Corinthians is that of a body. We all understand the body. It's a primary concern to each of us.

In verses 1-2, Paul challenges us to offer our bodies to God as living sacrifices. Now in verse 3, he begins to explain how that commitment is to be lived out. It is interesting to me that he did not talk first about personal morality and social

---

113 Bruce Bugbee and Beth Lueders, "Maximum ministry" (*Discipleship Journal*, Nov/Dec 1995 [Issue 90]). 60-62+.

ethics. God's first concern is how we function as a group of people called the church.

There are two primary principles in this passage. First, what we are in the body of Christ is given to us by God. It is not an achievement of spiritual greatness. Second, each member of the body is to function in his or her area of giftedness.

I. What We are in the Body of Christ is Given to Us by God

Paul repeats his emphasis three times on grace and receiving something as a gift in these verses. Verse 3a: *"For by the grace given me;"* and later, *"in accordance with the measure of faith God has given you;"* and in verse 6, *"we have different gifts, according to the grace given us."* "Grace" and "given" state emphatically that these abilities are not the result of some great spiritual attainment. God has designed and provided that every Christian, new and long-term, have a function in the church. We are not to "buy" our way out of our job through hiring more staff. Pastors have a function, and in a larger church there is a division of responsibility with several staff, but pastors do not displace spiritual gifts.

Our identity as New Testament believers is not in a family or racial sense as it was in the Old Testament. It is because we are "in Christ."[114] Our gifts and function in the church are tied directly to our being "in Christ."

II. Each Member of the Body is to Function in Their Area of Giftedness

Paul lists seven gifts. These are not offices or positions; they are things Christians do as they are given the ability to do them. Spiritual gifts and natural talents are not antagonistic. They work together. J. Oswald Sanders wrote, "Generally, the

---
114 Dunn, 733.

Holy Spirit imparts gifts that the recipient is naturally fitted to exercise, but He raises them to a new effectiveness."

A. Prophesying

The word usually refers to preaching God's Word, telling God's message, not foretelling some future event. The basic character of the gift is inspired speech generated by the Holy Spirit. It is not the product of a creative or analytical mind, though those faculties can assist in preaching. In the New Testament women are included in this gift.

There are different styles and forms of preaching. Narrative preaching and storytelling present truth in living form. Drama, films, and music can be forms of preaching. Teaching-preaching seeks to explain a biblical passage.

One who preaches is to do so in dependence upon God, *"in proportion to his faith."* It is a mathematical term and refers to the faith of the gifted person.

B. Serving

We get our word, *"deacon"* from this one. It is doing practical service for others. What is included? Most anything done around a church. Periodic work days to assist the custodial and ground crews; counting the offerings; assisting in secretarial work; making phone calls, or planning socials. Churches are able to accomplish to much with minimal resources is because of a vast network of volunteers. Each of us needs to help keep this campus clean and sharp. Our tape and CD ministry is conducted by servants. Our sound and tech crew are servants. Ushers, food preparation, mailings, and multiple other tasks are done by volunteers.

Outside of the church there are also many ways to serve the community and the needs of people and serve the Lord in the process. Churches have been in the middle of helping victims of natural disasters.

C. Teaching

The Word of God must be understood and explained. Obviously, not everyone has the time nor the skills to study the Bible in depth. God has resolved that by providing scholars, pastors, and lay teachers who are gifted to explain to us His Word. This is because of devoted biblical scholars who have language, historical and contextual skills have been published to bring enlightenment and understanding.

D. Encouraging

The word (*parakalon*) refers to coming alongside someone to impart strength. John used it of the ministry of the Holy Spirit to us. But we also need other believers to come alongside and give a word of encouragement and hope in the crises of life.

We encourage by praying for each other. This ministry requires that people let others know their needs. Small groups give opportunity to share with a few others on a more personal basis. Most churches provide a women's ministry of Bible study with small groups for discussion and encouragement. We are to encourage one another daily especially as we see the end coming (Hebrews 10:24-25).

E. Meeting the Needs of Others

The language means much more than simply giving money, though that might be a part of the giving. It includes food and assistance as well. Those who give are to do so in "a self-forgetful attitude, entirely innocent of any ulterior motive."[115] Thank you for your continued faithfulness in giving.

F. Leadership and Caring

The word means to give leadership, but it is not just managerial or administrative leadership. The structure gives a primary meaning of caring for others. It means to give guidance, direction, and protection that comes from a heart of caring.

Churches have always been hurt because there are so few who have the heart to lead, to take responsibility. Many people seem to want to be entertained, few are willing to take responsibility to lead a ministry. One of our working values is that *"the church is to be led by Spirit-controlled people who have leadership gifts, including administration, discernment, faith, leadership, shepherding/ pastoring, teaching and wisdom."*

G. Showing Mercy

This is to "tend the sick, relieve the poor, or care for the aged and disabled."[116] The demands of caring are more than the pastoral staff can manage. We need people of mercy to visit our shut-ins and to help when hardships strikes a family.

Application

What has to happen for this passage to become true in the life of a church? Here are five suggestions.

1. The late William Barclay wrote we must know ourselves and accept ourselves. Simply, we must know our spiritual gifts and our place in the Body of Christ. How do we make that discovery? It is both a personal and corporate

---

115 Black quoted by James D. G. Dunn, *Romans 2-8, Word Biblical Commentary, Vol 38* (Dallas, Texas: Word Books, Publisher, 730
116 Dunn, 731.

process. One helpful resource is the 'Networking' system that assists people in determining their spiritual gifts, passion for ministry, and style of relationships. There are several fine resources as well.

To accept ourselves is just as hard as knowing ourselves. Most of us aren't satisfied with the way God has put us together. We wish we were like someone else. My oldest brother was my hero as a child. During WW II, I wore a sailor suit because he was in the navy. He liked classical music, so I did too. When I entered the ministry, I nearly suffocated trying to be like him. I am not Charles Swindoll, Bill Hybels, David Jeremiah, Charles Stanley, or some other celebrity preacher. I'm Roy Price who has been *given* certain gifts. I have to accept who I am and what I am. That will help me accept you. The person who is fussing over who he or she is will also be critical of who and what other people are or are not. Every church needs the gifts God has given to each member and no one has all of the gifts.

2. Develop skills within the area of your gifts. A teacher needs to learn principles of teaching that helps to get the truth across. If you have manual abilities, develop them to the fullest.

3. The church needs to find a way for you to implement your gift. Most churches have a lot happening, but they need you to take initiative about your interests.

4. Each person must function. Each of us must do our job faithfully. A pastor is only one person with a mix of gifts. God never intended for pastors to do all the work of ministry, to try to meet all the needs of a congregation.

5. A spiritual gift is NOT to be used for personal prestige or benefit. God has given gifts to benefit His church.

Imagine the carpenter's tools holding a conference. Brother Hammer presided. Several suggested he leave the meeting because he was too noisy. Replied the hammer: "If I have to leave this shop, Brother Screw must go also. You have to turn him around again and again to get him to accomplish anything." Brother Screw spoke up: "If you wish, I'll leave. But Brother Plane must leave, too. All his work is on the surface. His efforts have no depth." To this, Brother Plane responded, "Brother Rule will also have to withdraw, for he is always measuring folks as though he were the only one who is right." Brother Rule then complained against Brother Sandpaper. "You ought to leave, too. You're so rough and always rubbing people in the wrong way."

Just then, the Carpenter from Nazareth came into the room. He put on his apron and went to the bench to make a pulpit for the preaching of the gospel. He used the hammer, screw, plane, rule, and sandpaper, and all His other tools. After the day's work with the pulpit finished, Brother Saw arose and said, "Brethren, I observe that all of us are workers together with the Lord."

I called a couple of people to get their impressions of their experience with the gift assessment tools we use. One said that though she had gone to church all of her life, she had never heard about or studied spiritual gifts. It was eye-opening to her and helpful. Another person commented that they found the results encouraging. It confirmed they were doing some things in sync with their gifts. They enjoyed going through the process and likely, you will too.

A dynamic and powerful church is one in which everyone functions in their area of giftedness. People in those churches respect and honor the gifts of others as co-workers with the Lord.

For your reflection:
- Which of the seven areas of gifting do you identify with?
- Where and how can you put your gifts to further God's work?

Do I Have to be GOOD to go to Heaven?

34

Romans 12:9-16

Eight Things a Christian Does

"The great principle of a life of victory and consecration. 'Be not overcome of evil, but overcome evil with good' (:10). This gives us the true secret of the life of faith. It is not by resisting evil directly that we overcome it so much as by receiving the life and power of Christ, and letting Him purify us by the expulsive power of a higher principle and a Diviner life.

"It is the bringing in of the light that drives out the darkness. It is the presence of the alkali that destroys the acid.

"The indwelling Spirit of Christ brings the exclusion of sin and the world. When the presence of God came into the ancient tabernacle there was no room for Moses, and when the Holy Spirit comes into the soul, He will dispossess the power of evil."[117]

Scripture: Romans 12:9-16

Main Idea: Having given our bodies to God and learned to serve Him with our spiritual gifts, there are moral and ethical behaviors Christians practice.

Romans is one of the apostle Paul's most structured letters. There is a logic to the development of thought. In broad strokes, in the first five chapters he defines how a person gains a right relationship with 'god. In chapters 6-8, the spiritual dynamics of Christian living are explored. In something of a parenthesis, Paul discusses God's relationship to the Hebrew

---
117   Simpson, 237.

people. With those matters behind him, chapters 12-16 talk about practical Christianity, how to live the life. First, we are to give God our bodies, then find our place of service by using our spiritual gifts, and now he identifies eight things that Christians do. Let's do this!

Introduction

Just so we don't get side-tracked in our thinking, the directives of the Bible for moral and ethical behavior are not given as steps to heaven. Rather, how we live expresses the reality that God has changed us on the inside. The inside life of the Christian is different than the inside life of a non-believer due to the personal presence of the Holy Spirit. This is NOT to say that non-believers do not live moral lives. Some religions place very stringent standards on their followers. Many irreligious people are highly moral. In fact, their high moral standard becomes a barrier to trusting Christ because they know they are good people. However, having received God's gracious forgiveness of sin and the incredible status of sons and daughters, there are things He asks us to do. Much of Romans to this point focuses on who God is and what He does. Now, Paul begins to outline behaviors God says we are to work at in our daily lives.

Now, let's see how our reporter's list lines up with eight things Paul says a person does who is in a right relationship with God and has given their body to God. This is not an exhaustive list of standards. It is only eight things that Paul chose to tell the believers in Rome they should do.

I. A Christian is to Love Sincerely (9)

The word for 'love' is *agapē* which is primarily used of God's love for humanity. Paul applies it to human relations here and in 13:10 and 14:15. This particular word appears only rarely outside of biblical literature. It appears, however, 116 times in the New Testament and 75 times in Paul's letters. James Dunn commented: "this is a word seized and taken over by the first Christians as they sought to find language to express their new experience of grace, a word filled with new content and significance by earliest Christian experience of God's love."[118] This, then, is a love placed in the human heart by God that will reflect in its behavior the character of God Himself.

This love is "sincere," which means to be without pretense or fakery. No hypocrisy. It is loving without wanting something back. Our sinful nature is polluted by a selfishness that is curable only by divine transformation. The result of the Spirit in our lives is love. Sincere love gives to meet another's needs, not to receive love, recognition, or security in return.

A basic human problem is that we don't know how to receive or give love without the corruption of selfishness. A question we need to ask is: 'Am I doing this because I'm wanting to get something out of it?' Are you in a relationship to get something or to give something? Fake, or insincere love, pretends to give love in order to get sex. Insincere love claims it feels our pain in order to get our votes. Sincere love simply gives what it can to meet the need of another person.

Our love is both to God and to people. We sing that we love God. Do we sing the songs in order to get something from God? Would we tell him we love Him if our world was falling apart, or would we be ready to curse Him and Christianity? Obviously, most of us came to God as sinners because we desperately wanted forgiveness and eternal life. Having come to Christ we can begin to grow out of selfishness. God wants our love. The first commandment is to love God with our whole heart, soul, mind, and strength.

---

118   Dunn, 739.

Loving God requires hating evil. We cannot love God and love sin at the same time. They are mutually exclusive of one another. In hating evil, we are to "cling to what is good." A better definition of sanctification could not be given. Paul makes a parallel statement in 1 Thessalonians 5:21-22. In both of these passages, the challenge follows a discussion of spiritual gifts. Spiritual gifts are not to be used deceitfully or for self-promotion.

Proverbs says God hates seven things (6:16-19). The list begins with "haughty eyes, a lying tongue, hands that shed innocent blood," and ends with a person "who stirs up dissension among brothers." If I cause dissension between two believers, God hates that action. Do we hate what God hates? Do we love what God loves?

II. Christians are to be Devoted to One Another (10)

"Devoted" means tender affection. It is a special word referring to family love. We are to love each other because we are family. I grew up in a family that had a lot of tension and arguments. However, overriding those conflicts was a loyalty and love because we were family. Family love seeks to "honor one another above yourselves." Paul said the same thing in Philippians 2:3, where he stated we are to "*do nothing out of selfish ambition or vain conceit, but in humility consider others better than yourselves.*"

The opposite would be grasping attention, wanting glory and honor, hogging the spotlight. Jeremiah told his secretary, Baruch, to not seek great things for himself. A mature Christian will pursue giving honor to others.

III. Christians are to Keep their Spiritual Fervor Alive (11).

The Message reads: "Don't burn out; keep yourselves fueled and aflame." Apollos was fervent in spirit. The root means to hesitate, to be slow or sluggish. Are you dragging your feet at serving God, making God or the church haul you around like a bratty little kid? You want to receive, you want the cotton candy, but you don't want to work for the Lord. Rather, we ought to be sweaty with serving the Lord. Orson Welles took a break in filming. The cameraman commented he should wipe the sweat from his forehead. He replied: "Horses sweat; men perspire; and (looking at the actress across the room) she glows." Our glow is the sweat of working for the Lord.

IV. We Are to be Joyful in Hope, Patient in Affliction, Faithful in Prayer (12)

Though these are obviously three different behaviors, they are related to one another. First, we have a hope of a future life of ecstatic joy and fulfillment as Jesus boldly promised. However, that is not life in the present. No matter how good our life is, we have problems and disappointments. Our promised future gives us joy regardless of life's experiences. A better day is coming.

When affliction does hit us, because we hope for a better day we can be patient—we can stand with our face to the wind. Hang in there, things will change, and one day, they will change dramatically.

Adversity carries some built-in benefits. Like the winds that carry an eagle to great heights, the winds of adversity enable a person to fly higher with God and gain a different perspective on life. An eagle's great wings enable it to soar above the harassment of lower skies and stay up longer. Our wings are faith and hope. Both are based upon the promises of a God of integrity.

Prayer enables us to be patient. Prayer gives strength to the wings of the eagle. Prayer keeps our eyes on the future and therefore our joy stays alive. One said, "Suffering colors all of life." The other replied, "But I propose to choose the colors." Prayer gives us the strength to choose to be joyful.

V. Christians are to be Hospitable (13)

There are two parts to this command. We are to "share with God's people who are in need." And we are to "practice hospitality." The two describe one basic behavior. The primary concern of the church is to take care of the needs of its own people. Through hospitality, people can break out of family webs and comfortable friendships to gain new friends. From being hospitable within the Christian community, we can move to opening our homes to our unchurched neighbors and friends.

VI. We are to Bless Those Who Persecute Us (14)

To bless someone who is wronging us is totally against the grain of human nature. It is fully within God's nature. Jesus demonstrated His own preaching on this when He hung on the cross, the most unjust act of any court in history. He prayed asking the Father to forgive those whose treachery put Him there and those who did the barbaric crucifying.

The negative form of "curse not" adds emphasis. Perhaps it had to be stated both ways, *"bless your persecutors,"* and *"bless and do not curse."* We are so bent on revenge by our depraved nature that we could easily twist the command to bless. We would say, "Bless you," and in our heart, add, "Damn you and your family." To bless and not curse requires us to forgive the wrong done to us. The idea of blessing comes out of God blessing His people. It is a bestowal of grace and peace and prayer for God to sustain and prosper[119].

The late William Barclay wrote: "There has been no greater force to move man into Christianity than just this serene forgiveness which martyrs in every age have shown."[120]

VII. We Are to Rejoice with Those Who Rejoice, and Mourn with Those Who Mourn (15)

The early church father, Chrysostom, wrote on this:

"It requires more of a high Christian temper to rejoice with them that do rejoice than to weep with them that weep. For this, nature itself fulfills perfectly; and there is none so hard-hearted as not to weep over him that is in calamity; but the other requires a very noble soul, so as not only to keep from envying, but even to feel pleasure with the person who is in esteem."[121]

VIII. We are to Live in Harmony with Each Other (16)

The "one another" narrows the application to the Christian community. An orchestra is harmonious when each player accurately plays what is written by the composer. It doesn't just happen, it requires work and patient practice. Just so, harmony in the church requires certain things:

- We need to accept the differences of temperament among us. That includes tolerating differences in tastes and desires.

- We must refuse to gossip or speak in a degrading manner.

---

119   Dunn, 744.
120   William Barclay, *The Letter to the Romans* (Philadelphia: Westminster Press, 1957), 181.
121   182.

- We must deal with one another in integrity and honesty. More than one Christian friendship has been torn apart by dishonesty.
- We too easily put a wrong interpretation on something we hear or see. Communication requires both accurate language and accurate hearing.

Again, a negative statement clarifies the line of thought, "don't be stuck-up". Pride destroys harmony. An egotist never fits into a group. Such a person wants everyone to be like them or to do it their way. Pride is based on the premise that people are not equal. Pride prevents us from accepting those who are lower in social position or of a different race as if inferior. It also prevents us from doing something we would consider below us. Conceit causes disharmony. The walls of racism and social snobbery can only come down when we acknowledge the biblical premise that all humankind is equal through creation, but not all ideas of God are equivalent.[122]

Conclusion

Beside each of the above, place a "*S*" if you feel it is a strength area, and a "*G*" if you feel you need to grow in that behavior. Under each category with a "*G*" write one thing you might do this week to help you grow in that behavior.

David D. Glass, the chief executive officer of Wal-Mart stores, when asked whom he most admired, responded: Sam Walton (Wal-Mart founder). He commented, "There's never been a day in his life, since I've known him, that he didn't improve in some way" (*Forbes Magazine*, Spring, 1988). Spiritual maturity will require a conscious effort on the part of the Christian to work on the 'growth areas' of his or her life. You have identified one or more of those this morning.

---

[122] See Ravi Zacharias, *Can Man Live Without God* (Nashville, TN: W Pub. Group, 1994) 141.

You have jotted down a possible strategy. Now let's pray and together ask God to strengthen us by His Spirit to work on them this week.

For your reflection:
- Celebrate the grace of God for the areas you marked as "strength" area.
- How will you begin to take some steps in the areas you identified as "growth" areas in your life?

Do I Have to be GOOD to go to Heaven?

35

Romans 12:17-21

When You Receive Evil

"'Do not repay anyone evil for evil'. (NRSV) The commands in verses 17-21 relate mainly to dealings with unbelievers. When people do evil against us, we are not to repay in kind, as much as we might like to (see also 1 Peter 3:9). Repaying evil for evil makes us participants in an evil economy. We will not be able to hate evil (12:9) while actively using it as a method of exchange with others. Instead we are to 'be careful to do what is right in the eyes of everybody' (NIV) (see 1 Peter 2:11-12). The word for *right* could also be translated 'noble' or 'honorable.' Paul is certainly not using the word *everybody* as it is used in the common expression 'Everybody's doing it.' Paul's standard for behavior was not common consensus, but godliness. The point being made here is that the behavior of believers must be such that no one can rightfully make a claim of wrongdoing. To commit the same *evil* that was committed against us makes us indistinguishable from the original offenders."[123]

Scripture: Romans 12:17-21

Main Idea: our response to personal abuse is not to seek revenge, but to find ways of doing good to the one who has hurt us.

---

[123] *Life Application Bible*, Romans 12:17

Introduction

Does anyone not understand the word, *"revenge?"* It means to do harm in return for a wrong received. The Jewish merchant in Shakespeare's "The Merchant of Venice," declared before the judge: "If you prick us, do we not bleed? if you tickle us, do we not laugh? if you poison us, do we not die? and if you wrong us, shall we not revenge?" We say, "I don't get angry, I just get even." Nothing is more natural to the sinful nature of humanity.

Try this on for revenge. A Philadelphia woman instructed her executor to take one dollar from her estate, invest it and pay the interest on the investment to her husband, "as evidence of my estimate of his worth." Another ex-wife bequeathed her former spouse one dollar to buy a rope to hang himself.

In the movie, "Schindler's List", Schindler sought to modify the Commandant's ruthless and arbitrary slaying of Jews. He drew a contrast between justice and power. He said that when a thief is caught and punished for a crime, it isn't a matter of power, it is justice. Power, he said, is when a person has the ability to hurt or destroy someone, but doesn't do it. It isn't power for a Larry Singleton to destroy someone weaker than him. He "wrote his own unique chapter in the annals of depravity when he chopped off the forearms of California teenager Mary Vincent after raping her, died of cancer in a Florida prison hospital."[124] It is justice for him to be punished for his crime in taking the life of another. Is it justice that John du Pont, heir to the du Pont chemical fortune, received a lesser penalty because the jury declared he was insane at the time he murdered the Olympic wrestling champion, David Schultz?[125]

---

124   http://www.sfgate.com/news/article/Lawrence-Singleton-despised-rapist-dies-He-2886703.php (accessed 03.08.17).

125   For story: http://www.nytimes.com/2010/12/10/sports/olympics/10dupont.html

> *"Do not repay anyone evil for evil. Be careful to do what is right in the eyes of everybody. If it is possible, as far as it depends on you, live at peace with everyone. Do not take revenge, my friends, but leave room for God's wrath, for it is written: "It is mine to avenge; I will repay," says the Lord. On the contrary: 'If your enemy is hungry, feed him; if he is thirsty, give him something to drink. In doing this, you will heap burning coals on his head.' Do not be overcome by evil, but overcome evil with good."*

In this last paragraph of chapter 12, Paul broadens his concerns from personal morality and relationships within the church to relationships outside the Christian community; *viz.*, when we receive evil. Christians were an endangered species that within the next ten years would be the target of a gay dictator, Nero, in one of the worst abuses and slaughter of innocent people in history. What is a Christian supposed to do when he or she receives evil?

I. The First Principle: Do Not Repay Evil for Evil (17-19)

The principle is stated first in positive terms:

A. Live at Peace

The Old Testament Hebrew concept of peace was a combination of an internal tranquility, and peaceful relations with God and with others. That is all inclusive in the greeting of *shalom*. An old English greeting of Christians was similar: "Good morning, brother, is it well with your soul?"

"Live at peace with everyone," is the simple instruction that enables us to "not repay evil for evil." Since Paul understood the sinfulness of the human heart, he added a double qualification. First, "if possible." It isn't always possible. Peace requires both parties to want it. Second, "as far as it depends on you" recognizes there are those times when

one cannot be at peace because the other party doesn't want it. So, if we cannot live at peace, neither are we to take revenge for wrong received. Put in the negative the principle is...

B. Do Not Take Revenge

There is a distinct difference between following the procedures of a legal system to obtain justice for wrong or evil, and seeking revenge. Revenge is "acting independently of or beyond the law".[126] A legal system is established by God, Paul says in the next chapter, to provide justice. Following the provisions of that system is not taking revenge.

The merchant in Shakespeare's play sought a pound of flesh as payment of debt. That's hardly looking for justice, but abusing the legal system to obtain the revenge of a deep-seated hatred. If legal justice is pursued, it must be in a spirit of forgiveness for the wrong received.

Western law has utilized the principle of *lex talionis* in establishing justice for wrongs committed against others and society. It is the *"eye for an eye"* principle. "The principle of *lex talionis* is to restrict the destructive effect of penal consequences and to secure a measure of restitution proportionate to the victim's loss".[127] In contrast, revenge seeks to bypass that process and inflict a measure of pain the victim determines is equivalent to the pain suffered.

Quoting from Deuteronomy 32:35, Paul appealed to let God have the vengeance. That sounds like God Himself is violating His grace to forgive, and seeking revenge. Rather, it acknowledges that God holds every personal attribute in perfect harmony. For Him to execute justice or vengeance is

---

126   James D. G. Dunn, *Word Biblical Commentary*, Vol. 38 (Dallas, Texas: Word Books, Publisher, 1988), 750.

127   John Macquarie, *A Dictionary of Christian Ethics* (London: SCM Press, 1984), 297.

not in violation of His mercy or His grace. Perfect law is only found in Him. The violation of His law requires His response.

Our problem in obeying Paul's command is a lack of true faith that God is sovereign and will really do what is right. We're afraid that He will be too soft, and we want the other person to hurt at least as much as us or a little bit more.

Proverbs 20:22 states: *"Do not say, 'I'll pay you back for this wrong!' Wait for the LORD* [YHWH—the faithful covenant keeping God] *and he will deliver you."* The promise of God's justice to correct wrong is either true or a lie. Faith requires we live as though they are true.

At the root of waiting on God is His longsuffering. This is a main theme of the Old Testament. Psalm 78 is an historical recitation of Israel's sins and God's patient and persistent grace. *"Yet he was merciful; he forgave their iniquities and did not destroy them. Time after time he restrained his anger and did not stir up his full wrath. He remembered that they were but flesh, a passing breeze that does not return"* (:38-39). Every one of us ought to be very thankful God is gracious and long-suffering. Were He not, we would all be hopelessly lost. That is how we are to respond to receiving evil.

Also, God has overcome evil with good, as we are commanded to do. The ultimate expression of this was the crucifixion of Jesus in which God sent His only begotten Son for the express purpose of overcoming evil. It required death on the cross. God sends rain on the just and the unjust. Contrast this biblical approach with the holy war idea, Jihad, of the Islamic religion.

II. The Second Principle: Overcome Evil with Good (20-21)

A. Do Not Allow Evil to Control Responses

The Bible consistently presents that behavior comes from the heart. The word for "evil" in verses 17 and 21, refer to intrinsic evil, or that the heart is the source of evil behavior. It is a worthless heart. Another word, *ponayros*, is hurtful referring to behavior that comes from and evil heart. The opposite of an evil heart is a good heart in verse 21. This is an intrinsically good heart. Right or honest behavior comes from a good heart.

"Do not repay anyone evil for evil;" "do not be overcome by evil." Any act of revenge is succumbing to evil in the same way as the person who did evil to us was overcome by it. We are only inviting the vengeance of the Lord against us in the same way we look for God's vengeance against those who have done evil to us.

B. Determine to Defeat Evil by Doing Good

Verse 20 is a quotation from the Septuagint translation of Proverbs 25:21-22. What is striking in Paul's use of the passage is his omission of the final phrase: *"and the LORD will reward you."* It could be a clue to a proper interpretation of heaping "burning coals of fire on his head."

My first impression of the phrase has been to see it as adding fuel to the final judgment God will bring upon the offender. With Paul's omission of "and the LORD will reward you," one could not think of using 'doing good' as a means of adding to the misery of the offender. Rather, the phrase seems to say that by doing good in response to evil, the heart could be changed and the offender won to Christ and to us.

Verse 17 says to *"not repay anyone evil for evil."* The word "evil" here and in verse 21 means was is intrinsic or the heart that produces worthless behavior. Another word akin to this (*ponayros*) refers to hurtful behavior that comes from an evil heart. The opposite of an evil heart is a good heart identified in verse 21. That is a heart intrinsic with good. It a right heart or honest heart and produces behavior that is "right" or good. It means to be sensitive to the views of others and carries the idea of beauty or worth. It is translated in other places as honorable. We are to think before we act by taking into full account all of the factors and points of view.

The last word of the chapter, "good," is in the present tense which indicates we are to pursue the good with a dedicated persistence. The first act of goodness is to forgive the wrong. Jesus showed us how by forgiving those who were crucifying Him.

I read the account written a number of years ago by Wurmbrand, a man who had been imprisoned by the communists for his faith. "I have seen Christians in communist prisons with 50 pounds of chains on their feet, tortured with red-hot iron pokers, in whose throats spoonfuls of salt had been forced, being kept afterward without water, starving, whipped, suffering from cold, and praying with fervor for the communists…. Afterward, [these same] communists came to prison, too.

"Now the tortured and the torturers were in the same cell. And while the non-Christians beat the former torturers, Christians took their defense. I have seen Christians giving away their last slice of bread (we had at that time one slice a week) and the medicine which could save their lives to a sick communist torturer who was now a fellow-prisoner."[128]

128 Richard Wurmbrand, *Tortured for Christ* (London: Hodder & Stoughton, 1999).

Application

New Age people deny the existence of evil, much like Christian Science. Shirley MacLaine wrote of evil in *Dancing in the Light* that "It doesn't exist. That's the point. Everything in life is the result of either illumination or ignorance. These are the two polarities. Not good and evil. And when you are totally illuminated, such as Jesus Christ or Buddha or some of those people, there is no struggle any longer."[129] Someone should have told Jesus that when He cried in agony on the cross, "My God, my God! Why have You forsaken me?" There He became sin to resolve the problem of evil that MacLaine says doesn't exist. Tell that to Mary Vincent, in 1978 a 15-year-old, who was mutilated and left for dead by Lawrence Singleton in Patterson, CA. Tell that to the millions of Jews who were crammed into cattle cars on their way to extermination in Auschwitz. Tell them, "Hitler wasn't evil, what he did wasn't evil. He was simply not illuminated." He was illuminated–by the same deceptive force that gave birth to New Age religion.

Jonathan Edwards, the great Puritan preacher and commonly acknowledged as one of the greatest minds America ever produced listed five vows as a young man. The fourth was "never to do anything out of revenge." Paul adds that we are to overcome evil with good.

Is it right to press charges when the police reports indicated the person had committed the crime? Most certainly. You might be involved in lawsuits; some might be seeking a resolve to conflicts. Pastors and lay staff are bound by law to report incidences of child and sexual abuse.

---

129   David K Clark; Norman L Geisler, *Apologetics for the New Age: a Christian critique of pantheism* (Eugene, Or.: Wipf & Stock, 2004, ©1990), 212.

At heart in this passage is our confidence that God alone is the final avenger of wrong, and maybe some of us will be surprised. We are to respond to offenders with kindness whether they are Christians or not. If we stoop to vengeance, we are being overcome by evil ourselves and in the same condition as the one who wronged us. If we seek revenge, we take away God's options of handling His enemies. When He gets vengeance, He does it right. If we try to get it, we'll likely botch it up.

While it is appropriate to seek justice within the legal system of our government, we must also settle the issue of our own need to forgive when wronged and to treat the offender with kindness.

It is right to expose sexual abuse to the legal process for the purpose of God working justice through law. An abuser should not be defended or protected. History and studies confirm, they don't stop with one offense. Unless they are caught, punished and worked with, they will continue their abuse.

What good thing can you do this coming week to the person or persons who have done evil to you? Some options might include to send a birthday, anniversary, or congratulatory card or some kind of gift. Exposing an abuser to legal authorities is an act of goodness. It is not good to let the person go on in their harmful and destructive behavior.

My wife and I have had to confront these Scriptural demands on a very personal level. I won't go into detail other than I have not wanted to bless the person who has brought tremendous hurt. The flesh wants to get even, not bless them. We are told to bless and curse not. We are told here to find a way of doing good to them. What are you facing? Were you the object of sexual, emotional, or physical abuse? Have you been cheated in business? Have you lost a job or a contract because of someone else's deceitful practices? Do your parents not understand you? Do you think they are too strict? What is the issue? Do you know someone who has been deeply hurt, who has received evil? How do you think you could best come along-side that person to encourage and strengthen them?

It is possible for the bowling ball of someone else's evil to knock down the pins of our life. More likely, we will be eaten up by our own inner passions of bitterness, anger and self-pity. God's gracious power will enable us to forgive. God's gracious power will enable us to conquer our drive to get even.

"Do not be overcome by evil. Overcome evil with good. As much as is possible, live at peace with everyone."

For your reflection:
- Everyone has been hurt at some point, or multiple times. If the offenses have been resolved, were any of these principles involved? What was the hardest for you?
- Who do you need to forgive?

36

Romans 13:1-7

The Christian's Relationship to Government

"Christianity started out with a most serious handicap in the eyes of Roman law, for the sufficient reason that its founder had been convicted and executed on a charge of sedition by the sentence of a Roman judge. The charge was summed up in the inscription attached to his cross: 'The King of the Jews' Whatever was the nature of the kingship which Jesus claimed, the one record of him known to Roman law was that he had led a movement which challenged the sovereign rights of Caesar. When Tacitus, many years later, wishes his readers to know what kind of people Christians were, he deems it sufficient to say that 'they got their name from Christ, who was executed under the procurator Pontius Pilate when Tiberius was emperor' [Tacitus, Annals, 15-44]. That adequately indicated their character."[130]

Scripture: Romans 13:1-7

Main Idea: Submission to governing authorities is commanded. Why? Because God is sovereign, which includes control of national leaders.

Introduction

Historian Will Durant observed, "In those days, the [Roman] government gave them bread and circuses. Today we give them bread and elections, but it is just a change in the

---
[130] Bruce, 219.

style of periodical amusement."[131] Thomas Jefferson wrote: "The whole of government consists in the art of being honest." Now that would be some change from today's norm. Who could qualify?

Speaking of politics... The senator was campaigning for re-election in a rural section of the country. His long-winded address had been going on and on, punctuated only by occasional gulps of water. During one of these very brief pauses an old farmer turned to his neighbor and observed in a loud whisper, "first time I ever saw a windmill run by water!"[132]

A basic premise of biblical interpretation is the necessity of understanding the historical context of a passage. This is certainly vital to our Scripture. What was Roman democracy and politics like? We cannot impose our own form of democracy on our understanding of this passage.

Biblical scholar, James Dunn, of England, wrote on this.

"Within the political structures of the Roman state the responsibilities and powers of government were clear. These responsibilities and powers were exercised by a few by right of birth, or connection, or wealth, or ruthless self-advancement. For the rest, the great majority, there was no political power and no realistic hope of wielding it. For modern commentators accustomed to the centuries-old tradition of developing democracy, the political realities of the ancient society, including not least the Roman Empire, are hard to grasp. It would not even have occurred to Paul and his readers that they could exercise political power in a Roman city, far less that they by their efforts might change its structures. All they could do was to live within the structures which existed, accommodate to them—as everyone had to—and seek to benefit from whatever rules or rights the governing authorities granted, such as Julius Caesar had granted the Jewish synagogues.

---

131 *Toastmaster*, p 135
132 Ibid., 183-4

So, Paul's opening exhortation was simply the common-sense wisdom of the great mass of the powerless living within the power structures of the corporate state."[133]

What is the Christian's responsibility to government? Democrat, Republican, Independent, Watergate, cynical, soft money.... Let's look at the opening statement which establishes the command of the Christian's basic responsibility to government.

I. Christians are Commanded to Submit to Governing Authorities (1-2)

"Everyone must submit himself to the governing authorities, for there is no authority except that which God has established. The authorities that exist have been established by God. Consequently, he who rebels against the authority is rebelling against what God has instituted, and those who do so will bring judgment on themselves."

A. Implications of the Command

The command defines an attitude. The grammar indicates a believer is to subject oneself, rather than being forced into subjection by political power or enforcement. Back in the mid-1960s, three out of four Americans said they trusted the federal government to do what is right all or most all the time, according to Gallup. In 1984 that figure had dropped to 44%. By 1994 only 19% had that kind of faith in the government.[134] The September 2015 Gallup survey 55% had little or no trust in the government. Submission is more than behavior, it requires an attitude of respect for the position, if not the person in office. That is lacking in our country today and explains the discontent and political battle of 2017.

---

133   James D.G. Dunn, *Word Biblical Commentary, Vol. 38, Romans 9-16* (Dallas, Texas: Word Books, Publisher, 1988), 770.
134   *Ministry Currents*, Jan-Mar 1994

A second implication is the basic difference in a democracy as opposed to a dictatorship. Democracy requires Christian involvement. Theodore H. White said that "although Christianity has never been the guarantee of a democratic state anywhere in the world, no democracy has ever thrived successfully for any period of time outside of Christian influence."[135]

Third, submission is to more than to the law, it is to the governing authorities. We are to submit to the people in the offices of power. The opening clause is a blunt charge by the apostle and is inclusive of authority whether political, parental, or secular authorities. Dunn wrote that the phrase "has the clear sense 'subject, subordinate,' and in the middle or passive, 'subject oneself, be subjected, subordinate'".[136] This is our responsibility, not something God does.

B. The Basis of the Command

"For there is no authority except that which God established." The foundation of Paul's argument is the sovereignty of God who works through authority in both civil and religious spheres. Elections, political power-plays, and all other authorities exist within His span of control.

C. Rebellion is Rebellion Against God

If we rebel against God-established authority, we are in rebellion against God himself. Does that preclude the right to protest? No because our laws grant that right. When the protests degenerate into property destruction and injury to others, it is out of bounds to the law of love and respect.

---

135   *Citizen*, April 20, 1992
136   Ibid., 760-761.

II. The Primary Role of the Government is the Safety and Welfare of Its Citizens (3-5)

The *Constitution of the United States* preamble states: "In order to form a more perfect Union, establish justice, insure domestic tranquility, provide for the common defense, promote the general welfare, and secure the blessings of liberty...."

That is why our government exists. Observation reveals we have drifted a long way from those roots because of social engineers who have ignored the religious and ethical values in which the *Constitution* was rooted.

"I don't know of any government program that's helped the family. I think every government program I know of, and I'm responsible for some, has ended up hurting families rather than helping them."[137]

Where has the experiment in social restructuring taken us? One writer expressed it well. "The reason homeowners have guns is that they have lost faith in the government to provide for public order."[138]

A. Rebels Should Fear

Fear of government is reserved for those who violate the law. Fear is a deterrent to evil. Our problem is the same as faced by ancient Israel. Ecclesiastes 8:11 states: *"When the sentence for a crime is not quickly carried out, the hearts of the people are filled with schemes to do wrong."* It seems to me that the courts have done more to facilitate crime than to deter it or to carry out justice. A part of this discussion is the place of civil disobedience. When can a person say with Peter, 'We will obey God rather than man?' We should have no fear

---

[137] Francis A. J. Ianni, author and professor of education at Teachers College, Columbia University [in *Family in America,* Aug 1992]
[138] "America must bite the bullet on society's decline, not guns" by Woody West. *Insight,* Jan 10, 1994 [Vol. 10, No 2], p 40

in going through customs, or the cars with Christmas flashing lights on the roof because we voluntarily function within the law. When we don't, we suffer the consequences unless there is an officer filled with grace talking to us.

B. The Civil Ruler is God's Servant

The word for 'servant' is *diakonos*, from which we get 'deacon'. James Madison said, "If men were angels, no government would be necessary. If angels were to govern men, neither external nor internal controls of government would be necessary."[139] Unfortunately, many governments aren't servants; they are demagogues imposing their desires and mind-set on their constituency. Because of the reality of sin, God established government as an agent of His wrath. Yet, if government fails to perform its God-given role, then the nation becomes subject to God's wrath. Submission by the citizen to government and the government to God, is required, not optional.

We have been blessed by many outstanding Christian statesmen. One was John Ashcroft who told how an old man accompanied his son to Washington, DC. The son had been elected senator and was to be sworn in.

"The father was eager that the son serve well. In a prayerful time of dedication, commitment, and devotion on the morning of the swearing-in ceremony, the elderly father told his son that 'the spirit of Washington is the spirit of arrogance, but the spirit of Christ is the spirit of humility.' He looked his son directly in the eye and admonished him with a clarity which went beyond speaking. He said, 'Nothing of lasting value in the world has ever been accomplished in the spirit of arrogance.'

---

139 quoted in *Insight*, Apr 4, 1994.

"As the group of friends and family assembled around the son to pray, the newly-elected senator noticed his father trying to get up off the sofa to join with the group in prayer. Noticing the father's struggle, the son turned to his father and said, 'Dad, you don't have to struggle to stand.' His father with weakness but clarity said, 'Son, I'm not struggling to stand; I'm struggling to kneel.'

"And he knelt by his son and prayed that the Spirit of Christ would be a mantle which would cover his son in humility so that he would have no regrets.

"That day," says Senator Ashcroft, "was the last day of my father's life. He died on his way returning home to Missouri. If you can freeze that frame for a moment—an ailing, aged father not struggling to stand but struggling to kneel and pray beside his kneeling son—you can observe a picture of what will help save America."[140] Would that we had more people with that kind of history serving in government. That is why you and I must pray.

III. The Rationale for Taxes (6-7)

A. Our Taxes Support God's Servants

The Old Testament economy was based on a theocracy in which God was the ruler. The money paid in tithes supported the priesthood and government. One author calculated the amount to be around 28% of a person's income. On top of that money, the people were asked to bring free will offerings to build or repair the temple facilities. That isn't too far from our own situation today.

---

140   *Intercessors for America Newsletter*, Dec 1995, p 3.

B. We Owe More Than Taxes

We are not only to pay our taxes, we are to pay respect and honor to those in position to receive it from us. There is a direct application to honesty in filling out our tax reports.

Application

The first step in Bible study is to attempt to understand what the Bible passage is saying and how it was understood by those who first read it. We gained a little insight into Roman politics in which Paul lived. However, we aren't in Rome. We live in the United States of America. Toward the end of the Twentieth Century a powerful political force called the "religious right" emerged. Many Christian people, aware of the spiritual drift and loss of moral foundation, thought that electing a Christian president would be the source of revival, of a spiritual renewal in America. They found out that it was an illusion. Jimmy Carter had his problems. The Reagan era came and no revival.

Writing on "God and Politics" and the disillusionment that followed the eighties, Charles Colson said: "I think the true explanation lies in our disregard for these two key truths: first, the solutions to all human ills do not lie in political structures; and second, it is impossible to effect genuine political reform solely by legislation. Many Christians, like much of the populace, believe the political illusion; this is, that political structures can cure all our ills…. What [government] does best is perpetuate its own power and bolster its own bureaucracies."[141]

Am I saying a Christian should not be involved in politics? Quite the opposite. As citizens in a republic, Christians have a power to shape government and culture

---

[141] Charles Colson with Ellen Santilli Vaughn, *Against the Night: living in the new dark age* (Gospel Light Publications, June 1999), 117.

by active involvement. It begins with voting. In spite of my spoken despair over the seeming hopelessness of the Washington mess—it seems to me good people get elected and when they get to Washington they catch a virus that attacks their brain and they lose basic powers of reason and ethical discernment—I still vote in every election. If you are inclined to political involvement, do it. But don't be blinded to think God will bring spiritual and moral renewal through national, state, or local government. That must come through God's people confronting personal sin, getting their consciences cleansed, and living as light and salt. Though many decry our national condition, too few are desperate enough to turn from their sin. The other vital expression of submission is prayer.

As we discuss this issue, there are other things to keep in mind. Dr. James Skillen, Executive Director for Public Justice, wrote in the *Evangelical Dictionary of Theology* on "Government". He pointed to two key biblical factors. First, there is no ideal biblical form of government. "Nowhere in the Bible does God put forward an ideal of monarchy or republicanism or some other political system as the unchanging truth for our aspiration."[142]

The second key factor is that the modern state "requires a thorough understanding of political and economic history, and thus the kind of education that we give our children is crucial."[143] My personal concern is that secularists, whose bias against Christianity is pronounced, have re-written the history of the United States to edit out the influence and role of Christianity both in society and in the lives of leaders. An

---

142   J. W. Skellen, "Government, the Biblical Witness", in *Evangelical Dictionary of Theology,* ed. Walter A. Elwell (Grand Rapids, Michigan: Baker Book House, 1984), 477.
143   Ibid., 479.

accurate portrayal of our history has to be found outside of public education textbooks.

When a government refuses to function by God's edict, then those in power, and the nation itself by extension, will come under his wrath. Mark Shields wrote in *World*: "It is an unwritten rule in Washington, DC: You have to belong to a church, but you cannot practice your faith."[144] We must live in submission and we must pray faithfully and fervently that God will raise up godly servants in government.

To summarize: name calling of the President of the United States is out; obedience to the law is in, so long as such law does not violate biblical principles.

For your reflection:
Look up the role of the church in the Underground Railroad during the Civil War and explain why that movement was not a violation of this Scripture.

---

144   Mark Shields, *World Magazine*, January 30, 1993.

37

Romans 13:8-14

God's Wakeup Call to His People

"Before the Lord Jesus comes back as the sun to light the new day, He will come back as the morning star to raise from the dead all who have believed in Him and to transform all living believers. After this will come the blackest hour the world has ever seen. The old proverb that the darkest hour is just before the dawn is borne out by this outline of prophecy. I cannot state too strongly that the key to understanding Bible prophecy is to realize that it not only concerns itself with the details of the age in which we live, but its prophecies have their fulfillment in the future. Trends are indicated, tendencies are pointed out, but the detailed march of armies and destruction of multitudes lies in the future. The seals of the Book of Revelation, the trumpets and vials, are all judgments to be visited upon this earth after the Lord has removed His own."[145]

Scripture: Romans 13:8-14

Main Idea: Because the coming of Jesus Christ is nearer than ever before, we must love our neighbor, wake out of our spiritual stupor, and live holy lives.

Introduction

We were sitting in a coffee roasting company enjoying a wonderful dark roasted cup of coffee and a healthy apple-fritter. A young male was talking with one of the two gals taking care of the business. The conversation was about

---

[145] Barnhouse, Vol. IV, "God's Discipline", 153.

romance and marriage. He said to her, "Do what you want to do—you know what I mean?" That is a fair summary of a basic premise that drives talk show conversation, the counseling office, as well as everyday talk. There are no absolutes to guide a person in making moral decisions. You are the only god there is, so do what you want to do. Don't be controlled by what happens to others or whether it is right or wrong, do what you want. As Christians, there are other factors to life's choices than merely what I want to do.

One of the greatest motivating forces in Christianity is the expectation of the return of Christ. It gives great hope when we fall into despair. It keeps us going when we want to quit. It enables us to step back and see a bigger picture. The second coming of Christ forces us to confront the reality that we will one day face God and will be accountable for life's choices.

In our Scripture, the second coming is God's wake up call to His people. Verse 11 reads: "And do this [the command to love in verses 8-10], understanding the present time. The hour has come for you to wake up from your slumber, because our salvation is nearer now than when we first believed. The night is nearly over; the day is almost here." If the "day" was nearer in Paul's time, how much more so today. Because Christ's coming is near, the burden on Paul's heart is that we love one another and that we clean up our act. He did not say since Christ's coming is near we should go out and win the lost. Why? The Great Commission commanding us to make disciples as we go about our daily activities has not changed. In the first chapter of this letter, Paul declared he was not ashamed of the gospel because it is God's power to save people. He devoted five chapters of this letter explaining that a right relationship with God is not the result of people keeping some moral code or following religious rituals. If people are lost and lost people matter to God, you would think his most pressing concern for his readers would be to get out there and get the job done.

Paul doesn't say that. He tells us to awake from our spiritual torpor and love one another. Wake up and live right. I think the issue is this. Jesus said the singular evidence of our belonging to Him was not our evangelistic zeal but our love for each other. When the world sees His reality in our ability to love in the middle of diversity, they will become open to His truth. That is what many call "contagious Christianity." In addition, why should anyone give a second thought to the message of Christ if there is no evidence of a changed life. If Christians carouse around in immoral living, booze it up, fight and squabble like everyone else, why should anyone take our message seriously. George Barna's surveys consistently state there is little difference in the behavior of Christians and non-Christians. That's a sad indictment.

God's wakeup call is for Christians to love each other and for us to live holy lives.

I. The Soon Return of Christ is a Wakeup Call to Love (8-10)

A. The On-going Debt of the Christian is to Love

One of the areas in which religion has excelled is writing lists of do's and don'ts. In fact, that is probably one of the first things that comes to a person's mind when they think of religion or church. In this paragraph, Paul followed the lead of Jesus in reducing all the laws that govern human relations to just 'one-rule living:' We are to love our neighbor as ourselves.

The immediate question that comes to our mind is, "Who is my neighbor?" Those who are familiar with the Bible will immediately think of Jesus' story of the Good Samaritan who came to the aid of the man left beside the road by robbers. Various representatives of the religious establishment refused to stop and give aid, but a despised Samaritan showed mercy and love. In that story, the crossing of racial boundaries is explicit. Others of you will think of the hurting within the Christian community. Paul's repeated call to love demands a wider inclusion of people. How wide?

Who are we to love? One writer pointed out two limiting factors. One is the word 'neighbor' itself. "The neighbor is the person encountered in the course of daily life who has a need which lays claim to the believer's resources."[146] The second is the limitation of the resources one has as a neighbor. God does not expect a person to bankrupt themselves to help all the hurting of the world. That is a demand beyond reason.

George MacDonald wrote: "A man must not choose his neighbor: he must take the neighbor that God sends him.... The neighbor is just the man who is next to you at the moment, the man with whom any business has brought you into contact."[147]

A second question is, 'What is love?' Stuart Briscoe wrote: "There is no doubt that love has its romantic and its sentimental aspects. That love has sexual connotations goes without saying, but the love of which Paul speaks is a choice to behave in a certain way, not necessarily because of romantic, sentimental, or sexual feelings, but simply because it is right."[148] The word is *agapao* which the love energized within a person by the Holy Spirit. He does not give impure love.

The rationale for one-rule living is love will not behave in a way that harms another person. As a result, through love a

---

146   Dunn, 783.
147   Bob Benson; Michael W Benson, *Disciplines for the Inner Life* (Nashville: Thomas Nelson Publishers, 1995), 330.
148   Briscoe, 238.

person fulfills—crams full—the law. Other Scriptures pour a lot of light on how love behaves. In Ephesians 4:2, Paul wrote that love is patient causing us to tolerate one another. At the end of the same chapter, he informs us that love forgives when wronged in the same way God has in Christ forgiven us. In 1 Thessalonians 5:11 we are to encourage one another and build each other up. Hebrews 10:24 tells us to find ways to stimulate one another to love and good works and all the more as we see the Day approaching. In Galatians 6:2, we are to carry each other's burdens.

Paul began his statement with the statement: "Let no debt remain outstanding, except the continuing debt to love one another." He tells us why he wants us to love, because one who *"loves his fellow man has fulfilled the law."* Some have attempted to use this statement as an absolute prohibition of debt. Money and indebtedness are not the topics of the passage. Nor does the language make that point. It is not so much a prohibition against debt as a statement to keep debt repayment on target. Don't be careless in ignoring your financial obligations. The sin is not in owing money but in failing to meet our obligations in paying our debts. What leads to that sin is another sin, that of consumerism, frenzied buying to fill some personal longing.

The late popular Presbyterian pastor from Philadelphia, Donald Grey Barnhouse, said "There is nothing morally wrong in renting a house to live in. The house is the property of the owner. The renter moves into the house. He does not own the house nor does he owe on the house. He owes the rent. He benefits from the capital which the owner has put into the house, and he is paying the interest, which is rent. Every rent day the tenant must pay the rent. This is the sense of our text, 'Owe no man anything.'"[149]

If you have gotten yourself so into debt you can't meet your obligations, don't blame it on God, or on your circumstances, or someone else. You may be a victim, but most likely you are only a victim of your lusts. Get out of debt. How can you win someone to Christ when you've robbed them by failing to pay your debts?

B. How Love Does and Does Not Behave

As is so often the case in the Bible, to enable us to understand the point, it is placed in a negative form so we will better understand it when stated positively. Paul cites four of the ten commandments. They deal with behaviors with one another: "*Do not commit adultery,*" "*Do not murder,*" "*Do not steal,*" "*Do not covet,*" and then he throws in the whole load, "and whatever other commandment there may be" are all summed up in the one-rule of love our neighbor as ourselves. What does that mean? Don't go to bed with someone other than your spouse [Jesus said if you look and lust you're an adulterer], don't murder [Jesus said if you hate, you're a murderer], don't steal, don't lust after stuff that isn't yours. All of those are unloving behaviors. Where do they come from? A heart separated from God and controlled by its own sinful nature.

The apostle John is in sync with the apostle Paul. "*Do not love this world nor the things it offers you, for when you love the world, you do not have the love of the Father in you. For the world offers only a craving for physical pleasure, a craving for everything we see, and pride in our achievements and possessions. These are not from the Father, but are from this world*" (1 John 2:15-16).

---

149   Barnhouse, IV, 127.

II. The Wake-Up Call is to Holy Living (11-14)

A. Motivation: The Return of Christ is Near

A particular word is used for time that refers to a set or proper time. A critical time for action, not simply the passing of normal time. There is a strong sense of urgency in the structure of the language. The day of our salvation is nearer than when we first believed. The tense of the verb, *'believed'*, refers to an act of commitment that began their Christian experience. A person doesn't slip into a relationship with God. There will be a time of developing understanding as a person seeks answers to their questions, but becoming a Christian requires a deliberate choice. Have you made that choice? Would you like to make that choice of receiving Jesus as your personal Savior and Leader? Do you want to participate in the wonderful day of release from this world and its degraded life to experience the joys of God forever? It is yours for the asking if you will believe in your heart Jesus died for your sins and rose again victorious over death's grip, and confess with your mouth Jesus is Lord. Believe on the Lord Jesus Christ and you will be saved.

B. Action: Shape Up and Live Holy

The moral climate of Paul's day was very similar to the pop culture of the United States. We are to "put aside the deeds of darkness and put on the armor of light." 'Put aside' literally means to excommunicate. His readers fully understood the meaning of getting kicked out of the synagogue or some other organization. We are to literally kick out certain behaviors so we can replace those behaviors with others.

There are three groups of two's. First, kick out orgies and drunkenness. 'Orgies' refers to carousing in letting loose. What helps us remove the barriers of restraint? Some form of drunkenness. This cannot be restricted to alcohol abuse, for the root, *methē*, means an intoxicant. Among the first things to go in drunkenness is moral restraint.

The second pair is immorality and debauchery. The word translated immorality means a couch and by implication a male sperm. It refers to sex outside of heterosexual marriage. Because of the sinfulness of the human heart in its search for sensual thrills, the inevitable result is excess, or debauchery. What is scary is the attempt of many to justify moral excess as acceptable behavior and appropriate depiction by the arts.

The supreme court nominee who was trashed by the liberal wing, Robert Bork, published his critique of American culture, *Slouching Towards Gomorrah*. A chapter is dedicated to illustrating the decline of moral restraint and sensibility as expressed in popular music, the cinema, and television. Remember those romantic lyrics of fifty years ago sung by Bing Crosby and Perry Como? Compare them with gangster rap language which is so filthy and subject matter so degenerate, I can't quote it in this audience. "Liberalism...," Borg wrote, "celebrates the unconstrained self, and savages those who would constrain."[150] After describing a confrontation of William Bennett and C. DeLores Tucker, a Democrat and head of the National Political Congress of Black Women met with the top Time-Warner executives to protest the filth they were marketing. The executives refused to read the lyrics out loud. They talked about finding "root causes" of crime and violence. That Tucker and Bennett were only talking about "symptoms". Bork reported that Bennett asked them "whether there was anything so low, so bad, that you will not sell it." After a long silence and a couple of "baloney" responses by Bennett to the hollow responses he was getting, Time-Warner chairman, Gerald Levin, objected

---

150   Robert Bork, *Slouching Towards Gomorrah, Modern Liberalism and American Decline* (HarperCollins; Twelfth Printing edition, June 1, 1996), 125.

to such language and walked out of the meeting. This from a man whose company published every vulgarity known. Bork's appropriate response to the statement, that offensive lyrics are the "price we pay for freedom of expression," was he "might as well have said that crack addicts are the price you pay for a free market."[151] We aren't approaching debauchery, we are embracing debauchery by listening to it and supporting it as we buy the filthy products. Every time we laugh at alley-cat humor we are affirming our own debauched mind.

Those four words—orgies and drunkenness, sexual immorality and debauchery—may leave many of us thinking we escaped, that we are okay. The next two might take us all in, "Not in dissension and jealousy." Those seeming innocent sins of the spirit are not so innocent. They are a part of the more gross behaviors of humanity. My wife, Sandra, commented, "Criticism and griping are viruses." They are highly contagious and are spread by breathing as we talk. How much griping and criticism have you participated in this last week? We are to excommunicate these viruses from our lives by nailing them definitively to the cross. Jealousy goes a step beyond dissension to mean a desire to destroy a competitor as Tanya Harding's attempt on Nancy Kerrigan years ago in ice skating competition for the Olympics.

If we aren't to live in those six descriptives, then how are we to live? We are to "clothe yourselves with the Lord Jesus Christ, and do not think about how to gratify the desires of the sinful nature." Don't even think about satisfying your sexual lusts. Do you have sexual lusts? Most people do. Do you fanaticize your lusts? Don't even think about it. Don't give forethought about how to satisfy them. If we don't think about our lusts, then, what are we to do? We are to clothe ourselves

---

151   Bork, 131.

with the Lord Jesus Christ. We are thrown back to Paul's previous discussion in chapter eight. There he told us that a mind-set on the flesh, the sinful nature, will produce death. A mind set on the Holy Spirit will bring life. We have culturally bought into the big lie that the way to life is through sensual indulgence that goes outside the lines. Can the Christian enjoy sex? The God who made us sexual is the God who wants us to enjoy all of its fragrant nectars. He established the boundaries for our protection, not to rob us of enjoyment.

There are choices to be made. The choice to excommunicate sin. The choice to clothe ourselves with Christ. We begin the Christian experience with a choice to believe in Jesus. We continue our walk with Him by making daily choices to throw out sin and do what is right through His gracious enablement. The picture of baptism is burial in the water in the death of our old life, and resurrection to a new life. The new life is lived in the power of the Holy Spirit.

Application

Verse 13 triggered the conversion of licentious Augustine, who became one of the greatest minds and most dynamic Christians of Christendom. 2 Peter 3:11-12: "Since everything will be destroyed in this way, what kind of people ought you to be? You ought to live holy and godly lives as you look forward to the day of God and speed its coming." 1 John 3:2-3: "*Dear friends, now we are children of God, and what we will be has not yet been made known. But we know that when he appears, we shall be like him, for we shall see him as he is. Everyone who has this hope in him purifies himself, just as he is pure.*"

Judge Bork, who does not profess a personal religious commitment, acknowledges in this book the necessity of a strong religious commitment by the majority of the population as necessary to halt our "slouch toward Gomorrah." "Whether the link between religion and morality can be demonstrated conclusively, as I have come to believe it can, it is true that the coming of trouble in our culture coincided with a decline in the influence of religion."[152]

The coming of Jesus is certainly nearer now than when Paul wrote. Even if it might be decades away, you could die this week. That reality is to move us to pay our financial debts. There is one debt we will never pay off and that is our debt to love each other. Are there people you need to encourage or strengthen? Is there someone you need to forgive?

Since the coming of Christ is near, we must excommunicate sin, clothe ourselves with the Lord Jesus Christ, and not think about how to satisfy our wrong sensual desires. Some of you need to go home and throw out the pornography, not just the slick magazines, but the soaps and cheap novels that titillate your lusts. Some of you need to kick out the critical spirit and karate chop your jealousy.

All of us need to keep our noses in the Book that will empower us to clothe our minds and wills with Jesus himself.

---

[152] 273.

For your reflection:
- Look up the following verses to see the consistent correlation of the return of Jesus to how we are to manage our lives today. Then, conduct a self-examination on areas the Holy Spirit is prompting change. We can be and do differently because of the indwelling presence of the Spirit Who imparts power to change entrenched patterns of behavior.
- 1 Corinthians 1:7-8; Colossians 3:4-5; 1 Thessalonians 3:12-13; 5:23; 1 Peter 1:13-16; 2 Peter 3:11; 1 John 2:28; 3:2-3
- Take particular note of the action words in each passage. What is the sense of urgency? Does this affect only a part of our lives or is it all inclusive?
- List the different words used to describe the quality of life and look them up in a dictionary to better understand how to apply them.

38

Romans 14

We Are Different, but We Don't Have to be at Each Other's Throat

"There has been much difference of opinion as to the source whence this weakness came and the background that gave to it its precise complexion. To be less positive than some exegetes have been would appear to be necessary. Rome was cosmopolitan and so was the church there. It may have been, and the evidence offers much to favour the thesis, that various types of weakness proceeding from different backgrounds and influences were represented in that situation which the apostle envisaged. It is not necessary to suppose that all within the category of the weak were characterized by the same kind of weakness. Some who were weak in one respect may have been strong in a particular in respect of which others were weak. The diversity may be the explanation of Paul's treatment. This passage deals with the question of the weak and the strong in a way that applies to every instance in which religious scrupulosity arises in connection with such things as those exemplified in this chapter."[153]

Scripture: Romans 14

Main Idea: In any size group of people, diversity is a given. However, in the church, it doesn't require conflict—we can get along. Paul lists six principles for getting along with others.

---

153 John Murray, *The Epistle to the Romans*, Vol. II, F. F. Bruce, General Editor, *The New International Commentary on the New Testament* (Grand Rapids, Michigan: Wm. B. Eerdmans Publishing Co., 1965), 174.

Introduction

We have two great children, a son and daughter, our son crossed the 60 line and our daughter is in her late fifties [2019]. They couldn't be more different even though both have the same mom and dad. That such is true in your family is a given, and amazing fact of life. Our subject is the family of the church getting along in spite of the diversity of personality, gifts, style and preferences.

Churches seldom fail because of outside pressures, but through internal conflict. Our nation most likely will not be conquered by another country. If it fails it most likely will be through the warring factions which too frequently become headlines. The curse of the church, Catholic and Protestant, has been its tendency to argue, to dispute over matters that are not clear-cut.

Even though the Bible states that the flesh produces anger, conflict and dissension, churches continue to succumb to the power struggles of carnal people who seek to impose their point of view. I have never personally experienced a church split. Most that I have read or heard about were not caused by substantive issues—by that I mean the fundamental core values of Christianity such as the Trinity, the person and work of Christ, heaven and hell, sanctification, or other like basics. Rather, a pastor may be on a power kick, or a group of people in the church don't like the service style, music, or some other non-essential thing.

Philip Van Auken wrote in *Clergy Journal* of three root causes of conflict in the church:

1. One source is people not feeling like group goals are their own. Goal-setting is something most churches do very well, but they often neglect to "sell" these goals to the grass-roots members. Leaders often don't become

aware of the undercurrent of resentment until non-cooperation or apathy becomes a problem.

2. A conflict may be ignited by one individual or group not being willing to defer some of their own goals for the sake of reaching larger goals that are more important to other groups or the church as a whole. An "us versus them" mindset robs them of any willingness to accept even short-term sacrifices to make long-range benefits possible.

3. Personality differences and immaturity on the part of members often spark conflicts in the church. Team efforts are frequently sabotaged by individual attitudes of stubbornness, mistrust, and insensitivity.[154]

Our Scripture lists the attitudes and behaviors necessary for a church to keep together even though there is great diversity. These principles are also directly applicable to the family unit. I have summarized the chapter in the sermon title: "We are different, but we don't have to be at each others' throats." The first principle involves an attitude that directs our behavior:

I. We Must Accept One Another (1a)

"Accept him whose faith is weak"

Godet wrote that this "denotes one whose faith falters (becomes weak) at a given moment and in a special case."[155] The conflict that Paul addressed could be expressed in traditional-liberal terms. Please do not put your political definitions on these terms, but allow me to use them according to the following definitions. The traditionalists were Jewish believers who held on to the religious practices of their Hebrew background, such as Sabbath and dietary restrictions, and

---

154   Philip Van Auken, *Clergy Journal*, "How to handle church conflict," Mar. 1992, p 44-45.
155   Reinecker, *Linguistic Key to the Greek New Testament*, 379

special religious days. They felt these had a valid place in the new movement of Christianity. The liberals of Paul's group rejected the Sabbath regulations, circumcision as essential to salvation, and the other religious cultural values and practices of the traditionalists.

At this point the scene can get touchy for Paul refers to the traditionalists as "weak", and the liberals as "strong". The traditionalists saw themselves as standing for principle but in fact their stand was a point of weakness of faith. To rigidly hold any church practices or traditions above the core values of the faith is weak faith. Any attachment of human works to a person's acceptance before God is a weakness of faith. Remember that Paul spent five chapters in this book carefully establishing the position that a right relationship with God is not the product of following religious practices or of trying to keep a moral code. We are made right with God by faith in the saving work of Jesus in His life, death, and resurrection.

The strong are to "accept" the weak without passing judgment on their position. The word, "accept", means to "take to one's self." It is used "of God receiving or helping man and of men receiving others into fellowship and companionship."[156] For strongly opinionated people to treat each other with that kind of civility and courtesy would take supernatural power and that is just the point. What God asks the believer to do is what He in grace has supplied through the personal presence of the Holy Spirit living in and through the human being. Our first principle for getting along is to accept one another.

---

156   Ibid. 379.

II. We Must be Non-judgmental in Non-essentials (1b-3)

Accept him whose faith is weak without passing judgment on disputable matters. One man's faith allows him to eat everything, but another man, whose faith is weak, eats only vegetables. The man who eats everything must not look down on him who does not, and the man who doesn't not eat everything must not condemn the man who does, for God has accepted him.

I am using the term *non-essentials* define the word, "disputable matters." What are disputable matters? In this specific context, disputable matters refer to vegetables versus meat as a diet. Today, it might be illustrated by the question that so many people ask: Why are there so many denominations? It is because of disputable matters, things in which the Bible gives flexibility of interpretation. What do I mean? The mode of baptism: whether sprinkling, pouring, or immersion. The doctrine of last things, whether the church will be translated before, during or after the tribulation or whether the millennium is literal or spiritual also fall into this area. Style of worship, day of worship, ministry program, dress codes for church, or bringing in a cup of coffee, are "disputable matters."

The problem is when you have been told all of your life that you are the special chosen people of God and God's people are circumcised, God's people eat vegetables, you don't give that up very easily. It became a crisis of identity for both the Jewish converts and Christianity itself. The Jewish believers felt very justified in bringing to the table their traditions which were their *"boundary markers."*[157] Paul told the so-called liberal to not despise the traditionalist, and the traditionalist to not condemn the liberal.

---
157   Dunn, 811-13.

In the same way, people today have grown up in church with the identity markers of certain rituals, the recitation of the Apostles' Creed, hymns, rules of behavior and dress that are not biblical mandates, and other personal preferences. The weakness is the tendency to make those boundary markers of their church experience, the boundary markers of Christianity itself. Those who reject those things are not to despise those who hold those positions, nor are those who hold those positions to condemn a different group of preferences.

III. We Don't Own Other People, God Does (4-11)

"Who are you to condemn another man's servant?"

Here is a fundamental argument in this debate: *We do not own other people and so have no business judging someone who belongs to God.* Beyond that, Paul says these things don't cause a person to stand before God. It is arrogant of us to judge others when viewed from this perspective. Yet we don't think of it that way. We have our personal convictions about things and sometimes we even feel heroic about protecting the church from decay. *"We're standing for what is right,"* we say to ourselves and probably to sympathizing friends. *"Why those scandalous new people; we never did it that way before. What is this church coming to, anyway?"*

In Paul's illustrations, the one who eats meat gives thanks to God and eats. The one who abstains, thanks God for his vegetables. "If we live, we live to the Lord; and if we die, we die to the Lord. So, whether we live or die, we belong to the Lord." It is really simple, isn't it? Why do we have to complicate it? It seems we have to for all the wrong reasons, one of which is control, and another is the arrogance of *"I'm right, and everyone should live by my rules."*

In verses 9-11, Paul reminds us that the very reason Jesus came, lived, died, and rose again was to gain ownership of people He saves. He is the judge before whom all of us will stand, so we ought to get out of each other's face.

IV. Each Person is Accountable to God (5, 12)

There are two statements that relate to this point:

(5) "Each one should be fully convinced in his own mind."
(12) "So then, each of us will give an account of himself to God."

In non-essential matters, it is a personal position before God that must be definitive. A number of years ago I wrote the following as an attempt to establish moral boundaries without degenerating into legalism. Here is a summary of behavioral standards as I attempted to express at the time. I was strongly influenced by Frances Schaeffer's *True Spirituality*.

> "We feel the following statements summarize the kind of life God expects of His people. We view these as guidelines as well as goals of attainment which serve to remind us to be holy as He is holy. We affirm that believers are called by God to live a disciplined life under the Lordship of Christ and in obedience to His Word. Such a life requires daily Bible reading and prayer, regular personal witnessing and fellowship with other believers. Specific attention should be given to establishing personal standards of behavior based upon Romans 12-16, Ephesians 4-6, Colossians 3 and James. The basic issue is to love God with our whole heart, soul, mind and strength and our neighbors as ourselves. Unthankfulness and covetousness are inconsistent with loving God and our brother. The Christian should abstain from all appearance of evil. In love for his brother, behavior that causes another to stumble should not be continued, nor should the believer allow anything to form a habitual mastery of him other than Jesus Christ. We are to give ourselves to the pursuit of a life pleasing to God."

The final resolution of this issue is every individual will stand before God to account for themselves. You are going to stand before God for *your* life, not someone else's. We are not to live *for* one another, we are to live *for* God.

V. Each Person is Responsible to *Not* Put a Stumbling Block Before Others (13-16)

At the same time that the liberal is not to despise the traditionalist and the traditionalist is not to condemn the liberal, neither is to be guilty of throwing stumbling blocks into the path of the other. A *stumbling block* is an opportunity to take offense. An *obstacle* is a snare, a stick that causes one to stumble into a trap.

Note in verse 15 that if one believer caused a fellow believer *distress* by eating meat, then they were not acting in love. This principle goes contrary to the radical individualism of our day that claims personal rights without regard for the group. A society can't hang together with everyone only concerned for themselves, neither can a church, and neither can a family.

VI. We Must Keep Our Focus on Core Values (17-23)

Paul listed some core values of Christianity. He stated in verse 17, the "kingdom of God is not a matter of eating and drinking, but of righteousness, peace and joy in the Holy Spirit." Righteousness here means as much our relationship with others as it does our relationship with God. God is concerned about honesty, fairness, and love in the workplace and the home. It matters to God. He doesn't want His people cheating in school or business. He wants us to learn to live in peace, to get along with each other, which will require deferring our personal rights. The thrust of this whole chapter is the title of the message: "We are different, but we don't have to be at each other's throats." Let's get along. And our lives ought to be full of joy.

What does this mean? Verse 19 tells us to "make every effort to do what leads to peace and to mutual edification. Do not destroy the work of God for the sake of food." May your church never bite the dust as a church divided over non-essentials.

Applications

Each one of these points is applicable to unity in the family.

1. Family members need to accept each other and not try to reshape each other. Wives need to accept their husbands and husbands their wives. Brothers need to accept sisters and sisters their brothers. Now, that may seem impossible, but God is the author of the impossible.

2. Families need to cut each other some slack in non-essential items. One of the key issues for parents is to draw the right lines of battle. Often parents make minor things major and then they undercut the ability to make the major issues important. Parents need to agree on what their core values are and what things are "non-essential".

3. Parents also need to remember they don't own their children, God does. Parents are to manage what belongs to God. We are stewards. That attitude will communicate respect for the dignity of the children. In the same way, husbands don't own their wives. Spousal abuse flows out of the unbiblical idea that a husband owns his wife.

4. Families need to remember they will individually stand before God to account for their lives and no one will be able to play the victim game. If you mess up in

breaking God's laws, you will be held accountable for your choices and you won't be able to pass blame on to someone else or the government.

5. Family members shouldn't try to trip up each other and get each other in trouble.

6. Families need to keep right priorities. Getting money and accumulating things aren't listed as a core value. Righteous living, obedience to God's Word, being people of peace and not conflict, and living joyful lives are core values. I don't get it, but a lot of people I look at seem like they would crack their skin if they laughed. We are to be joyful. Let's lighten up and act like we are walking with the God who loves us and is blessing us.

Which of those six areas do you need to work on in your relationships within the church, and which do you need to work on at home?

For your reflection:

- Think about an instance of church conflict in your experience. How did it affect your attitude, your relationship with the Lord, and with that congregation? What role did you have in the conflict and how do you think it might have been avoided?

- What are areas where you think your church quibbles over "non-essentials"? Is this helping or hurting the church? How might it be addressed in a constructive way?

39

Romans 15:1-7, 13

Learning to Accept One Another

"Paul continues his discussion from chapter 14 on how believers should relate to one another, especially when there are disagreements on matters of opinion. There is no question that a variety of opinions on many matters will be represented in any church—and the church in Rome was no exception. Paul uses "strong" and "weak" to describe the believers. "Strong" believers are those who understand their freedom in Christ and who are sensitive to the concerns of others. They realize that true obedience comes from the heart and conscience of each individual. "Weak" believers are those whose faith has not yet matured so as to be free of some of the rituals and traditions. "Strong" believers can function in a variety of situations and be influences for good; "weak" believers find that they need to stay away from some situations in order to maintain a clear conscience. But both are still *believers*, and both are still seeking to obey God. As long as these matters of conviction do not entail disobedience to God, strong believers must not look down on their weaker brothers and sisters, and weak believers must not judge and condemn the freedom of stronger brothers and sisters (14:1-12). Also, strong believers must not flaunt their freedom in a way that hinders the spiritual growth of the weaker brother or sister (14:13-23). Our best example for dealing with others in the church is Jesus Christ. We should imitate him."[158]

---

158   *Life Application Bible, ibid.*

Scripture: Romans 15:1-7, 13

Main Idea: The key to unity in the church, enduring in our faith, and encouraging one another, is giving total, unconditional acceptance to each other through the enabling of the Holy Spirit.

Introduction

Max Lucado wrote, "Some time ago my wife bought a monkey. I didn't want a monkey in our house, so I objected.

"'Where is he going to eat?' I asked.

"'At our table.'

"'Where is he going to sleep?'

"'In our bed.'

"'What about the odor?' I demanded.

"'I got used to you,' said my wife. 'I guess the monkey can, too.'

"Getting along with others doesn't begin by demanding that others do what we want, but in accepting that we aren't so perfect ourselves."[159]

Accepting one another requires accepting warts as well as smooth skin, those who aren't so beautiful as well as the beautiful, those who are going through problems as well as those who seem to have it together. The church hasn't always done well with that, and neither has the home.

All through church history, conflicts have plagued the church. The issues have varied widely from theological differences to personal dress. Paul stated it was a matter of accepting one another.

The problem Paul faced with the Romans is discussed in chapter 14. Some Christians felt the Old Testament Hebrew kosher rules no longer applied in the new Christian community.

---
159   Max Lucado, *New Man*, Nov/Dec 1995, p 18.

Others felt those old rules were still valid and that it was totally wrong to eat any meat and so only ate vegetables. Another dynamic of this problem was addressed in Paul's letter to the church at Corinth. The meat sold in the marketplace had been offered as a sacrifice to idols, in essence, as demon worship. In addition, some Christians in Rome wanted to respect the Old Testament holy days while others said it didn't matter what day it was—every day is a day God has given.

Two thousand years later, the church faces the same type of thing. At the turn from the nineteenth to the twentieth century, most fundamental churches condemned the radio as the devil's box. A controversial issue today is whether the 19th century hymn, the 20th century gospel song, Maranatha Scripture choruses, or the contemporary rhythmic, guitar driven and electronic music is acceptable for the church. To keep the folks happy, many churches are offering different venues with various music styles.

Paul used the word "strong" to refer to people who said, "Food is food. What a person eats has nothing to do with being made right with God. That is ours as a free gift of God's grace. Furthermore, it was openly sold and so had nothing to do with worshipping idols." "Weak", refers to people who said, "The Old Testament food regulations are an inherent part of the worship of a holy God and distinguish us as His people. That meat has been a part of demonic worship. You can't be a Christian and eat that stuff."

The position of those who were strong was that the grace of God had no strings of performance attached to salvation. The weak said it is a distortion to think such things aren't an elementary part of Christianity.

Rather than discussing these matters, I will talk about accepting personal weaknesses and the weaknesses of others as a community of believers. The key to unity in the church, to enduring in our faith, and to encouraging one another is giving total, unconditional acceptance to each other through the enabling of the Holy Spirit. That is what God has done for us in Christ. Also, there is a direct application of these principles to the home.

I. The Church is a Place Where Strong People Lend a Hand When Others Fail (1, 7)

> *"Those of us who are strong and able in the faith need to step in and lend a hand to those who falter, and not just do what is most convenient for us"* (Peterson, The Message).

A. Who is Strong and Who is Weak?

Paul is not talking about how much a person is able to bench press when he spoke of the strong helping the weak. The word refers to "powerful people." The implication is of a power to dominate others, not of physical strength. In this specific instance, it means people who more thoroughly grasped the concept of God's grace.[160]

The man who wrote this was Mr. Strongman, Paul the Apostle. How strong was he, really? He described himself as weak and subject to discouragement. He told the Corinthians he had not come to them as a skillful orator but rather in "weakness and fear and with much trembling." He was a personal demonstration of God's grace working in power in a weak person, **not** an example of the superman who strides through life with it all together.

I've viewed David as the consummate man. He wrote of himself: "I am poor and needy, and my heart is wounded within me. I fade away like an evening shadow; I am shaken off like a locust" (Psalm 109:22-23).

---

160   Dunn, 837.

We want our leaders to be strong. In fact, they are weak like us. All of us are a combination of strengths and weaknesses. Leaders have public responsibilities, they have heavy accountability, but they also have weaknesses. Even though they have weaknesses, they are to lend a hand to those who struggle and not reject them.

B. Jesus' Acceptance of Us is Our Standard for Accepting Others (7)

"Accept one another, then, just as Christ accepted you."

Here's my working definition of grace. Grace is a word God uses in the New Testament to describe everything He has done to provide for our weaknesses, sin, failures, and limitations. A popular definition is *unmerited favor*—God's goodness to us that we do not deserve. We accept grace in God's gift of salvation. We often do not accept grace for our personal needs or weaknesses. In Jesus God has met our deepest needs for significance, security and being loved as a free gift of grace. We do not have to look to any other person to make us feel good about ourselves or to be accepted.

I have known that to be true intellectually, but all throughout my life I have tried to prove my worth by achieving highly. The church has put a premium on performing well, especially on those who are "platform people."

In August, 1991, I found my emotional tank had run dry. I had read articles and listened to discussions about burnout. I considered it something of a cop-out until I found myself fighting to survive the deadness in my inner life. During the previous two years I struggled to prepare sermons and to be "up" for Sunday. I felt I was ineffective as reflected through a declining attendance and financial struggles. I did not wish to put my burdens on the congregation or others. I thought that if

I kept hanging in there, I'd come around the bend and be back to my old self. I pled with God to strengthen me in my inner self. However, my fatigue continued.

Sandra and I went to a counseling center in southern California that specializes in pastors and their wives. During a month of intensive counseling and reflection, I learned a little of what was behind my workaholic habits. Christians who don't drink can piously condemn substance abusers while abusing their families and personal lives in work orientation. I could excuse taking on additional positions or study programs as a part of my serving God. In reality, I was caught in a trap of seeking to gain a sense of worth and approval from other people that can only be found in Christ.

Robert McGee wrote in *Search for Significance*:

"We strive for success, driving our minds and bodies harder and farther, hoping that because of our sweat and sacrifice, others will appreciate us more. But the man or woman who lives only for the love and attention of others is never satisfied—at least, not for long. Despite our efforts, we will never find lasting, fulfilling peace if we have to continually prove ourselves to others."[161]

That was Roy Price. I lived by the motto: "He who dies having done the most, wins." Seeking significance in work was one of my weaknesses. What are yours? Denying we have any is only fooling ourselves and limiting us from experiencing God's grace that provides for our weaknesses.

Again, McGee in *Search for Significance*:

"I have great worth apart from my performance because Christ gave his life for me, and therefore, imparted great

---

161   Robert S. McGee, *The Search for Significance* (Houston, Tex.: Rapha Pub., 1994), 11.

value to me. I am deeply loved, fully pleasing, totally forgiven, accepted, and complete in Christ."[162]

I encourage you, moms, dads, kids, and others, to learn that statement and repeat it frequently. It will help you accept your true worth and value. You and I do not have to prove our worth to anyone. You have worth, not because of what you do, but because Jesus has given you value. That is our significance.

II. The Purpose of Acceptance is to Build and Encourage (2-4)

> *"Strength is for service, not status. Each one of us needs to look after the good of the people around us, asking ourselves, 'How can I help? That's exactly what Jesus did. He didn't make it easy for himself by avoiding people's troubles, but waded right in and helped out. 'I took on the troubles of the troubled,' is the way Scripture puts it* (The Message). (4) *For everything that was written in the past was written to teach us, so that through endurance and the encouragement of the Scriptures we might have hope"* (NIV).

None of us will be able to make the progress we could make in our personal lives until we find a few other people who will give us total and unconditional acceptance. We need others to help us see our weaknesses and be honest about ourselves because we tend to deny our weaknesses. Other people can gently hold us accountable for our attitudes and behaviors. In the safety of a trusted relationship, we can face our needs and learn God's supply for those needs. There are two sides to this. I need to be willing to be transparent. Others must be willing to accept my concerns with integrity and stand with me. The church should be a place where weak people are accepted. The home ought to be a place where unconditional

---
[162] *Ibid*, 61.

acceptance is given to children. Kids should not be given the concept that their worth is tied to performance.

Our role as friends is to accept one another, **not** to fix up the other person. Most of us—especially pastors—think we know how to fix others. When someone shares a need, a weakness, a problem, thirty-nine fix-it solutions are offered. Acceptance is allowing someone to talk about what is going on in the inside without offering some formula to fix it.

The Holy Spirit and the Word of God are our primary fix-it sources. We are to offer total and unconditional acceptance of one another which gives the Spirit room to work. I hesitate to refer to the Bible because many have grown up in a Bible church. We can throw verses at people like dartboard champions. There is a time when sharing a related verse is appropriate, but that comes along with the full communication of total and unconditional acceptance of a person and their weaknesses. Such an acceptance of the person is not to be confused with an acceptance of their behavior, which might be sinful. By understanding grace appropriately, we can distinguish between the person and behavior.

Several years ago, a Christian therapist served as a trusted friend for me. I had not been willing to look at my workaholic behavior and the damage it was doing to my marriage and to me until the pain became so great I was forced into it. Confronting that matter, and other issues, was not easy, but it enabled me to begin to change. It is important to understand that real inner change is the product of the Holy Spirit, not of our efforts to change ourselves. Pain brings us to the place where we are willing to look at the stuff on the inside and bring our garbage to Jesus who has the power to do something with it. Other people who totally and unconditionally accept us can help facilitate our taking action.

We are to accept one another so that the Lord can fix us, not so we can fix each other. However, we are to bear one another's failings. This is the same word used in the Greek Old Testament in Isaiah 53 of the Suffering Servant, Jesus, who bore our sicknesses. Paul also used the word in Galatians 6:2. To bear others' failings and not please ourselves requires those who are strong in the grace of God to not force their freedom on others. It means to not attempt to fix up others by setting them straight. It means to be patient and tolerant of the differences of maturity level within a body of Christians.

III. The Goal of Acceptance is Worship (5)

"May the God who gives endurance and encouragement give you a spirit of unity among yourselves as you follow Christ Jesus, so that with one heart and mouth you may glorify the God and Father of our Lord Jesus Christ. Accept one another, then, just as Christ accepted you, in order to bring praise to God."

Worship is more than expressing praise to God. It is being honest with our feelings. It is facing our weaknesses and failures. It is bearing others' failures in prayer as we hold them before God. As we are honest about ourselves and experience the fullness of God's grace to meet our deepest needs, we will bring glory and praise to God. Then our songs of praise will flow out of true heart experience, not just some formal religious ritual.

McGee gave five elements needed for emotional healing.

1. Honesty—being aware of our needs;
2. Affirming relationships. We need another with whom we can share the inside stuff;
3. Right thinking—each of us has an elaborate array of defenses which cause us to deny we have a problem or need;

4. The Holy Spirit—God is the only one who can fix what is wrong on the inside;
5. Time—we don't change with one prayer or one visit with a skillful counselor. It takes time to change.[163]

Conclusion

Janice Sue Zeiler wrote of the vital role parents have in expressing acceptance. In her instance, her father failed to affirm her love:

> "I remember when I was five or six years old having a big writing tablet on which I could do block printing."One day I took a sheet of tablet paper, folded it in half, and wrote 'I love you' on the inside. I put my dad's name on the outside, covered the sheet with hearts, and set it on his dresser. I had made a valentine for him, and it wasn't even Valentine's Day! Eagerly I anticipated what I thought would be an enthusiastic response. It never came.
>
> "The next afternoon I discovered the valentine in the wastebasket. 'This has to be a mistake,' I thought. 'He must not have seen it.' I lifted the valentine from the trash and carefully stood it up in the center of his dresser. My heart was pounding the next day when I checked the wastebasket. It was there again! Only this time it was crumpled with some other papers.
>
> "'He must not have liked it!' I thought. 'Or maybe he didn't see it.' I smoothed out the creases as best I could and placed the valentine on his dresser once more. I made sure that it was very conspicuous so that this time he would see it.
>
> "The next day Dad called me to him. I remember feeling very shy. 'Will you quit putting that note on my dresser?' he demanded. 'I already know that you love me!'

---

[163] . *Ibid.*, 32-34

"When I became a Christian, I thought about finding that valentine in the trash and about how hurt and angry I had felt. Why hadn't my dad reached out in love to me?

"Then I thought about Jesus. Jesus had put a valentine on my dresser. It had my name on the outside, and on the inside it said, 'I love you.' The lettering was not with a pencil; it was written with blood. It cost Jesus His life to send me His valentine. I'm glad that I didn't crumple it and throw it away."[164]

I read that story and thought how could a dad do that to a six-year-old. What an emotional cripple! The home must be a place where acceptance and unconditional love are experienced. Yet, even when that is present, we must understand, our value does not come from others, but from the Lord. Moms, you will never find your full significance in mothering. Nor will you find it in a career or someone else. It is found only in Jesus and your acceptance of who you are in Him. The same is true of your children. The power enabling us to give unconditional love and acceptance is the Holy Spirit.

> If I could look through Your eyes,
>
> I'd see there's no way to impress You, and I wouldn't even try.
>
> I'd stop try'n' to prove I'm worthy, and I'd take off the disguise, if I could look through Your eyes.
>
> And I would see that I'm precious, and I would know that I'm prized;
>
> I'd know your love never changes, if I could look through your eyes.
>
> Andrew Martin

---

[164] Janice Sue Zeiler, *Decision*, Feb. 1994, p 42

My benediction for you mothers and women, is beautifully stated in verse 13:

"May the God of hope fill you with all joy and peace as you trust in him, so that you may overflow with hope by the power of the Holy Spirit."

Oh, Let the Son of God enfold You
With His Spirit and His love
Let Him fill your heart and satisfy your soul
Oh, let Him have the things that hold you
And His Spirit like a dove
Will descend upon your life and make you whole

O Jesus, Come and fill Your lambs
O Jesus, Come and fill Your lambs

Oh, come and sing this song with gladness
As your hearts are filled with joy
Lift your hands in sweet surrender to His name
Oh, give Him all your tears and sadness
Give Him all your years of pain
And you'll enter into life in Jesus' name

John Wimber

Dear Jesus, our Lord and God,

When you healed the bleeding woman, a woman who had been bleeding for 12 years, we know you were showing us how great your mercy and power are and that you are sensitive to the needs and sorrows of women.

Lord, we beg for your healing and enlightenment for women who bleed physically—whether it be because of disease or illness, self-inflicted suicidal wounds, or the injuries of abuse or rape, and especially for the blood shed because of abortion, both the mother's blood and that of her unborn child.

We plead for your love, Lord, to lift up and cradle the girls and women who suffer from bleeding hearts—those whose emotional pain only your love can heal—whether it be from abandonment, sexual or physical abuse, or from the loss of a loved one, or the inability to love themselves. We also ask that your love envelop those women so desperate for love that they turn to prostitution, adultery or other forms of promiscuity.

Knowing that your abilities are infinite, dear Jesus, we ask that you also place a healing hand on those women who are mentally abused or abusers, and on those who waste the mental abilities you've given them—either through their own choices, the will of others, or because of lack of opportunity. We also ask your guidance for those who use their minds to justify sin and poor choice, to rationalize away you and your commandments.

We pray for those women and girls who are destitute, with nowhere to turn, for those who are discriminated against because of gender, or race, ethnicity or religious beliefs, because they are too heavy or too tall, too smart or too uneducated.

Finally, dear Jesus, we ask that you place your hand in the hand of those girls and women who are trying to walk your path, who sometimes feel alone in their right choices, and just need to feel your presence to continue to do your will. We ask you to keep their families whole and their souls full of your grace.

As a father scoops his little girl up in his arms, protecting and loving her, may you, with your Heavenly Father, surround girls and women with your love, so our faith in You never falters.

Prayer given by Carolyn Ratto at 1997 National Day of Prayer

For your reflection:
- Would you describe yourself as a strong or weak Christian? If weak, how can you become stronger? If strong, is there someone you might help strengthen? How would you go about that task?
- Am I covering up things on the inside that I need to face?
- Do I have one or two other people with whom I can share my struggles?
- How can I better "lend a hand" to help someone whom I know is struggling?

40

Romans 15:14-22

The Competence of the Church

"Paul assures the Roman Christians that the teaching in his letter has not been given because he imagined they were incapable of teaching one another. He is well aware of their moral and intellectual quality and what he has written is more by way of a reminder of what they already know than by way of instruction in the elements of Christianity. Moreover, although he is not the founder of their church, he is the apostle to the Gentiles, and it is in that capacity that he had written to them. He views his apostleship as a priestly service and his Gentile converts as the acceptable offering which he presents to God."[165]

Scripture: Romans 15:14-22

Main Idea: God has invested in His church (the people) all of the tools necessary for them to fulfill His commission of evangelism and personal growth.

Introduction

Dr. Diane Komp is a pediatric oncologist who teaches and practices at Yale University School of Medicine. She told about attending a medical conference "where physicians of different disciplines exchanged ideas on difficult tumor cases. The case at hand was that of a baby who had broken all the rules.

---

165   Bruce, 244.

'Are you sure you had the right diagnosis?' asked the radiotherapist of the pathologist. 'I've never seen this particular tumor respond that way. You must be wrong.'

"'No, I'm not wrong!' responded the somewhat indignant pathologist. 'I know that tumor when I see it.'

"The radiotherapist, looking elsewhere for an explanation of the unexplainable, turned to the chemotherapist managing the case. 'That chemotherapy must have done the job.'

"'Don't look over here for the explanation. We only use a radio-sensitizing dose. Besides, the tumor was growing through the last course of different drugs. Are you sure it wasn't the radiation therapy that did the job?'

"'No way. This tumor has never gone away like that before.' He turned half-joking to the radiologist who had interpreted the scans. 'Are you sure those are the right films?'

"'Yes, they're the right x-rays! You can tell from the comparison to the old ones that it's the same child. Only the tumor is gone.

"'It doesn't make sense,' the radiotherapist kept repeating.

"The minutes of that conference simply reflected the lack of a known medical explanation for the disappearance of the tumor. The medical records did not reflect other activities on her behalf. Teams from a local church fasted and prayed daily for Bethany, two by two. Many other family friends prayed for her tumor to go away."[166]

---

166   Diane M. Komp, M.D. *A Child Shall Lead Them* (Grand Rapids, Mich.: Zondervan, 1993).

Our focus is the competency of the church as God's gifted people to carry out the mandate He has given us to bring people into a personal relationship with the Lord Jesus Christ and help them become His fully devoted followers. The competency is based on God's equipping His people to do what He has mandated we get done. Where God determined signs and miracles were appropriate, they have taken place historically as well as today. The primary point is not the miracle but our functioning as God has gifted us to serve Him. When each person in the church is responsive to God, the church is to itself and in the community what God wants it to be.

I. A Description of a Church Qualified for Ministry (14)

A. First Qualification: They Are Full of Goodness

The word for goodness is used in Galatians 5:22 as a fruit of the Holy Spirit. Paul used it in a similar sense in Ephesians 5:9 as behavior demonstrating a person is a child of the light. It means just what it says, a person is filled with virtue or what is good. The dictionary defines 'good' as "having the right qualities, excellence" (*World Book*). What determines 'right'? God does. One of His attributes is goodness. J. I. Packer wrote, "Goodness, in God as in man, means something admirable, attractive, and praiseworthy."[167] Another clarified that "the word 'good' is the most comprehensive term used when praising excellence of something."[168] Paul said the people in the church at Rome were full of goodness. It is a basic quality for ministry. A second qualification for a ministering church...

---

167 J. I. Packer, *Knowing God*, (Downers Grove, Ill.: InterVarsity Press, 2010),145.
168 D. J. Miller, "Good, the Good, Goodness" in *Evangelical Dictionary of Theology*, ed. Walter A. Elwell (Grand Rapids, Michigan: Baker Book House, 1984), 470.

B. Second Qualification: They Are Complete in Knowledge

One commentator felt the first two of these phrases were simply an overstatement according to conventional courtesies of that day.[169] How much knowledge makes complete knowledge? Those to whom Paul wrote did not even have the New Testament. They were new believers in Jesus and certainly were not seminary or Bible college trained people. Yet, Paul stated they were full of knowledge. What they had was enough for the task of evangelizing and growing in their faith, Christ's mandate for the church. If people wait until they have a certain level of knowledge so they feel comfortable, they will never get to the task of serving God.

The Princeton Religion Research Center disclosed [c. 1995] that basic beliefs are about the same as they were 50 years ago. In 1947, 95% of the population said they believed in God. Now it is 96%. In 1947, 73% believed in an afterlife. Now it is 71%. Ninety percent prayed in '47 and the same is true today. Forty-one percent attend church regularly. The paper stated: "One clue as to why religion in America remains broad but not deep is the continuing fact that the American public's knowledge of religious fact and dogma remain at the Sunday School level."[170] Even though many have an elementary knowledge of the Bible, they ought to use what they have and then get more.

Whereas 75% felt religion was "very important" in their lives in 1952, that figure had declined to 57% in 1994. A large gap exists between what people say they believe and how they live. You have enough goodness and knowledge to give yourself in service to God and others. A third qualifying characteristic of a ministering church…

---

169 Dunn, 866.
170 *Emerging Trends*, Vol. 19, No. 4

C. Third Qualification: They Are Competent to Instruct One Another

Perhaps the most important of the three statements is this one. Psychologist and popular writer, Jay Adams, based his book and counseling theory on this verse. He called it 'nouthetic counseling' based on the Greek word, *nouthēsis*, found in this verse. Strong defines this word as "to put in the mind, *i.e.* to caution or reprove gently." One Greek scholar referred to it as "to put sense into." It occurs eleven times and is often translated as "admonish" or "warn". Adams prefers the word, 'confront' to describe the meaning of this word.

Jay Adams lists three elements in this form of counseling. First, a problem must be recognized, confronted and overcome. Second, confronting the problem is done with words—we encourage, reprove, blame, and warn each other. Third, the motive is to benefit the other person.[171]

Every biblical, evangelical church is fully competent to carry out this ministry. However, a paid staff or 20% of the congregation cannot accomplish the task, every believer in the Lord Jesus Christ needs to find their place and begin to serve. Networking is one tool among others designed to assist in assessing a person's spiritual gift mix, passion, and personality style.

In Paul's day, the church met only in homes and did not have the central church campus and celebration of worship. The small group is the most appropriate forum the church offers for believers to help each other grow. I have held for many years that most of the problems I have become familiar with in counseling could be handled in a supportive small group setting. There are some issues that need other

---

171   Jay Adams, *Competent to Counsel: introduction to nouthetic counseling* (Grand Rapids, Michigan: Zondervan Publishing), 44-49.

professional input, but the run-of-the-mill issues people go to counselors about could be resolved as Christian friends, committed to each other, can help resolve and facilitate personal growth.

Christian counselor and author, Larry Crabb, wrote in *Effective Biblical Counseling*: "When it is operating biblically, the body of Christ provides individuals with all the necessary resources to appropriate their significance and security in Christ."[172] He proposed three levels of counseling that can take place in the local congregation. Level 1 is "Problem Feelings". Through simple biblical encouragement and love problem feelings can be replaced with "Biblical Feelings". Everyone can participate on this level. He explained that "someone in your class is aching about a husband who drinks every night, a daughter who is defiant and probably immoral, a bank account that's dwindling, a job in jeopardy, a marriage on the rocks, a perverted sexual desire which floods the mind with bizarre fantasies during the singing of 'Holy, Holy, Holy,' or feelings of guilt or emptiness from which death seems welcome relief, and so on and on.... The majority of people who are experiencing personal anguish can be tremendously helped by the warm, genuine interest of people who care."[173]

Level 2 deals with "Problem Behaviors" that through the exhortation of Scripture are replaced with "Biblical Behaviors". The third level confronts "Problem Thinking" that through the enlightenment of biblical thought, problem thinking is replaced with "Biblical Thinking". "A Level III counselor will look underneath the wrong behaviors into the thought world, expecting to find wrong assumptions about how to become significant and secure. These erroneous beliefs are

---

172   Larry Crabb, *Effective Biblical Counseling* (Grand Rapids, Michigan: Zondervan, 1977), 164.
173   *Ibid.*, 165-166.

the culprit. They have produced wrong behaviors which have in turn produced the wrong feelings."[174]

I have shared this model with you, and Jay Adams' comments, to illustrate that two high-profile Christian counselors have accepted the competency of the church to fulfill its primary mandate of helping people become mature believers.

Next, Paul is an illustration of a qualified servant. To say the church is fully competent to carry out its ministry, in no way disqualifies those God calls to full-time Christian service. Pastors, evangelists, missionaries, and others are a valid part of God's program. Four things characterize a qualified servant.

II. Paul is Himself an Illustration of a Qualified Servant (15-22)

A. A Qualified Servant Has Been Given Placement by God (15)

Paul said his ministry was a product of the grace of God at work in him by the Holy Spirit. God must call any valid minister to His service. The ministry is far more than a vocation someone chooses because of the work environment or ideal of helping people. Those things will not hold a person in the saddle for the long haul. As a gift of His grace God calls people to serve Him.

B. A Qualified Servant Has a Priestly Duty (16a)

Paul chose a word that referred to a temple-worker or official. "The verb here means that Paul was willing to make sacrifices as did the priests of the Old Testament.... The sacrifice has nothing to do with animals, but that which is precious to self."[175] Jesus alone was the singular sacrifice for

---

174   Ibid., 181-182.
175   Spiros Zodhiates, *The Complete Word Study Dictionary: New Testament* (Chattanooga, TN, 1992), 764.

sin and that once for all time. As a result, there is no more sacrifice for sin. Paul's sacrifice was giving his life to serve the Lord.

C. A Qualified Servant Produces the Result of Obedience to God (16b, 18)

The product God looks for in evangelism is a life growing in obedience to Him. Evangelism is much more than getting a person to acknowledge a need of a Savior or to say a prayer. The prayer of repentance of sin and faith in Jesus Christ is to move a person to begin obeying God in daily life. Anything short of that fails to meet biblical standards of evangelism.

God wants us to obey Him. If you are a true believer, you have an inside motivation to please God. If that is not present, you are likely playing a religious game with yourself. You aren't fooling God because He knows you.

D. A Qualified Servant is a Vehicle of Jesus Christ (17-22)

The only boasting Paul was interested in was boasting about what Jesus Christ had done through him.

- Paul's work was to lead "Gentiles to obey God".
- The tools Paul used to accomplish his task included signs and miracles produced by the Holy Spirit. The word for 'power' is the same used in Acts 1:8 where Jesus told His disciples they would receive 'power' when the Holy Spirit came on them. It is a power enabling them to carry out Jesus' commission to make disciples.

A review of the history of missions is that God has often accompanied the preaching of the gospel with miracles to authenticate the message when it was first delivered to a group of people. The pastor in China told my wife and me that people are frequently healed in answer to prayer. God is establishing His authority in a country that has been in darkness for so long.

Theologian, J. I. Packer, wrote, "Our expectations with regard to seeing the power of God transforming people's lives are not as high as they should be." He identified three references to power through the Holy Spirit in the New Testament. First was through "signs and wonders" (miracles in nature and healings). There is no apparent cause for these kinds of events except that Almighty God is showing His power. Second, Christ not only did powerful deeds but His words were powerful, too. The same is true of Paul. The New Testament emphasizes that God's power transforms lives. The message has power, and the messenger has power, but, third, there is also power at work in those who believe to affect a dramatic change."[176]

- Paul's passion was "to preach the gospel where Christ was not known, so that I would not be building on someone else's foundation" (20).

Though vast areas of the world have heard the gospel, there is still an incredible number which have no knowledge of Christ. May God continue to call men and women to go to unreached people-groups with the good news of Jesus. Many areas are closed to traditional missions work. People go there with creative endeavors to live and love for Jesus. Translation workers are part of reaching the yet unreached world with God's grace. Most of the unevangelized cities of more than 500,000 are in China. Missionaries can't go to China but Christians with expertise can.

---

[176] J. I. Packer, "The empowered Christian life" by J. I. Packer. *Faith & Renewal*, Jan/Feb, 1992, p 3-9.

Application

You can minister on level one by opening your heart and mind during conversations for opportunities to share someone else's feelings. It doesn't take sophisticated training, just a caring heart.

Packer stated that believers are meant to be channels through which God's power flows first into our own inner being and then into the lives of others. It always remains God's power, though. He is the one who exercises and possesses it. We must never try to have that power in order to use it the way we choose to. Paradoxically, God perfects His strength in our weakness. The more aware we are of our weaknesses, the better. Even Paul had a "thorn" that God would not remove. Yet He gave Paul the power to go on. This pattern indicates what God will most likely do for us. Then in the end we can say with Paul, "I can do all things through Christ who strengthens me" (Philippians 4:13). "That," says Packer, "is the fullest expression of the empowered Christian life."

Every one of us can experience that empowered life.

Think about it this week:
- I think my spiritual gifts would include _____ and I ought to look to serve God in _____
- What personal weakness is a place where God can demonstrate His power in your life?

**Crabb's Model for ministry within the church:
Level I: Problem Feelings-ENCOURAGEMENT-Biblical Feelings
Level II: Problem Behaviors-EXHORTATION-Biblical Behavior
Level III: Problem Thinking-ENLIGHTENMENT-Biblical Thinking

41

Romans 15:23-33

Looking to the Future

"To preach where Christ was already known would not have been disgraceful, since there the initial disgrace had been endured and overcome. But where Christ was not yet known, there the dishonor would have been new (for the Apostle) and so all the harder to bear. This the Apostle had in mind when in Romans 1:14 he said: 'I am debtor both to the Greeks, and to the Barbarians; both to the wise, and to the unwise;' and again in 1:16: 'I am not ashamed of the gospel of Christ.' This is to say, I regard this as my ministry of glory (*to preach the Gospel*); indeed, I seek my glory in that of which other, because of the disgrace (*involved*), are terrified. So also in 15:17 he says: 'I have therefore whereof I may glory through Jesus Christ in those things which pertain to God.' He means to say: (*I glory in Jesus Christ before God*), though in the world I am dishonored by (*wicked*) men. In the same way we read in Psalm 119:46: 'I will speak of thy testimonies also before kings, and will not be ashamed.' That is I am not ashamed, but regard it as my glory to speak of Thee, (*O God*).[177]

Scripture: Romans 15:23-33

Main Idea: Paul always had his eyes on the future. Our future is bright with service to God and the community.

---

177   Luther, 218.

Introduction

"At the dawn of the New Year [2013], almost two-thirds of Americans are pessimistic about the overall direction of the country, with 70 percent saying they lack confidence in the federal government to improve things in 2014, a new poll shows.

"The Associated Press-GFK survey found that 63 percent of respondents believe the country is heading the wrong way, while 35 percent said it's heading in the right direction. One percent didn't answer the question."[178]

What do you think the future will be like? Will Tesla cars replace GM as the main US auto manufacturer? What will space exploration look like in 2035? Will the U.S. be a has-been nation? What will your life be like in 2020? What percentage of the population attend an evangelical church? What will services be like—what kind of music style?

Faith Popcorn, a futurist, said [back in the nineties] "Globalnomic thinking will emerge because the current system is broken at virtually every level." A one-world mind-set fits biblical prophecy. Are we really close to the Second Coming of Jesus Christ? To escape the increasing stresses and dangers of our lives, Popcorn said we've made our homes "armored cocoons." Technology enables us to obtain nearly everything we need via telephone and computer. Virtual reality technology promises to give us access to many experiences and adventures without ever leaving home, making it unnecessary to develop social relationships.[179]

---

178   http://www.washingtonexaminer.com/poll-most-americans-pessimistic-about-countrys-future/article/2541502 (accessed 08.03.16)

179   Faith Popcorn, Gerald Celente, and Michael Tobias, "What's next?", *Psychology Today*, Jan/Feb 1995 [Vol. 28, No 1], p 34-39.

Paul was a futurist in the sense that his eye was always on tomorrow. He did not live in the regrets of past failures or problems, but always on the potential of bringing the knowledge of Jesus Christ to people. In this passage, we will see four characteristics of Paul's ministry. Each of us will be challenged to evaluate our personal lives in light of these characteristics.

I. Four Characteristics of Paul's Ministry (23-33)

A. Paul's Strategy Was Future Oriented (20)

"It has always been my ambition to preach the gospel where Christ was not known, so that I would not be building on someone else's foundation."

Paul wrote a similar statement to the Corinthians about ministry matters. He wrote,

"By the grace God has given me, I laid a foundation as an expert builder, and someone else is building on it. But each one should be careful how he builds. For no one can lay any foundation other than the one already laid, which is Jesus Christ. If any man builds on this foundation using gold, silver, costly stones, wood, hay or straw, his work will be shown for what it is, because the Day will bring it to light. It will be revealed with fire, and the fire will test the quality of each man's work. If what he has built survives, he will receive his reward. If it is burned up, he will suffer loss; he himself will be saved, but only as one escaping through the flames" (1 Corinthians 4:10-15).

This passage informs us that as a foundation-layer, Paul set goals to go to other places where the gospel had not been preached. His goal was Spain.

B. He Understood the Mutual Support of the Community of Believers (25-27)

He had stimulated the church in Macedonia to give to the poor believers in Jerusalem. His rationale is stated in verse 27: *"For if Gentiles have shared in the Jews' spiritual blessings, they owe it to the Jews to share with them their material blessings."*

It is important we understand the setting of this comment. The Jewish believers were excommunicated when they converted to Christ. Excommunication carried with it an economic embargo in which Christian converts could not buy or sell in the Jewish marketplace. They were literally cutoff from daily commerce. Following Christ carried very serious economic consequences. The community of believers was to stick together and help out when another got into difficulty. I wonder how many of us would be Christians if it cost us our job, if we couldn't buy food in the grocery stores. That is what Jewish believers faced in the first century in Jerusalem. The old prophet spoke of how believers will help one another in times of need in the future. Isaiah 66:19b-20, *"They will proclaim my glory among the nations. And they will bring all your brothers, from all the nations, to my holy mountain in Jerusalem as an offering to the LORD...grain offerings, to the temple of the LORD in ceremonially clean vessels."*

This theme runs throughout the New Testament. One of Paul's great words was *parakaleo*. A good translation is 'encourage.' In various forms, he used it 30 times. It means to come alongside and impart courage. For example, he wrote in 1 Thessalonians 5:11: *"Therefore encourage one another and build each other up, just as in fact you are doing."* Three verses later he said we are to *"encourage the timid, help the weak, be patient with everyone."*

A second great word he used also appears in verse 11—'build' [*oikodomeo*]. It literally refers to a contractor or one who builds houses. It means to build up another person. We can do that by confirming and empowering one another.

A third characteristic of Paul's ministry was prayer.

C. The Foundation of His Ministry Was Prayer (30-32)

"I urge you, brothers, by our Lord Jesus Christ and by the love of the Spirit, to join me in my struggle by praying to God for me. Pray that I may be rescued from the unbelievers in Judea and that my service in Jerusalem may be acceptable to the saints there."

He specifically asked prayer that he would be rescued from the unbelievers in Jerusalem. The account of Paul's visit begins in Acts 21. A conspiracy to kill Paul in an ambush was overheard by Paul's nephew who informed authorities. At nine o'clock that night, the Romans took Paul to Caesarea accompanied by 400 soldiers and 70 horsemen (23:12-24). God answered the prayers of the church at Rome.

D. He Practiced a Team Ministry (32)

"...so that by God's will I may come to you with joy and together with you be refreshed."

Of significance in this statement is the *humility* required to make. We think of Paul as the great apostle. He saw himself as tired and needing to be refreshed by the fellowship of fellow Christians.

In addition, it speaks of his *transparency*. Fatigue was inherent in his statement. He was at the top of the heap, but he was also willing to acknowledge personal needs.

II. Four Characteristics of Ministry at Church XYZ

A. It Must have a Strategy of Ministry

There are two parts to a good over-all thrust of ministry. One is the Great Commission in which Jesus told us to make disciples as we go about our daily experiences. The mission is to bring people into a personal relationship with the Lord Jesus Christ. That assumes, of course, that the person seeking to bring another person to Christ has that personal relationship. I can't invite you to share in something I don't know about. It also means that each person is very intentional about commitment to lost people. They matter to God and they should matter to us.

The second part of that ministry is the Great Commandment. Jesus summed up all the hundreds of laws of the Old Testament into two basic points: We are to love God with everything in us, and we are to love one another like we love ourselves.

Dann Spader in his book, *Growing a Healthy Church*, outlined a strategy in a pyramid metaphor. A church can orient its entire ministry on the pyramid of win, build, equip, multiply and send. Spader argues these five ingredients summarize how Jesus carried out His ministry. That is a good template to follow.

Strong growth requires reaching large numbers of unchurched people. Many people do not have a religious background, others have a little. How do we reach unchurched people? We reach them through our daily experiences. Every body of believers needs to find a strategy that is culturally relevant and prayerfully and persistently work at reaching those have yet to commit their lives to Jesus. If motivated by love, cynicism can be penetrated. To tell our own story of how we came to Christ and what He has done for us is hard to reject.

However, it has been proven that we can't argue someone into faith.

B. It Must Have a Vision

The vision is that by fulfilling the mission the church will become a community of believers who love God with all they have, and also love one another as they love themselves.

How is that kind of community developed? One way community is built is through small groups where true fellowship can take place and people care for each other.

In addition, a very strong educational program for children, youth, and adults will aid in that development. Finally, corporate worship will build a strong community.

C. Prayer Is Foundational

Prayer is not an appendix, though many treat it that way. Why? Is it because we seldom see anything happen as a result of prayer? One of the curses of the American disposition is instant everything. People tap their toes waiting for the microwave to finish. We are antsy and if God doesn't immediately jump to our requests, we assume prayer doesn't work. There is far more to prayer than putting an ATM card into God's big machine and getting something out. Prayer is more for fellowship with God than for asking and receiving. If prayer isn't fellowship with the Lord, we will become shallow and hollow in our spiritual life.

D. It Must be a Team Ministry

A church will never be or do what God has placed it here to do unless each member buys into team. The church is you. You are key to the church fulfilling its reason for existence. The staff exists to facilitate the membership, not to take the member's place. Ministers in God's church are the members. Pastors are coaches and shepherds to encourage, build, and equip the membership for ministry. '*Encourage*' and '*equip*' must be themes permeating every area of ministry.

Application

Paul concluded the chapter in verse 33 with a benediction: "The God of peace be with you all. Amen."

The same four characteristics of Paul and the evangelical church should have a place in your personal planning. Are you future-oriented, or are you focused on the past, the 'good old days'? Where do lost people fit in your life?

You, too, are to *encourage and build* other people. Every person can be a part of these extremely important behaviors. Have you encouraged anyone lately? Are you helping to build someone else? My wife has written a great slogan as a daily reminder: "Be the reason someone smiles today." A great testimony in dour times.

Where are you in your *prayer* life? Is it only a series of give-me requests? How much time do you spend learning from God in His Word, or fellowshipping with Him? How often do you pray specifically for your church pastor(s)? I hope you are a part of the *team*. These concepts are not oriented to a certain size of congregation. A downside of a larger church is people can come, sit, soak, and sour. They can be anonymous and uninvolved. Any church is a team ministry. For the church to reach its potential will require personal involvement. A characteristic of a dynamic churches is lay participation. People serve with joy.

Think about it this week:

- Where does service to the Lord and the community fit into your current plans for the future?
- What gifts/talents has the Lord given to you that can be used in your church?
- Is there a regular time when you get with other believers to encourage each other and pray?

Do I Have to be GOOD to go to Heaven?

42

Romans 16:1-16

The Church is Made Up of Ordinary People

"Rome was the capital of the empire. As Jerusalem was the center of Jewish life, Rome was the world's political, religious, social, and economic center. There the major governmental decisions were made, and from there the gospel spread to the ends of the earth. The church in Rome was a dynamic mixture of Jews, Gentiles, slaves, free people, men, women, Roman citizens, and world travelers; therefore, it had potential for both great influence and great conflict. The Romans had built a tremendous system of roads between the various major cities of its vast empire, so movement by people from place to place was not unusual. As Paul preached in the eastern part of the empire, he went first to the key cities—Jerusalem, Antioch in Syria, Philippi, Corinth, Athens, Ephesus. Along the way he met many believers who eventually ended up in Rome. The fact that Paul knew the whereabouts of so many of his friends and co-workers gives us a glimpse into the interest this great missionary had in the people to whom he ministered and who ministered to him. This final chapter reveals a treasury of friends Paul expected to see in Rome. Paul had not yet been to Rome to meet all the Christians there, and, of course, he has not yet met us. We too live in a cosmopolitan setting with the entire world open to us. We also have the potential for both widespread influence and wrenching conflict.

We should listen carefully to and apply Paul's teaching about unity, service, and love."[180]

Scripture: Romans 16:1-16

Main Idea: The people whom Paul greeted were not super stars, they were ordinary people.

Benjamin Franklin said, "all mankind is divided into three classes—those that are immovable, those that are movable, and those that move." The church is included with all three groups present. In my experience, church movers have seldom been the wealthy and powerful. They are ordinary people who are passionate for God and His church and devote their time and resources to carry out the mandate He has given. The church in Rome had an interesting mix of people, and I'll guess your church does as well.

Introduction

The April 21, 1997 edition of *Time* magazine featured the most influential people in America. "Among this year's 25 are good influences and dubious ones, public personalities and players so private you may not have known they were pulled up to the game board, much less that one of the pieces was you" (40). Number one on the list was Tiger Woods. His segment began with: "He has been likened by overheated journalists to Jesus, Mozart and Gandhi, and his father Earl Woods has said, 'Tiger will do more than any other man in history to change the course of humanity'" (41). As we now know, those were overblown expressions of adulation.

When listing the greatest influencers of history, one website began with Aristotle followed by Jesus Christ. Others included Galileo Galilei, Sigmund Freud, Charles

---

180   *Life Application Bible Commentary*

Darwin, Elvis Presley, Louis Pasteur, Walt Disney and George Washington among others.[181]

When Paul wrote to the little church at Rome, he sent greetings to people whom he knew. The listing of names with comments relevant to them indicates the relational, people-centered heart of Paul as a pastor of people. Those identified were not on the cover of the Roman *Gazette* as the "most influential people in Rome." In the long run, that little band of believers had a greater impact of the future of western civilization than did Caesar, the senators, and entertainers. What kind of people were they? What might Paul say about the people in your church, whether a mega church or a small congregation? I don't know, but following is some input from a pastor of over sixty-years' experience.

I. The Special People in Rome Were Ordinary People

A. Phoebe

Some suggest that Phoebe carried this letter of Paul to Rome. She was a deaconess, or as the *NIV* reads, *a servant*. The *NIV* note states she probably held a specific office. Cenchrea was a seaport town located six miles east of Corinth.

B. Priscilla and Aquila

Close friends of Paul, they were also tentmakers. When Paul visited Corinth Aquila, who was a Jew, had recently arrived from Rome. Claudius had ordered all Jews to leave the city. Paul's account is "they risked their lives for me." They also hosted a *'house church'*. This devoted couple later traveled with Paul to Ephesus. When Apollos came to that city, Priscilla and Aquila heard this dynamic speaker and discerned a lack of understanding. Acts 18:26 reads, *"they invited him to their*

---

[181] http://list25.com/25-most-influential-people-in-history-by-attribute/ (accessed, 10.25.2017).

home and explained to him the way of God more adequately." At some point, they returned to Rome.

C. Other Key People

Epenetus was Paul's first convert in Asia who now lived in Rome.

Mary worked very hard for the church in Rome.

Andronicus and Junias were relatives of Paul. The phrase, *"they were outstanding among the apostles"* can mean apostle is used in a wide sense, or it can mean they had an outstanding reputation among the apostles.

> *Verses 8-15 read: "Greet Ampliatus, whom I love in the Lord. Greet Urbanus, our fellow worker in Christ, and my dear friend Stachys. Greet Apelles, tested and approved in Christ. Greet those who belong to the household of Aristobulus* [he might have been the grandson of Herod the Great and brother of Herod Agrippa I]. *Greet Herodion, my relative. Greet those in the household of Narcissus who are in the Lord. Greet Tryphena and Tryphosa, those women who work hard in the Lord. Greet my dear friend Persis, another woman who has worked very hard in the Lord. Greet Rufus, chosen in the Lord, and his mother, who has been a mother to me, too. Greet Asyncritus, Phlegon, Hermes, Patrobas, Hermas and the brothers with them. Greet Philologus, Julia, Nereus and his sister, and Olympas and all the saints with them."*

There are several points that were emphasized to me from this list.

- Was Paul significantly influenced prior to his conversion by these members of his family who were "in Christ before I was"?
- The church grew and matured because of teamwork, not superstars.

- Women had significant roles of ministry in the church. Commenting on this, Dunn wrote: "Not least in significance is the number of women who evidently assumed roles of some prominence in the Roman churches… So far as this list is concerned… Paul attributes leading roles to more women than men in the churches addressed. We cannot rule out the possibility that the more restrictive rulings on women's participation in leadership probably reflected…a second or third generation reaction against the…earlier years" (900).
- The church crossed Jew, Greek and Roman cultural and ethnic lines.

II. How a Local Church Chooses Leaders

My experience has been mostly within the framework of the Christian and Missionary Alliance, an evangelical denomination, and these thoughts come from that experience. The bylaws of a local congregation usually outline requirements for offices and the process of choosing. For example, in my last pastorate, several requirements were listed for the office of elder. Elders were to be elected from the male membership; they shall emulate the conditions listed in 1 Timothy 3:1-12 and Titus 1:5-9. "The Biblical role of the Elder will be to: shepherd the flock and lead through example, teach and exhort, refute those who contradict truth, manage the church of God, and pray for the sick." "The management and control of the affairs of this church shall be vested in a Board of Elders, (this Board shall legally be called the Board of Directors)."

There are five points about leadership that I would add to the above.

A. Elders Must Have a Personal Walk with God

A non-negotiable is the elder's personal relationship with God. He must lead by example in consistent personal fellowship with God, reading the Bible, praying, and listening to God. Of course, a man should never be chosen if there is any doubt about his faith in Jesus Christ. He must be a believer.

B. Elders Must Practice Personal Stewardship

First, that means a man who at present is involved in ministry. No man should go from non-ministry into a position that controls ministry. That makes no sense. The elder position is not for power, prestige or control, it is for ministry and those who aren't in ministry should not be in a control position.

Second, practicing personal stewardship means he not only gives to the Lord's work, he must give to *this church's ministry*. God's standard is a tithe, or 10%. Jesus said that where a man's money is his heart is. I will raise some hackles, but I'm willing to ride out the storm. This is a line in the sand for me. I have very deep convictions about this issue, and I am weary of serving in churches that have walked on eggshells in this matter. A man should not be in leadership deciding how thousands or millions of sacrificial giving by God's people is spent if he doesn't himself give to his church. How are we going to know? Giving records can be looked at by legally authorized people. If there is no record of giving, they will not be processed. Therefore, if you don't give, and you don't want anyone in leadership to know it, then don't allow your name to be brought to the nominating committee. The privatization of giving by our culture is one of our sins. It has hurt the church. I have served where well-heeled men were elected to this highest position in the church only to find later that they didn't support the church. We aren't electing men to manage other ministries, we are electing men to manage THIS ministry. If they don't give here, they may be godly men, but their heart is not in their church.

My wife and I tithe to our church and then give beyond that to other ministries s we have means. I have a vested interest, not because I am a pastor, but because my money is tied up here. Everyone who tithes, or more, will have that same level of interest. If one doesn't give, the commitment will NOT be there.

C. Elders Must Have a Heart for Lost People

Christians in leadership should be injecting God into their friendships and sharing Christ in a clear, concise way. They should seek to develop strategies for their own peer community; for example, teachers reaching teachers, lawyers reaching lawyers, retailers reaching retailers, drivers reaching drivers, families reaching their neighborhoods.

Those in leadership need to lead by example.

D. Elders Must Be Committed to Their Church's Strategy of Ministry

Nearly all churches in the 21st century have developed a mission statement and leaders should champion the mission and strategy of accomplishing the end results. If a leader doesn't agree with who and what a church is they should not seek a leadership position.

E. Elders Must Be Gifted as Leaders

One value statement reads: "The church is to be led by Spirit-controlled people who have leadership gifts, including administration, discernment, faith, leadership, shepherding/pastoring, teaching and wisdom." If a person doesn't have one or more of these gifts in their mix, he/she should not be in the position of leading. That is no reflection on his spirituality. God designed different people for different roles.

What is a leader? Some define leadership with the general term, *influence*, which makes everyone a leader. Everyone influences someone else and some more than others do. However, there are specific gifts that are leadership gifts. They are enabled by God to provide direction for His church. In Paul's letter to the Corinthian church, he listed various gifts in chapter 12.

Administration means to steer and carries the idea of directing an organization. *Networking* assessment defines the gift as "the divine enablement to understand what makes an organization function, and the special abilities to plan and execute procedures that increase the church's organizational effectiveness. Clarifying goals and developing strategies or plans; organizing people, tasks, and events; managing details carefully and thoroughly; helping organizations or groups become more efficient."

In Romans 12:8, Paul challenged leaders to lead. There the word means to stand before or preside. Another assessment defines the gift as "the divine enablement to instill vision, to motivate, and to direct people to accomplish the work of ministry. Taking responsibility for directing groups; motivating and guiding others to reach important goals; managing people and resources well; influencing others to perform to the best of their abilities."

Those two gifts in particular are obviously leadership gifts. Including discernment, faith, and wisdom makes sense because those functions are essential in making right decisions that affect the work of God in a community. Two other gifts can be included: pastor [or shepherding] and teacher. Since the primary work of the church is educational, it only seems logical that the leadership group should include that perspective. Ideally, there would be a balance of those gifts, or representation of each gift, on the board of elders at any given time. However, that probably isn't feasible. If there are only vision casting gifts, there will be a lot of motivation from the board and not many people getting involved. If, on the other hand, the board is over-loaded with teaching types, there will be no vision and the church will flounder.

The obvious conclusion is that every person considered for a leadership position should know what their gift mix is.

Conclusion

What should you do? Some bylaws ask the congregation to submit to the nominating committee names of people they would like considered for leadership. Permission to do so should be received from the individual under consideration.

Max Lucado was quoted on a calendar: "Reliable servants. They're the binding of the Bible. Their acts are rarely recited and their names are seldom mentioned. Yet were it not for their loyal devotion to God, many great events never would have occurred."[182] "Greet one another with a holy kiss."

For your reflection:

You will be of great value to your church as you pray for your pastoral and lay leaders. Ask the Lord to give them insight, wisdom in decisions that will direct the future of the congregation, and that they will be sensitive to the promptings of the Holy Spirit in their personal, business and ministry.

---

182   Max Lucado, *God Came Near: the chronicles of Christ* (Portland, Or.: Multnomah Press, 1987), 66.

Do I Have to be GOOD to go to Heaven?

43

Romans 16:17-24

God's Ultimate Objective

"*Then those who feared the LORD spoke with each other, and the LORD listened to what they said. In his presence, a scroll of remembrance was written to record the names of those who feared him and always thought about the honor of his name*" Malachi 3:16.

"This chapter is a page from the book of life, and it give us an idea of how the records of our life will appear when the books shall be opened. The long genealogical tables which we sometimes pass over in reading our Bibles are by no means dry and uninteresting. To the divinely taught mind they are chapters from the book of remembrance, and some day others may read our names, as we are reading theirs. They tell us how God appreciates and remembers the lives and services of His children, and discriminates, with loving fidelity, between the better and the best.

"This chapter forms the climax to the principle which have just been unfolded in the previous pages, and we see them here in action and practice."[183]

Scripture: Romans 16:17-24

Main Idea: The goal of the gospel is that all people might believe and obey Him, the only wise God.

---

183   Simpson, 285.

Introduction

David Seamands, author, pastor, and seminary professor told of a newly licensed pilot flying his plane on a cloudy day. He was not experienced at instrument landing. When the control tower was to bring him in for a landing, he started thinking of the hills, towers and the buildings in the area and panicked. In a calm and stern voice, the command came: "You just obey instructions; we'll take care of the obstructions."[184]

We come to our last study in Romans. This is the first time in forty years of preaching I have made it through this great letter. In the last three verses of the letter, Paul summarized God's purposes in all He has done for humankind, that everyone might believe and obey Him. Before we examine those verses, let's look at the instruction on how to keep the church on target to accomplish this great purpose of God. Paul gives two strategies in verses 17-19.

I. How to Keep the Church on Target (17-19)

A. Avoid Problem People (17-19)

Society has problems because there are child-molesters, murderers, thieves, and addicts that will rob and destroy to buy another fix. The church has problems because it is composed of people who are contentious and cause trouble for the whole group. How can the church keep on target when there are ego-driven people who assert their will, when there are evil beings of incredible power totally set against God's agenda, and when fallible humans are responsible for its operations? Paul gives two basics.

One strategy is to *"watch out for those who cause divisions and put obstacles in your way that are contrary to*

---

184   David A. Seamands, *Living with your Dreams* (Wheaton, Ill.: Victor Books, ©1990), 79.

the teaching you have learned. Keep away from them." The primary source of the church's failure has never been the opposition of godless forces, though they have been great. The church has failed because of people who are determined to follow an agenda not mandated in the Bible. The Modernist/Fundamentalist division in the early part of the 20th century is an illustration. Many churches are stalemated because people in control don't want to obey God's command to take His gospel to others. To them, familiarity and tradition are more important than confused and lost sinners finding a Savior.

Proverbs 6:19 states that one of the seven things detestable to God is *"a man who stirs up dissension among brothers."* Though that may refer to family members, it also applies directly to the family of the church. Paul knew conflict first hand. He was the target of abusive conflict resolution when stoned by religious leaders in the Jewish community. Factions arguing over the leadership of Paul, Peter, or Apollos tore the church in Corinth. He encountered conflict when he first entered the ministry and leaders questioned his authenticity. On one occasion, he took on Peter in a face to face conflict. Conflicts are inevitable in a church, but there are people who do not care about the mandate of the church, they are out to control and impose their agendas. Those people are to be shunned. Isolation will cause them to go elsewhere.

Paul Cedar, former President of the Evangelical Free Church and former pastor of Lake Avenue Congregational Church, wrote that most contributing causes of conflict originate with sin and the work of Satan. Conflict over leaders and ministries is a major problem in churches today, as it was in Corinth. Personality conflicts emerge as a serious problem in many churches, affecting personal lives and the church's ministry. There are single-issue people who seem unable to see any other point of view than their own. Divisive people, with critical and contentious attitudes, do great harm to the church, as do chronically angry people and those who lust for power.[185]

Marks of a divisive person:
- Full of "I" language and plans. Paul wrote "by smooth talk and flattery they deceive the minds of naïve people." No offence, but people are gullible. Divisive people flatter their way into acceptance. Watch out for flattery, the person probably has an agenda.
- Makes a peripheral issue central.
- Crosses the line from issues to character attacks.
- Pretends to be spiritual by using pious language, but is full of hatred.
- Is more concerned about what is wrong with the church than what is right.
- Longs for power, but can't produce when they have it. When they have power, they divide the church.

A second way the church can keep on target is to…

B. Be Wise About Good, Innocent About Evil (19-20)

"Everyone has heard about your obedience, so I am full of joy over you; but I want you to be wise about what is good, and innocent about what is evil. The God of peace will soon crush Satan under your feet."

The word for 'innocent' means *'unmixed'*—it is a person who is one thing. 'Evil' means something that is intrinsically worthless (*kakos*). 'Good' is something worthy of admiration. Susanna Wesley was the mother of seventeen children including John and Charles Wesley, the founders of the Methodist Church, also enjoyed a wealth of wisdom. She wrote: "Would you judge of the lawfulness or unlawfulness

---

[185] Paul Cedar, "The cost of conflict" *Moody*, April 1994 [Vol. 94, No 8], 11-15.

pleasure, or the innocence or malignity of actions? Take this rule: Whatever weakens your reason, impairs the tenderness of your conscience, obscures your sense of God, or takes off the relish of spiritual things—in short, whatever increases the strength and authority of your body over your mind—that thing is sin to you, however innocent it may be in itself."[186]

Evil is at its malignant worst when it appears innocent. This week, we renamed the Tower building, at a former church, the 'Ant Palace'. Periodically we get inundated with an ant attack as we did this week. We have a flying truck service that comes to our rescue. They put food out that the ants will feed on, take it back to their home where it will do its deadly work and hopefully free us from infestation. Sin is like that. It appears good, we take it only to find the bitter poison of death.

The word for wise is taken from the Greek word for the Sophists. The word means 'clear' and is used in that pure sense here. However, in Greek culture it degenerated to refer to a clever but misleading argument, and argument based on false or unsound reasoning (*A History of Philosophy*, 55). The word 'sophistication' has this at its root. It means "to make experienced in worldly ways; cause to lose one's natural simplicity and frankness, make artificial." The Bible says the heart is deceitful and desperately wicked, who can know it?

The face of evil on our culture has these marks of sophistication:

- There are no absolutes. All so-called truth is relative.
- Sex is a sport. There is more fun outside the lines than inside.
- Religions are all the same, only surface differences.

---

186   Donald Grey Barnhouse, *Romans, Vol. 4, "God's Glory"* (Fincastle, Virginia: Scripture Truth Book Company,1964), 156.

- Satan is good. He is not a personal being, but a façade given to evil.
- People are basically good. Bad behavior is a result of a person's environment or because one is a victim.
- The way to happiness and fulfillment is through money.
- Spiritual advisors are simply gifted people who can help you make decisions that will bring you happiness and success.

We are to be innocent about evil, and wise, or clear, about what is good. Our best resource for understanding the good is the Bible and a personal walk with God in the Holy Spirit. The Bible is a lamp to our feet and a light to our path. The Holy Spirit has been sent by God specifically to lead God's people into the truth and away from evil. God is the absolute, the truth and the source of all truth. Anything contrary to Him is evil. The problem is not with God but with rebellious, arrogant and sinful people.

Our assurance is that God will crush Satan under our feet, a fulfillment of a promise found in Genesis 3:15. Paul gives us confidence of the "final triumph of good over evil, of God over the most powerful force of evil that affects this world."[187] Now we come to the primary verses that close this letter.

II. Understanding the Basics of the Gospel (25-27)

A. Life Change is God's Work, the Gospel is His Means (25)

"Now to him who is able to establish you by my gospel and the proclamation of Jesus Christ, according to the revelation of the mystery hidden for long ages past..."

The first concept that leaps out of this verse is that God is *able* to make us into people that bring honor to Him. Getting

---
[187] Dunn, 907.

us established is His job. Not only does God bring forgiveness, he make us mature in Christ. Peterson translated this: *"All of our praise rises to the One who is strong enough to make you strong."* Phillips reads: *"To him who is able to set you on your feet as his own sons."*

Jesus said to Peter, "I have prayed for you, Simon, that your faith may not fail. And when you have turned back, strengthen your brothers." You and I can be comforted that Jesus is the same today and as concerned about us as He was about Peter. He is able to establish you.

God uses preaching as His tool to accomplish this work. Elsewhere Paul said preaching was foolishness to many. People think the same today, but it is God's means of causing us to grow in our walk with Christ. Preaching centers on the gospel which was at one time a mystery, but no longer. God made known to humanity who He is, what He is like, why we need Him, and how we can know Him. It was not the random discovery of enlightened men, but the revelation of God.[188]

Part of the good news I am to preach is that God not only forgives sin and gives eternal life, but He also resolutely turns us toward right behavior instead of sinful living. God gives us the power to be different. Jesus is the answer to the deepest human needs.

B. The Gospel Has Been Around for a Long Time (26)

"But now revealed and made known through the prophetic writings by the command of the eternal God..."

The reason people in Old Testament times did not understand the gospel is because it was locked up in what Paul

---

[188] John Calvin, *Commentaries on the Epistle of Paul the Apostle to the Romans* (Grand Rapids, Michigan: Wm B. Eerdmans Publishing Company, 1955), 554.

called a 'mystery'. It was a secret that God unlocked when He sent Jesus to become our Savior.

C. God's Goal is Faith and Obedience to Him (27)

"So that all nations might believe and obey him—to the only wise God be glory forever through Jesus Christ! Amen."

Today is Father's Day. While this is not specifically a sermon to dads, this last verse has direct application. God's goal is for those who become His children through faith in Jesus to also obey Him. Love and obedience are two sides of the same coin. A child who loves their father will also obey him. False love says the loving thing but doesn't do the loving thing. When Augustine said, "Love and then do as you please"[189], he was referring to the way true love behaves.

What does God want us to obey? There are hundreds of statements that could be viewed as commands. They are imperatives, not suggestions. God tells us to…

- not be hypocrites like the religious leaders (Matthew 6:8);
- not judge one another (Matthew 7:1);
- be ready for Jesus' return (Matthew 24:44);
- be merciful (Luke 6:36);
- not fit into the world's mold but be transformed from the inside out (Romans 12:2);
- affectionately love and care for one another (Romans 12:10);
- learn to get along and think alike even though we disagree with each other (Romans 12:10);

---

189   Barnhouse, 149.

- hang in during the tough times (Romans 5:3-5; 1 Corinthians 15:58, James 5:7);
- to not link up in covenant relationships with unbelievers (2 Corinthians 6:14);
- be controlled by the Holy Spirit, not substances (Ephesians 5:18);
- obey our parents (Ephesians 6:1);
- control our sexual lust (1Thessalonians 4:4-5)
- respect those who are over us in the Lord (1 Thessalonians 5:12-13);
- keep doing the right thing and not give up (2 Thessalonians 3:13).

These are a few of God's expectations. Jesus said that every biblical requirement is summed up in just two commands—love God with everything in us, and love one another as we love ourselves. If we do those two things, we will not violate any of the hundreds of commands given in the Bible.

Wisdom speaks in Proverbs (8:32-36) and says, *"Now then, my sons, listen to me; blessed are those who keep my ways. Listen to my instruction and be wise; do not ignore it…. Whoever finds me finds life and receives favor from the LORD. But whoever fails to find me harms himself; all who hate me love death."* What does Wisdom say to sons? *"Listen, my son, to your father's instruction and do not forsake your mother's teaching* (1:8). Thirteen times Proverbs links fathers and sons in a teaching/learning role. Obviously, it assumes that dads will teach, that they will be in the home to do so. Divorce is not assumed in the Bible like it is today in our society. Sons, 99.9% of the time, obeying your father will bring good results in your life. There are times when dad isn't right in something, but obeying him anyway is right. The only time you should not obey your father is when he demands you to disobey a clear command of God. Even then, there is a right and a wrong way to approach the issue.

We don't always understand the why behind God's commands, but we can know that they are right and will bring the best results in our lives.

Application

I have referred to a great Bible teacher who was pastor of a large Presbyterian church in Philadelphia during the middle years of the 20th century, Donald Grey Barnhouse. He told the story of the young son of a missionary couple in Zaire who was playing in the yard. Suddenly the voice of the boy's father rang out from the porch, "Philip, obey me instantly! Drop to your stomach!" Immediately the child did as his father commanded. "Now crawl toward me as fast as you can!" The boy obeyed. "Stand up and run to me!" Philip responded unquestioningly and ran to his father's arms.

As the youngster turned to look at the tree by which he had been playing, he saw a large deadly snake hanging from one of the branches! At the first command of his father, Philip could have hesitated and asked, "Why do you want me to do that?" Or he could have replied, "In a minute." His instant obedience saved his life.

God's objective is obedience, not because He is a tyrant, but because sin is deadly. We delay or disobey to our peril. What are you now doing that you know God has told you to stop? Why don't you? Do you need reinforcement because the temptations are pretty strong? Is there someone with whom you can share this problem so they can stand with you?

Some time ago a man confided in me his battle with pornography and said he would get a friend to check up on him. I asked if I might periodically ask him how he was doing and he agreed. Do you need that kind of help? We can walk with one another down the path and face the dangers together instead of alone. The good news is that God is able to make you strong as you determine to be a godly man.

For your reflection:
- It seems that a critical attitude comes fairly easily. There are a lot of Monday morning quarterbacks. A willingness to be part of a solution, requires patience, time and a controlled tongue. How would you grade yourself?
- It is also easy to drift spiritually. Hebrews chapter 3 warns about the danger. How are you managing your life to avoid becoming spiritually slothful?

Do I Have to be GOOD to go to Heaven?

Conclusion

In the preface I wrote: "The core theme of Paul's letter to the Roman house churches is that heaven is a free gift we cannot earn and do not deserve, but it can be received. We do have to be good to go to heaven. The question is whose goodness qualifies a person." I hope you are able to definitely answer that a person is guaranteed eternal life in heaven based on the goodness of the Lord Jesus Christ, the God-Man, the second person of the Trinity. He laid aside His divinity, became fully human and lived a perfect life without sin. At the hands of Rome, He was nailed to a cross. There He received the full sin of all humanity suffering the wrath of the Father that we sinners might stand before a holy God clothed in His righteousness.

God now offers to us complete forgiveness as a gift of grace we have neither earned nor deserve. To receive the gift, one must turn away from self-righteousness, acknowledge their guilt of violating the good laws of God and place their trust in Jesus alone as Leader and Forgiver of their lives. It is a personal choice every person must make. None of us had a choice in our birth. To be born again into God's family requires a personal choice. How is this done? Jesus commended the man who cried out, "God be merciful to me a sinner." I would add to that, "Jesus, I receive you as my forgiveness. Come into my life and change me into the person that pleases you in thought, motive and act. Thank you for hearing my prayer." 1 John 5:11-13 reads:

> *"And this is what God has testified: He has given us eternal life, and this life is in his Son. Whoever has the Son has life; whoever does not have God's Son does not have life. I have written this to you who believe in the name of the Son of God, so that you may know you have eternal life."*

Bibliography

GENERAL

Augustine, "Confessions," *Devotional Classics*, Foster & Smith, HarperSanFrancisco,1993.

Barclay, William, *The Letter to the Romans*. Philadelphia: The Westminster Press, 1957).

Barnhouse, Donald Grey, *Romans,* Fincastle, Virginia: Scripture Truth Book Company, 1952.

Barnhouse, Donald Grey, *Romans: Expositions of Bible Doctrines Taking the Epistle to the Romans as a Point of Departure*, Vol. 3. Fincastle, Virginia: Scripture Truth Book Company,1959, "God's Heirs."

Barnhouse, Donald Grey: *Romans* Vol I, Part 2, Fincastle, Virginia: Scripture Truth Book Company,1953.

Baxter, J. Sidlow, *A New Call to Holiness: A Restudy and Restatement of New Testament Teaching concerning Christian Sanctification*. Grand Rapids, Michigan: Zondervan Publishing House, 1973.

Baxter, J. Sidlow, *His Deeper Work in Us: A further enquiry into New Testament teaching on the subject of Christian Holiness*, Grand Rapids, Michigan: Zondervan Publishing House, 1967.

Benson, Bob; Michael W Benson, *Disciplines for the Inner Life*, Nashville: Thomas Nelson Publishers, 1995.

Bork, Robert, *Slouching Towards Gomorrah, Modern Liberalism and American Decline*, HarperCollins; Twelfth Printing edition, June 1, 1996.

Bounds, E. M., *His Works on Prayer* Electronic Edition STEP Files Copyright © 2007, QuickVerse. All rights reserved.

Brand, Paul, Philipp Yancy, *Pain: The Gift Nobody Wants,* London: Marshall Pickering, 1994.

Briscoe, D. Stuart, *Romans*, Waco: Word, 1982.

Bruce, F. F., *Romans, Tyndale New Testament Commentarie*s, revised edition Grand Rapids, Michigan: Wm B. Eerdmans Publishing Co., 1989.

Bruce, F. F., *The Letter of Paul to the Romans: Tyndale New Testament Commentaries*, Grand Rapids, Michigan: Inter-Varsity Press,1989.

Calvin, John, *Commentaries on the Epistle of Paul the Apostle to the Romans,* Grand Rapids, Michigan: Wm B. Eerdmans Publishing Company, 1955.

Carnell, Edward John, *An Introduction to Christian Apologetics,* Grand Rapids, Michigan: Wm. B. Eerdmans Publishing Company, 1948.

Chrysostom, John (345-407), "Dead to Sin", *Devotional Classics,* edited by Richard J. Foster & James Bryan Smith, Harper: San Francisco, 1993.

Clark, David K; Norman L Geisler, *Apologetics for the New Age: a Christian critique of pantheism,* Eugene, Or.: Wipf & Stock, 2004, ©1990.

Colson, Charles with Ellen Santilli Vaughn, *Against the Night: living in the new dark age,* Gospel Light Publications, June 1999.

Crabb, Larry, *Effective Biblical Counseling* (Grand Rapids, Michigan: Zondervan, 1977), 164

Crabb, Larry, *Inside Out: Real Change is Possible If You're Willing to Start from the Inside Out,* Colorado Springs: Navpress, 1988.

Cranfield, C. E. B., *The Epistle to the Romans: a critical and exegetical commentary,* Edinburgh: T. & T. Clark Limited, 1987.

Dunn, James D. G., Romans 1-8, David A. Hubbard, Glenn W. Barker, General Editors, *Word Biblical Commentary, Vol. 38,* Dallas, Texas: Word Books, Publisher, 1988.

Elwell, Walter A., ed., *Evangelical Dictionary of Theology,* s.v. "Martin Luther", R. W. Heinze, Grand Rapids, Michigan: Baker Book House, 1984.

Emerton, J. A., C. E. B. Cranfield, general editors, *The International Critical Commentary of the Holy Scriptures of the Old and New Testaments, Romans, Vol.* 1, Edinburgh: T&T Clark Limited, 1975.

Geisler, Norman, *Kindred Spirit,* Autumn 88 To verify." *Leadership,* Fall 1990.

Gordon, A. J., *The Ministry of the Spirit.* Philadelphia: American Baptist Publication Society, 1894).

Halverson, Richard C., *Prologue to Prison: Paul's Epistle to the Romans,* Los Angeles, California: Cowman Publishing Company, Inc., 1964.

Hodge, Archibald Alexander, *Outlines of Theology*. London: Banner of Truth Trust, 1972.

Ianni, Francis A. J., author and professor of education at Teachers College, Columbia University [in *Family in America*, Aug 1992 "America must bite the bullet on society's decline, not guns" by Woody West. *Insight*, Jan 10, 1994 [Vol. 10, No 2].

Inrig, Gary, *Hearts of Iron, Feet of Clay*. Chicago: Moody Press, 1979.

Kerr, Hugh T. and John M. Mulder, *Conversions*, Grand Rapids, Michigan: William B. Eerdmans Publishing Company.

Komp, Diane M., M.D. *A Child Shall Lead Them*, Grand Rapids, Mich.: Zondervan.

Lewis, C. S., *Mere Christianity*, New York: Harpers, 1952.

Life Application Bible Commentary: Romans Copyright © 1992 by The Livingstone Corporation. Electronic Edition STEP Files Copyright © 2002, Parsons Church Group, a division of FindEx.com, Inc. All rights reserved.

Luther, Martin, Translated by J. Theodore Mueller, *Commentary on Roman*s, Grand Rapids, Michigan: Kregel, 1954.

Macquarie, John, *A Dictionary of Christian Ethics*. London: SCM Press, 1984.

McGee, Robert S., *The Search for Significance*, Houston, Tex.: Rapha Pub., 1994.

Meyer, A. W., quoted by John Murray, *The Epistle to the Romans, The New International Commentary on the New Testament*, F. F. Bruce, General Editor, Vol. I, Grand Rapids, Michigan: Wm B. Eerdmans Publishing Co., 1959.

Miller, D. J., "Good, the Good, Goodness" in *Evangelical Dictionary of Theology*, ed. Walter A. Elwell, Grand Rapids, Michigan: Baker Book House, 1984.

Mounce, R. H., "Gospel", *Evangelical Dictionary of Theology*, Walter A. Elwell, ed., Grand Rapids, Michigan: Baker Book House, 1984.

Murray, John, *The Epistle to the Romans*, Vol. II, F. F. Bruce, General Editor, *The New International Commentary on the New Testament*, Grand Rapids, Michigan: Wm. B. Eerdmans Publishing Co., 1965.

Packer, J. I., *Knowing God*, Downers Grove, Ill., InterVarsity Press, 2010.

Payne, Ed, *Biblical Reflections on Modern Medicine*, May 1995.

Rienecker, Fritz /Cleon Rogers, *Linguistic Key to the Greek New Testament*. Grand Rapids, Michigan: Regency Reference Library, 1980.

Robertson, Archibald Thomas: *Word Pictures of the New Testament, Vol. IV,* Nashville, Tennessee: Broadman Press, 1931.

Schaeffer, Frances A, *How Should We Then Live? : the rice and decline of western thought and culture,* London : Marshall Morgan & Scott, 1980.

Simpson, A. B., *Christ in the Bible Series, Vol.* XVII, Harrisburg, Pa: Christian Publications, Inc., n.d.

Skellen, J. W., "Government, the Biblical Witness", in *Evangelical Dictionary of Theology,* ed. Walter A. Elwell. Grand Rapids, Michigan: Baker Book House, 1984.

Sproul, R. C., *The Holiness of God*, Wheaton, Ill.: Tyndale House Publishers, 1985.

Swindoll, Charles, *Living Above the Level of Mediocrity.* Edison, NJ: Inspirational Press, 1995.

Tozer, A. W., *The Knowledge of The Holy.* New York: Harper and row Publishers, 1961.

Tozer, A. W., *The Pursuit of God,* Harrisburg, PA: Christian Publications, 1982.

Tozer, A. W., *Total Commitment to Christ,* Camp Hill, Pennsylvania: Christian Publications, 1995, Quick Verse.

Tozer, A. W., *Man: The Dwelling Place* of *God: What it really means to have Jesus Christ living in You*, compiled by Anita M. Bailey, Christian Publications, Camp Hill, PA 17011, 1966, Chapter 10, "The Old Cross and the New".

Wiersbe, Warren W., *Be Right: A practical guide to discover how to be right with God, yourself, others,* Wheaton, Illinois: Victor Books, 1978.

Wood, Skevington, *Life by the Spirit.* Grand Rapids, Michigan: Zondervan Publishing House, 1963.

Wuest, Kenneth S., *Wuest's Word Studies: From the Greek New Testament*, Vol. One, *Romans,* Grand Rapids, Michigan: Wm. B. Eerdmans Publishing Company, 1955.

Wurmbrand, Richard, *Tortured for Christ,* London: Hodder & Stoughton, 1999.

Yager, Dexter and Ron Ball, *The Marks of a Millionaire*, Wheaton, IL, Tyndale House Publishers.

Zacharias, Ravi sermon: "Why I am Not an Atheist Quoted" by Ravi Zacharias, *A Shattered Visage: The Real Face of Atheism*, Brentwood, Tennessee: Wolgemuth & Hyatt, Publishers, Inc., 1990.

Zacharias, Ravi, *Can Man Live Without God?*, Nashville, Tenn.: Harper Collins, 1994).

Zodiates, Spiros, *The Complete Word Study Dictionary New Testament* Chattanooga, TN: AMG Publishers, 1992).

JOURNALS

"An editorial on sin." *National & International Religion Report*, Jan 27, 1992.

Brown, Harold O. J., *Religion & Society Report*, April 1992.

Bugbee, Bruce and Beth Lueders, "Maximum ministry", *Discipleship Journal*, Nov/Dec 1995 [Issue 90].

Colson, Charles, *World Vision*, Dec/Jan, 88.

Colson, Charles, *World*, 7/1/89.

Crabb, Larry, "Finding God", *Today's Better Life*, Winter 1993, Vol.3, No2.

Intercessors for America Newsletter, Dec 1995.

Lesheid, Helen, *Discipleship Journal*, Nov/Dec 1990 [Issue 60].

Lucado, Max, *New Man*, Nov/Dec 1995.

Marston, Robert, "Experiencing the Presence of God During Times of Need: a case study," *Journal of Pastoral Care*, Fall 1990.

Ministry Currents, Jan-Mar 1994 *Citizen*, April 20, 1992

Packer, J. I., "The empowered Christian life" by J. I. Packer. *Faith & Renewal*, Jan/Feb, 1992.

Phillips, John, "Exploring Romans: The Gospel According to Paul" *Moody Monthly*, 1969.

Popcorn, Faith, Gerald Celente, and Michael Tobias, "What's next?", *Psychology Today*, Jan/Feb 1995 [Vol. 28, No 1].

Shields, Mark, *World Magazine*, January 30.

Tapia, Andres, "Abstinence: The Radical Choice for Sex Ed," *Christianity Today*, Feb. 8.

Today's growing prayer movement signals hope for the world" by David Bryant. *National & International Religion Report*, Mar 6, 1995, Vol 9, No 6.

Tozer, A. W., "I Have Been Crucified," *The Alliance Witness*, 12/6/72.

Van Auken, Philip, *Clergy Journal*, "How to handle church conflict," Mar. 1992.

Zeiler, Janice Sue, *Decision*, Feb. 1994.

INTERNET

For story: http://www.nytimes.com/2010/12/10/sports/olympics/10dupont.html.

http://www.sfgate.com/news/article/Lawrence-Singleton-despised-rapist-dies-He-2886703.php (accessed 03.08.17).

http://www.washingtonexaminer.com/poll-most-americans-pessimistic-about-countrys-future/article/2541502 (accessed 08.03.16).

About the Author

Roy C. Price, DMin, DPhil, is a graduate of Westmont College in English Literature, Luther Rice Seminary (ThM, DMin), and Oxford (now Omega) Graduate School, USA, www.ogs.edu (DPhil in the Sociological Integration of Religion and Society). He presently serves as Adjunct Professor of Pastoral Theology and Polity at the A. W. Tozer Theological Seminary, Redding, CA.

Dr. Price served various pastorates with a missionary attitude. His ministry included experience in rural, suburban, urban, and international congregations. He served in several regional elected positions of his denomination and two terms on the Board of Directors of the national organization of the Christian and Missionary Alliance. He also served on the Board of Regents of Oxford Graduate School, USA.

Significant articles have appeared in Leadership magazine, Christianity Today, and the Alliance Life magazine. Roy and Sandra live in northern California near their grandchildren.

www.ingramcontent.com/pod-product-compliance
Lightning Source LLC
Chambersburg PA
CBHW030132170426
43199CB00008B/40